OF TIME AND PUNISHMENT

A MEMOIR

J.D. MATHES

This is a true story.

Names have been changed, and some have been left out altogether to give them plausible deniability. For that same reason, some details like locations and timing have been altered to protect others.

But my role in the crime and how I was caught are true.

Printed in the United States of America

Permissions
Stephen F. Austin State University Press
P.O. Box 13007, SFA Station
Nacogdoches, TX 75962
sfapress@sfasu.edu
936.468.1078

ISBN: 978-1-62288-282-3

First Edition
Production Manager: Kimberly Verhines
Designer: Karina Chacon

"You're released but your custody calls
And I want to be free
Don't you want to be free?"

David Bowie, "Hallo Spaceboy"

As always, for the Girl Posse

Contents

PART I

RELEASE DAY, 1986

"Oh, let the sun beat down upon my face
With stars to fill my dreams
I am a traveler of both time and space
To be where I have been"

Led Zeppelin, "Kashmir"

Lynne, my ex-wife, pulled her car in front of the prison's administration building. I walked down the concrete steps. The US Army T-shirt with a bald eagle I wore when I was arrested now fit tight across the shoulders and chest. It felt like being a kid after a growth spurt, but we couldn't afford new clothes yet. I put my cardboard box in the backseat of her car. A cone of incense burned in her ashtray, and the smoke drifted out. As I got into the front, I heard, like some cruel dream, the Pink Floyd song, "Wish You Were Here," playing on the car radio. I started weeping as if I'd made landfall after years adrift. She touched my arm and said it'd be okay. I was free now. I shrugged, not feeling free at all. She shifted her old '76 Celica, splattered with hippie and rock 'n' roll bumper stickers—one cautioning, "I Brake for Hallucinations"—into first and popped the clutch. It backfired and smoked as she shifted gears, making guards flinch and inmates look wistfully to the desert.

How long ago had it been when the marshals had parked in front of that old clapboard building, bringing me here to finish my sentence? *Summer last year*, I thought. All the months collapsed like a dark star in my brain into this moment. On the hillside, built into the bluff like ancient cliff dwellings, were several barracks and buildings, all a faded yellow with brown trim like Fort Knox or Fort Irwin or Fort-Fucking-No-Where, a frontier outpost the Army forgot about. At the summit of the bluff, a still operational radar dome shone in the late morning sun. Three vultures hovered into the wind above it. I looked away from the searing whiteness of the dome and toward the open road.

At Terminal Island, a medium-security place of high fences and barbed wire in the Los Angeles Harbor, I was told this place in the Mojave Desert was a Federal Prison Camp. These minimum-security prisons picked up the nickname Club Fed for the reputation of being like mini resorts for white-collar criminals, but here, it was more like being in the Foreign Legion in North Africa. Sure, the only block wall stood around the staff housing, and the only fence in sight stretched around the radar installation, but where was anyone going to fucking go in this march-or-die landscape?

I wiped the tears away and got ahold of myself.

Braless in a sundress, and I knew Lynne didn't wear panties, so my hope swelled. Reading my mind, the first thing she said was, "I know it's been a long time, and I'd fuck you, but I'm with someone now. Been married a month." I cursed my timing and the misfortune of a month as I felt my cock hardening under my jeans.

I smiled. "Not even a blow job?"

"Especially not a blow job. I'd get that thing in my mouth and then need it between my legs. You know how I am."

I nodded. Indeed, I did.

Blue feather earrings matched her eyes, and her eyes always looked bright as if everything amazed her. Part of her beauty was everything did amaze her. She existed in a state of wonder. She had an air around her eyes and lips as fragile as spider silk, powerful enough to withstand forces of nature but helpless to the ravaging boots of ignorant boys. She acted the street kid who rebelled in school and the courageous activist, even being arrested every Easter for crossing the boundary of the nuclear test site north of Vegas. But still, something ran under her surface like the two sets of razor scars on each wrist she covered with bracelets. Pale slash marks from the two times life overwhelmed her sense of wonder and the future failed to give her any expectation that life was worth sticking out. On my release day, my state of wonder had been crushed as well as any sense of the future. What else could I manage then?

It was nearly overwhelming to be riding in a car with a beautiful woman whom I had once slept with night after hot night and to consider what was next. The halfway house for sure, but what of the act of living, of getting a life? From Clark County Jail, I was transferred to Federal Correctional Institution, Tucson. Behind the rows of fences and rolls of concertina wire, inside the cement and block walls with a slit for a window, I watched sunsets blister the sky beyond the brutalist administration building. I began learning meditation from a heroin-smuggling Buddhist. The days gave way to the eternal sunshine of sulfur-colored lights. I measured each breath like an alchemist searching for the right combination of elements to create gold from lead.

"Remain in the present," the heroin smuggler had said. Suffering was an illusion. Life was an illusion, and I was the agent of my own misery. The past did not matter. The future did not matter. But of course the future mattered, and so did the heavy past in ways my thin philosophy failed to account.

Now in the Celica hurtling down the highway, I used deep breathing to keep my erection down and bring the desire to a standstill. In my cell, I'd meditate on my bunk after lights out, easing the longing in my groin, my ache for touch. I believed I was mastering self-control. Desire, the heroin smuggler told me, was all an illusion. That was a lot easier to think without a woman sitting so close, smelling of spring, sandalwood incense, and hemp, racing and more radiant than the desert sun.

Hot wind rushed through the passenger window, and bits of desert sand stung my face. The eye-searing July sun bore down with a weight, and the steady whir of tires on asphalt lulled me into a trance of shifting sand and sky. I stretched my stiff legs and pushed back into the seat, letting some air flow under me. Lynne tapped her finger on the steering wheel, humming along to the thumping intro of Led Zeppelin's "Kashmir." The Indian fusion rock song was one of her favorites as it made rock 'n' roll mystical and sought something transcendent. When the music crescendoed and Robert Plant's voice began to soar, her gaze strayed beyond the road to the horizon's far mountains for a moment.

The highway markers ticked by. Fast cars passed us going from LA to Vegas. A couple, all glittering diamonds and gold in a Mercedes convertible; a gasoline big rig with its tanker shimmering like a mirage of water; and college boys in a station wagon hurtling like a green rocket ship for the far planet, Party. Lynne and I had not come from LA to party like the Rat Pack. Not anything so cool or hip.

We drove Highway 58 out of the prehistoric Lake Mojave until it dead-ended at I-15 west of Barstow. Bluffs and mountains of ancient magma chambers stripped of volcanic glory lay unsheltered under the wind, the sun, and the stars. I'd stared out at various forms of this geologic order for a lifetime and felt their silence and hardness. I watched as seasons of light passed color and shadows over this landscape.

As a kid, my dad took us across deserts and mountains, chasing gold and the legends of treasure. The vastness expanded like the distance between vultures spinning circles and their shadows on the ground. My child's eyes began to take in the horizon and wonder what was over it. We think we see so much further than we really do. I remembered my childhood wonder at a land charged with the sacred. What kept the vultures circling on high? Magic or physical processes? Thermals of air rising from the heated desert or a gift granted from the gods of flight? Maybe both. Because in the stories we use to make sense of the world, isn't there room for them? Another thing for the boy hiking alone across the desert to see was himself both exposed and ignored. So much light and expanse and dryness, where everything appeared open to view, but where everything remained hidden.

The desert hid the military and the ghosts of nuclear testing, the sprawling miles of gunnery ranges and landing strips for bombers and space shuttles fenced off with wire, and the Army's National Training Center where I'd ridden in tanks, training to fight the Soviets. Peppered throughout were ancient petroglyphs along footpaths haunted by shaman on vision quests and spirit animals waiting for someone worthy. A few decades before, borax miners loaded and drove thirty-seven-and-a-half-ton wagons with teams of eighteen mules and two horses by the shadow of the prison where I sat. From up on the prison mountaintop, I looked off either side of history. In the distance to the southwest, I watched the astronauts of my boyhood dreams drop out of the sky and land the space shuttle after the sonic boom rolled out of space, rattling windows. The land still bore the ruts of the mule trains. I imagined those poor mules groaning in their harnesses. The ones collapsing under the lash and the sun were cut out of their train, and their carcasses were left for scavengers and sand to hone their bones to relics. In all directions, ancient desert dwellers had lived, now long gone except for their stone and earth artifacts, petroglyphs, and their lonely spirits wandering the land.

In geologic history, even the petroglyphs are only a superficial and brief encounter. Perhaps I couldn't control my own life until I could see the ancient desert as it once was. Here, an inland sea and rivers created a lush landscape, and if you look, you can find its story in the marine fossils and minerals of the seabed that had once been living creatures. The long wearing of time dried it out and transformed islands into mountains and seabed into desert flats. I envisioned the landscape as it was before the arrival of humans who would tease out meaning and mystery. I learned of other deserts in Sunday school where Old Testament prophets preached feverish warnings to people who ignored them and paid the price. Places where angels descended to the earth and whirlwinds or crackling bushes aflame were the mouth of God in the wilderness. When did I first become aware of the desert as this other place? This place to seek and suffer and to hopefully find answers. A place to find grace and redemption, or the illusion of it because if life is an illusion, then so is enlightenment.

At I-15, we cut down to Barstow. Lynne clicked on the blinker, turning onto the highway off-ramp. We rattled into town in her fastback Celica, where she treated me to my first restaurant lunch in a dingy cafe. "I figure you could use a taste of the free world right about now," she said.

A young waitress handed us menus. She had a mound of red hair and a southern drawl that flowed from her red lips like refrigerated honey. The first woman's voice I'd heard not a relation or an employee of the prison system in almost two years. Her name tag said Rose.

I asked for a cheeseburger with fries, and Lynne ordered a salad and a Diet Coke.

Lynne mentioned her accent didn't fit with Barstow, and Rose smiled and said she was an Army wife from Fort Irwin. Married out of high school and then here four months later.

"Barstow's a long way from the fort," I said.

She said she made enough in tips to supplement her enlisted husband's meager salary, making the 50-minute one-way drive worth it. They were saving for a house for when he got out of the Army. She whisked away to put our ticket up on the metal wheel in the window between the front and the grill. An old man in an apron and a white T-shirt turned gray snapped the ticket down. He canted his head to see around the cigarette sticking out of his mouth and squinted through smoke to read it.

A half hour later, the plate clacked in front of me. Rose said, "Enjoy."

I savored the moment. Funny how the small things I'd pushed out of my mind came rushing over me. The place was like so many other cafes I'd been to or worked at along so many desert roads. I became aware of perfume drifting along with the smell of fried food, bleach, cigarette smoke, and dust shed off boots and jeans. Perfume, a small strand of something beautiful. I felt how a bloodhound must feel catching the scent of the lost girl he was searching for out past the garbage dump. It made me think of trips up dirt roads past the old mine, past our dump, and into the foothills where me and my first girlfriend parked and watched car lights on this highway stream through the summit to Vegas and back after we'd had sex. The smell of her hair in the desert evening like something out of a fairy tale.

I squirted mustard and ketchup on the bun and squished it down on the pickle, limp lettuce, and tomato. I picked up the burger. Pretty average diner fare by all standards, but the nonstandard anticipation made my stomach growl. My first bite broke the spell. I'd had better in prison. For a second, I wondered if I might get sick. Rose came around and filled my tea. "Y'all alright?"

I nodded and smiled at the sound of her voice. "Where you from?"

"Washington County, North Carolina."

I tried to think of something else to say, but nothing came to my mind except what it'd feel like to wake up pressed against her naked body and its luscious warmth. I imagined, in those seconds as she stood there, cupping her breasts from behind as we came into consciousness, becoming aware of the world and a new day of possibility, wanting to linger in the sensation. If life were an illusion, like the imagination, then it was a visceral illusion.

Lynne wiped her mouth with a napkin. "How long you been out here? Must've been a big shock to come from there to here."

She laughed in that charming way I always assumed coy Southern belles laughed when asked to dance by men they'd rather not dance with. "Well, let's just say the desert's not for us. We had hoped for Germany."

Germany. Every armored crewman's wet dream except for those guys who thought they could score cheaper hookers in Korea. "Dude, your poontang to dollar ratio is kick-ass over there, and they clean your room." What else was important to teenaged men? I too wanted to go to Germany. I had no idea of the possibilities the Army presented a poor boy from the desert until after I'd had my brain reorganized by drill sergeants.

I'd been a tank gunner in the Army National Guard. Even though we were essentially the "well organized militia" of the state for state emergencies, we also fell under the command of the president for national service, like being called up to reinforce regular Army units in war zones or other federal emergencies. And because of this, we went to basic and advanced training in a military occupational specialty and trained with active-duty units on field exercises. My Guard unit went to Reforger, the massive joint NATO field exercise to show the Soviets we were serious and had the hardware, personnel, and logistics savvy to kick their asses. I'd missed out on going to Officer Candidate School (OCS). I wondered, at what point had I wanted to be an officer? I didn't. I was ordered to take the test. I passed the test with an exemplary score, as I always scored exemplary on tests, and went at the first sergeant's urging because a suggestion from the senior noncommissioned officer of the company was as good as an order.

Rose continued. "Plus, this fort isn't like the posts back home that are all by towns. This one is so far out and is so…"

"Desolate," I said, filling in her pause. "But the humidity back East is killer." I'd lived all my life in the desert except for some time in Kentucky and Ohio as a little kid and the four and a half months in Kentucky for basic and armor training. What I remembered most: sweat. A walking-around, eye-burning sweat that soaked T-shirts and underwear as you put them on. And the rank smell of recruits stuffed into barracks all sweating from physical exertion and fear.

"My skin dries out so out here," Rose said. "I like the warm, humid evenings when lightning bugs pop up. I am amazed how much there isn't around here and how far it is to get anywhere that is the least ways bearable."

"How much longer you have?" Lynne asked.

"Three years." Her voice trailed away as if the desert had swallowed it.

"At least he can get a skill to use in the outside world," Lynne said.

"He wants to be a police officer, but he's an infantryman, so we'll see."

My skill set from the Army included marching, being yelled at, making beds, folding clothes, being a top gun armor crewman, and an abiding hate for communism and Russians without any logical reason other than I was told to. "Do you hate communists, private?" "Yes, drill sergeant!" "Why, private?" "Because you told me to, drill sergeant! Kill Russians, drill sergeant!" I was the fool who wore the "I'd rather be killing communists" T-shirt. I shook my head as I thought about it. I'd have to throw that rag out. I often thought of young Soviet and Warsaw Pact recruits yelling, "Kill capitalists! Kill decadent Westerners!"

"Three years will be a lot of tip money," I said to her.

She looked out the window to the street. "The worst of it is I won't see my family till we can get back. None of them can afford to come out here. Like we been sentenced to Siberia without all the snow." She laughed again, but this laugh was what I imagined Southern belles sounded like when they said they wished they still lived in the Antebellum South—except for slavery, of course…polite laugh.

A guy in a trucker hat and plaid shirt lifted his coffee cup to get her attention. She excused herself and made her rounds with coffee pot in hand. I thought of her in three years. The shine would really come off being out West. How many months until she started looking at the highway out of town as an escape? There wouldn't be a shortage of truckers and traveling men passing through, offering her a ride over the horizon and out of exile, all desiring to run their fingers through her red hair lit by parking lot lights.

Lynne smiled. "I hope they make it." She took a forkful of salad.

She could have been talking about a past us.

I finished my burger. The clock on the wall behind the counter was a starburst with arms radiating out in some fifties design of what they thought futuristic back then. An antique store relic tarnished with the smoke of cigarettes and grilled food. The future was right then. The gold hands clacked. I felt the urge to go before another minute clicked like the snap of Death's bony fingers.

We drove out of Barstow, leaving Rose to fill the emptied coffee cups and iced tea glasses like an aproned Sisyphus—soup or salad, fries or fruit cup—until her husband finished his enlistment. Rose seemed too young to be married, but then I was not even twenty and Lynne was eighteen, still in high school, when we staggered into the Justice of the Peace in downtown Vegas. When I looked at Rose, I felt ancient, emerging out of the desert after searching for gold or a god but returning with empty saddlebags and faithless. She greeted me as the first sign of civilization with her coffee pot and order pad, the wife who followed her soldier husband to the bitter frontier.

Even though I was a part-time citizen soldier, it wove its web through Lynne and I's marriage. Although I volunteered for a lot of temporary duty assignments with regular Army units, we'd never had to relocate, not to Germany, not to Korea, not to Planet Irwin outside of Barstow in the Mojave Desert. But it took us both far from home.

We got back in the Celica. Lynne pushed the cassette tape back into the player. "Kashmir" took back up where it had left off when we stopped. We descended on the highway over low-ranging rocks sharpened on the whetstone of the wind cutting south of Death Valley. I'd migrated all over the American Southwest and its deserts my whole short life, even while incarcerated: county jail in Vegas to Tucson, to Phoenix, to Lompoc, to Terminal Island, to end at Boron Federal Prison Camp far out in the Mojave Desert. How long can a place hold on to you?

"Let me take you there…" Lynne sang the dreamy last lines of the song. Her blonde hair flew about, catching sunlight and wind like brass bullet casings flying out of a .50 caliber machine gun. She owned every Zeppelin album and had taken me to see *The Song Remains the Same* about a dozen times. She could recite all the dialogue and sing the live versions with all of Robert Plant's ad-libs, which she added when the studio version of the song played. *The song doesn't always remain the same*, I thought.

I watched other cars headed to Vegas and tried to imagine what they were all thinking and doing. Did they all have the hope of being big winners, or were some more modest in their aspirations? A small winner still wins. Restraint and a steady will? Restraint might just be staying home. A Honda CBR1100 crotch rocket, the rider bent over the tank as if he were protecting it from vultures overhead, flew by doing at least 100 mph. *Go like hell*, I thought, *because you control a lot less than you think you do.*

We drove out of the Soda Mountains and into the desert's low-lying hills past Zzyzx Road before they tapered onto the hot plains of creosote and cactus. Along this highway, another reminder of my youthful promise idled under the sun. Baker, California was a blot along the highway for weary travelers to stop and ogle at the World's Largest Thermometer, which we high schoolers joked was the world's largest rectal thermometer. The sign announcing The Gateway to Death Valley came into view as we drove. *Indeed*, I thought, *"Abandon all hope, ye who enter here."* I'd finished going to high school there. I was bussed down thirty-some miles with other kids whose parents worked at the rare earth mine in the mountains looming above the California and Nevada state line.

The highway sign warned us the first off-ramp for Baker split off in a mile. "You want to stop?" Lynne asked.

"No. Not exactly like I'm the triumphant alum returning to spread the glory and dispense advice to the graduating class."

She laughed. "Well, you could probably give them some advice. Soap and showering type stuff." She snorted, laughing hard at her own joke.

Her laugh made me want her more. "Right. And don't sleep on your stomach."

She shook her head, laughing.

"Did I mention not pissing on the electric fence?" Conditional wisdom.

"Oh, stop it." Her smile and the look out of the corner of her eyes warmed me. *This is freedom*, I thought.

I didn't want to walk back into an old school anyway. I'd spent my childhood on the move, leaving schools and landscapes and not coming back. As my dad always said, I didn't forget anything there to go back for.

As we hurtled down the freeway, I knew Lynne loved me deeply, even without a sweet fling in the back of her Celica. After all, when an ex-wife comes to fetch you hours away in another state on your release date, there must be a little something in her heart that isn't just obligation or nostalgia. We had learned what it was to be married and hit the rocks of bad faith and addiction as we lived fast and would maybe die young, but now we'd begun to learn what it was to be divorced and still be in love in some odd way.

Lynne tapped the steering wheel. The off-ramp for Baker appeared. "Are you sure you don't want to stop? I mean, they have a Bun Boy restaurant, or is that too painful from your recent experiences?" Lynne smiled.

"Ouch."

"That's what I said my first time too."

Lynne kept driving past the congregation of highway-side businesses, leaving them behind like a boomtown after the lode-bearing ore was gone. The desert stretched ahead of us. I longed for the miles I'd hiked in the deserts and over broken rock mountains with no destination in my mind but the bend in an arroyo or the crest of high ground.

I first became immersed in the desert during the summer between fifth and sixth grade. My parents decided to chuck the suburbs to make a homestead where we would live off the land. We'd driven down a few times to walk the forty acres in Southeast Arizona, camp out for the night, and get back so my dad could be back at work as a municipal judge. As soon as the school year ended, we moved into tents and began digging the foundation for the adobe house my dad envisioned. He left behind his judgeship and worked odd agricultural jobs to make car and land payments and buy food and clothes. I spent many hours walking or just sitting in the desert, exploring, and discovering an awareness of myself in a larger world. It puzzled me to think I felt this out there, apart from civilization and people. We lasted a year and a half before the bank forced us off the land.

The cassette tape auto ejected. I flipped it over to play the other side. Lynne smiled at me, and the whiteness of her teeth slowed the world a second. I had bought her the smallest diamond the store had for a wedding ring to replace the cigar band we used at the Justice of the Peace. I had also given her an opal I'd carried out of the Superstition Mountains when I was in the fourth grade and carried with me as we knocked about the West. What small, semi-precious things had I managed to hang on to over time?

We climbed the last mountain ranges in California before Nevada. The highway cut between the Clark and Ivanpah Mountains. At the summit, the town of Mountain Pass had been carved out on the north side of the interstate. It was both the last summit before Californians descended into Nevada and forgetfulness and the first summit to climb after leaving Vegas. Although no one warns you, you shouldn't look back.

We neared the summit of these mountains created from volcanism and the long grind of tectonic plates. A tough land that can break tough people. Above us, the sun erased the shadows. When I read *Paradise Lost*, I imagined Satan and the other fallen angels fell like lightning through a landscape like this. All of a summer's day can feel like an eternity. Blasted and scorching hot, with winds whipping sand into the air powerful enough to strip the skin from your face. Everything bears menace—sharp edges, thorns, and spikes, fangs and stingers filled with venom. Out here, heatstroke can make you delirious and hallucinate talking animals or visions of spirits rising in the heat waves, speaking warnings against your death in an afternoon. You can die between lunch and dinner, before the cooling night, under a hypothermic sky and the starlit heavens you will never reach.

The rare earth mine at Mountain Pass was the last mine I'd lived at. The place where I'd left home for Los Angeles after high school. Now the company was laying off workers, scaling back to skeleton crews. They'd shipped off most of the single-wide trailers where miners and their families had lived. Where I, my girlfriend, friends, and others we knew from school had lived for a couple of years. All that was left were some scattered trailers among the empty lots stretching to the mountains of discarded earth and stone, most everyone dispersed over the country. Even still, the mine was lit during the day, exhaling steam and dust from its superstructures and buildings. Further out, the dump at the base of the foothills still brimmed with decades of household trash and discarded possessions that didn't fit into a moving van. This gutted land. Why do we believe the stories where we can put things back to the way they were? Filled-in mining pits will always be mining pits.

As we passed, I looked toward where my family still lived despite the mine being abandoned by degrees. Their mobile home out of sight behind the bowling alley and some trees. I couldn't bring myself to stop there. As odd as it sounded, I needed more time before I could face them. Face anyone else I'd known. So Lynne picked up speed and we crested the summit.

PART II

HALFWAY TO NOWHERE

"The only prisoner is always in, not knowing what he's done."

Richard Hugo, "Degrees of Gray in Philipsburg"

Lynne steered her Toyota off the interstate and into the streets of North Las Vegas. Heat waves shimmered off the blacktop, and nobody walked or hung out along the sidewalks except for a couple of people in the shade of a liquor store. Only an hour from Mountain Pass, me and some friends used to drive to Vegas for concerts at the Aladdin Casino Theater on the Strip or drag races northeast of town by Nellis Air Force Base. But when high school ended, I didn't want to live or go to college there. I wanted to go to Los Angeles where my friends, Adam and Jane, who were a brother and sister from my first high school at Eagle Mountain, lived.

We'd planned to be roommates and go to college. But that fell apart a week after I'd arrived. Unable to afford an apartment in Los Angeles on my own and not wanting to live in my car, I called a friend named Blaine who let me stay in his garage in North Vegas until I could afford an apartment. Blaine was a good but strange guy, sleeping in a homemade plywood coffin to remind himself of his mortality every night, and if he died in his sleep, they'd only need to hammer the lid on and bury him. It looked like one in an Old West tintype, painted black with a skull carved onto the lid. Like me, he didn't drink, so he helped me avoid that high school peer pressure.

Even without my LA plan, Vegas never came to mind as a place to go after graduation. It always felt like a transient town for tourists and gamblers, not a place to start college or start a career unless you were going into gaming, the hospitality industry, or organized crime.

We drove along East Owens Avenue, looking for some side street where the halfway house was supposed to be. The area hadn't changed much, but why would it? No one invested in poor areas with majority Black populations.

We found the street. Lynne dropped me off in front of the halfway house. She waved and told me to call her and we'd do lunch. I watched as her car backfired, smoked, drove up the street, and turned the corner. The halfway house looked like any old apartment complex in a declining working-class neighborhood, with all the doors facing each other across a grassy courtyard with a couple of poplar trees. A block wall screened it off from the street, and two wrought iron gates stood on either side of it. I squinted against the summer sun, feeling out of sorts in a familiar land. Blaine's house was only a couple of blocks from here. I'd also gone to the community college a bike ride away, further northeast, on Cheyenne Boulevard.

No sidewalks lined these streets where knots of two to three teenagers stood in their youthful poses of toughness. They reminded me of guys I'd been in the county jail with. Apartment buildings and some old houses with faded and flaking paint or cracked and water-stained stucco made up the run-down block. It looked on the verge of being abandoned or bought up by developers to plow a freeway through or erect a stadium. Some yards had tended lawns, and others had let weeds go to seed and die standing in the Vegas heat.

For a moment, I imagined I stood in front of my own apartment and was not a heartbeat away from being a fugitive. If those inside thought I was dragging my feet or thinking about running, a call was all it'd take to bring the cops. Would they understand that I was only taking a moment to feel the place around me, to feel free before I stepped back into the system of checks and punishment? I might be some guy waiting on a ride from a woman to go on a date. What would it be like to go out again? A hunger filled me for life that I'd kept suppressed. I'd come so far and just wanted to be in the delusion that I was on a street with no particular place to go, with no one waiting on me to arrive, and not subjecting my body to the State once again. I walked up and pulled open the wrought iron gate. It squeaked on its hinges so sharply I winced.

I entered the office, which looked like any rental office of an apartment complex, but here, government employees supervised us like prison guards in street clothes.

I set my cardboard box on the counter. A tall Black woman with an afro, red business skirt and red blazer over a white blouse, sensible shoes, and no jewelry looked me up and down. She had the air of a den mother who knew which kids were the fuckups, and you always thought it was you even though you hadn't done anything. She introduced herself as Ms. Randall before searching my box. It held Colgate toothpaste, a toothbrush, a pocket comb, a plastic soap case with a bar of white prison soap in it, shower shoes, deodorant, two disposable razors, a notebook with a black government pen, a transistor radio with an earpiece, and a piece of cardboard from a legal pad with the yin and yang symbol drawn in black ink on one side. On the other side, I'd written dates on it, starting in the upper left-hand corner since I'd been locked up. I'd drawn little asterisks next to some dates, meaning Lynne had come to visit.

I showed Ms. Randall my papers, and she told me how to sign in. She explained the rules, that curfew was at 9:00 pm, and in time, I could apply to remain out over a weekend if I had someone to house me. She took out a urinalysis kit. "You need to fill this cup to here." She pointed to the line. "Don't get smart and overfill it. Just enough to get the test done."

She waved over a skinny man with thinning gray-black hair from a desk in the back. He sported a thin moustache like the lines on a topographic map and had the smile of a guy who thought he was in on the joke. "This is Mr. Lopez. He will accompany you."

I shrugged. He showed me to a restroom and stood in the doorway, looking at me while trying not to look at me. I stood staring at the cup, trying to will myself to piss.

The old guy smiled as he turned on the faucet to a trickle. "A little mood music."

"I never was good at performing in front of an audience."

He chuckled. "We can't leave here until you do."

I finally managed to fill the cup to the bottom line and set it on the back of the toilet. The old guy took it and screwed the cap on it. He noted the date and time, applied the security tape, sealed it in a bag, and had me sign the label on the bag. I washed my hands and went back out.

Mrs. Gutiérrez, a short, heavy woman, came from an office in the back. The bangs of her black hair were feathered up, and her long nails gleamed red. She looked at the breathalyzer on the desk. "Didn't you administer the breathalyzer?"

Ms. Randall looked at her with cool indifference. "He don't smell of booze."

"That doesn't matter. Everyone must be tested when they check in." She took the breathalyzer off the desk and, after prepping it, held it up to me. "Just blow until I tell you to stop."

I put my lips to the little tube and blew. When Mrs. Gutiérrez was satisfied, she took it and wrote something on the form. She looked me up and down. "Let me warn you now. We tolerate no trouble here. You will be sent back if you can't follow my rules."

I regarded her and nodded at the full weight of the federal government in her ID badge.

Ms. Randall escorted me out of the office and toured me through the apartment. She had me sign a form about the condition of the premises. I noted a crack in the wall opposite the couch above the TV, the leaking faucet in the bathroom, and general shabbiness of the furniture. Before leaving, she told me to ask if I had any questions. I said I didn't, but if something came up, I would. She lowered her voice like I was back on the yard. "Do not cross Mrs. Gutiérrez." She tilted her head to make sure I got her meaning.

I nodded. I knew.

"There's time to go food shopping before curfew. Don't aggravate me by being late."

I stowed my cardboard box in my bedroom. The bunk wasn't much different from a barrack's bunk. There was a chest of drawers and a closet with no hangers. I looked out the window. A concrete path cut between the halfway house and another old apartment complex.

I sat on the couch. A dingy, slapped-together place with all the charm of a rent-for-afternoon-flings hotel on the seedy side of town. An hour ago, Lynne had dropped me off at this North Vegas address with a kiss on the cheek and an invitation to come visit her and her new husband when I got a pass. It was sweet of her to have kept visiting me in prison. She was always a better person than I had ever given her credit for when our marriage became a casualty of drugs, alcohol, and adultery. Maybe she was looking for atonement by helping me out. I don't know for sure, but I was happy to believe she was a compassionate person.

The sun's rays slanted crossways through the gaps in the curtain. The sun still had a long way to go before reaching the horizon. I was free to leave for a few hours, but I sat and thought about the probability of running into someone I knew. The odds of them being in this part of the city were pretty slim, if they hadn't left Vegas altogether. There might've been people who'd recognize me from the news casts a year and a half ago when the BATF agents arrested me at the armory out of the battalion commander's office or the countless times the feds marched me back and forth from court. I'd been away a while, but still, I wasn't ready to chat up any old acquaintances or have any confrontations.

Outside the office was a payphone. I needed to call my parents and let them know I'd made it. I'd have to call collect as I didn't have a phone card. At the phone, I took a breath as I picked up the receiver. My stomach knotted as I pushed the zero and the operator came on. Within a few minutes, the phone on the other end rang. My youngest brother, the third son, picked up and accepted the charges. I said, "Hey," to him, and he asked how I was doing. We hadn't spoken in over two years, and now it was strange to hear his post-pubescent voice on the other end. Like I'd called the future. My younger brother, the second son, had graduated high school and joined the Navy to be a SEAL. My sister was seven years younger than me, so I felt even more distant from her since I last saw her. I had no idea how they were doing in school or what they wanted to do other than the news I got in sporadic letters like from a distant aunt who didn't travel from the Old World.

He rounded up dad, who was glad to hear I made it okay. We made a plan for him to meet me on Saturday to bring some clothes, a couple of books, some towels, and any other things he might happen to think of as he packed. I told him I'd like to have my daypack, the one I had for school and probably still had schoolbooks and my last homework assignments from college.

I thanked him for getting my stuff. They'd packed up my apartment after my arrest and took it to Mountain Pass. Dad said they had ransacked the place. When he'd gotten there, the doorknob had been busted with a sledgehammer and the door left open. He didn't think anything was stolen. The manager kept the deposit.

I'd seen mom and dad once when they came to visit me at Boron last summer. They sat across from me. The old man in his plaid work shirt, jeans, and sun-weathered face as if he'd just stepped off a horse after scouting ahead for the wagon train. Mom with her blonde hair curled, discrete makeup, nice blouse on for visiting, and all the quietness of a woman still coping with her oldest son's fuckups. Their eyes scanned me like a stranger. They scanned the others, no stranger than me as they had thought they'd known me but were now not so sure who I was. They hadn't seen me in over a year. What changes did they see in my face?

They made chit-chat. My dad said, "Least you ain't in Nam," and I thought I'd rather have been given the choice to go to Nam or not. Like one of the guys on my cellblock who chose Nam the first time he ran afoul of the law like in the Bruce Springsteen song, "Born in the USA." He went Ranger and survived long-range reconnaissance patrols and booby traps and time-stopping firefights. He wished he'd had the chance to go to war the second time instead of sitting in a cell. They didn't really know me. Maybe dad and I just knew different horrors and talked past each other. Maybe he thought he was cheering me up. They talked about how my siblings were doing. How things were at the house. Grandma was still gardening and canning. They told me how life went on. How things changed all the time but didn't. They only asked if I was okay in a general way and never probed for specifics. Some shit was better left unknown. I'd said, "Fine."

Dad said he'd be at the halfway house around 4:00 pm. He handed the phone off to my mom. She asked if I had enough food in the apartment. She'd send leftovers along with dad to make sure I wouldn't go hungry. I told her I was planning on grocery shopping after our talk. We said our goodbyes and I hung up the phone.

My mom grew up the youngest child, with two older brothers, of a widowed mother. Her father died from tuberculosis in 1947 when she was a baby. My grandmother had been a nurse and had left her Oklahoma farm to move to Arizona, but when her husband died, she went to secretarial school and then got a job with Maricopa County instead of going back to the family farm. A single mom with three kids, she still managed to get her kids fed and to church every Sunday at the local Methodist church. My dad had grown up in Covington, Kentucky, the second son of seven boys with little prospects. He dropped out of high school and joined the Air Force to escape the alcohol-induced poverty of his parents. The Air Force stationed him at Luke Air Force Base, and he somehow ended up on a blind date with my mother. They were opposites, and they endured teasing from my future uncles, both former Navy men who served on aircraft carriers in the 1950s, about how the flyboy with the smooth southern drawl had flown away whenever he was delayed hitching a ride from the base. They married in 1963. I was born in May 1964, and just after my first birthday in June 1965, he deployed to Vietnam as a helicopter door gunner. He'd be shot down five times but still returned in one piece. My mom stayed with her mother, and I kept the company of two resilient single mothers. That year, I learned to read, and something I can't quite put my finger on happened that made me always identify more with those two women than anyone else.

When my mother said goodbye on the phone, it was the same voice exhausted from migraines and misbehaving boys I heard. The voice of a woman worn the way a stone is worn by wind and water, still there but contoured by the troubles of her life.

I regarded the phone, thought how it closes distances but opens gulfs between us. I needed to get food for dinner and the next few days. I'd need breakfast before going out to look for a job. I needed to act like a normal citizen again and escape institutional thinking. I wanted to cook for myself and not have someone else on an assembly line cook my food and serve me. I wasn't sure what to get, but I figured to cruise around the store to see what hit me. I left the apartment and signed out under Mrs. Gutiérrez's suspicious gaze.

Litter, tumbleweeds, and dirt blown in from out of town filled the gutters. Graffiti decorated some walls and the sides of stores. Neon casino and bar lights blinked nonstop. I wondered if my favorite bartender still served up cocktails at my favorite bar where Lynne and I drank underage. I wondered what Lynne was up to now.

Some dudes in front of a liquor store panhandled me. "Help a man out. Spot a brother some change." I automatically sized them up. Ever since being jumped in county lockup, I gave strangers space so I had a chance to fight back.

A guy from my unit, whom I went to basic training and armor school with, lived in this neighborhood or close to it. He claimed to be a pimp and a Playboy Blood. He had a Playboy bunny with one ear up and the other folded down tattooed on his bicep that looked like an angry kid had carved it into his flesh with a ballpoint pen. I always thought he wasn't serious about being in a gang, just posing. What gang member joins the National Guard for college money? He was a disciplined soldier and dependable. We all called him Private Playboy anyway. Decades later, a professor of English at East Carolina University, told her students to quit acting like gangsters in her classroom because gangsters weren't worried about their GPAs. I laughed but thought of the good soldier, Private Playboy. He could have been both. Why not?

At the store, I cut through the parking lot, measuring people as if going into a prison dining hall. In the past, my concern had been idiot drivers. Now it was the potential for mayhem where people gathered and the warning signs I'd learned to spot, like sudden movements—an arm raised too fast—or an inmate's lowered gaze, bloodless face, and body tensed with attack. Funny how terror binds itself into a person's DNA.

The automatic doors whooshed open, and the light and noise gave me pause like when I was a kid entering a carnival. Where do I go first? In the supermarket, I wandered the aisles, making great looping circles. A black-haired chick berated her boyfriend in rapid machine-gun bursts of Spanish. I loved the sound of her words and the frenetic pace of the language and wished for a second to be on the cuss end of that conversation, but only for a moment. The cart's wavering wheel made me force it to turn. I still wasn't sure what I wanted. I felt out of sync, like a time traveler who found himself in a not-too-distant future. A time and place not totally alien, but just unfamiliar enough to be disorienting. I hadn't been around people in street clothes, people with money, people who were women, and kids—loud and racing and crying and screaming for treats.

"Mom, I want chips now!" The mom hauled off and slapped the crusty snot right off the face of her eight-year-old in front of racks and racks of chips.

"That'll learn you."

Not likely, I thought. I bet the kid's face had been struck harder in the past, and given where I'd just come from, slapping the shit out of kids didn't necessarily slap the bad or the madness out of them. It'd just be pushed down, festering for the want of a needle to lance it.

I looked at myself in the mirrors on the upper part of the wall reflecting the store. I tried to see through to the other side where security was surely sizing me up. In the racket of a market in full clean-up-on-aisle-five mode, old people tottered in the middle of aisles, men slouched around the frozen food, and women jockeyed carts like chariots in *Ben-Hur* for the cashier line.

The women, though. Trying not to look like a freak, I breathed in deeply as they passed me, taking in their smell like the traces of faded desire and hope. Housewives, college coeds, women off work in pantsuits with heels clicking like the seconds on a biological bomb, some on welfare, some choosing between name brand and store brand, some with hair up in a quick afternoon ponytail, some sprayed and lacquered, some fat, some skinny, some in between. Old, young, middle-aged. I had missed the presence of women, the sounds of their voices, their laughter rippling the air like egrets over still water, and their touch.

In the frozen foods section, I tossed some frozen pizzas into the cart. The door frosted over as a cold mist breathed out. When it closed, I saw my reflection in the whitened glass. My big shot at normalcy. Had I ever been normal? I felt stoned and uncaught and something else, that the world watched me from behind the mirrors above, in security camera footage broadcast on the news. Undercover officers tailed me and reported back to a command post. Good citizens trying to keep their community safe from fuckups like me. Someone waited for me to ball it up and send me back. "I'm sorry, but you tried to use an expired coupon for Hungry-Man TV dinners. You'll have to come with us downtown." The system was full of people who'd been back home, minding their own business, and landed back in prison because some cop had a hard-on for them, some dickhead probation officer, some "friend" with a grudge, some ex with a dull axe in need of an edge. Walking down a street, the police pulled up in their shiny prowl car. "You in violation, son. Come with us. We got a few questions for your no-good ass. You know anything about a Spilotro?" Then along with those worries, the low-grade fever of paranoia that someone I slighted or fought with in the county jail or prison still had it out for me and waited for me in an unguarded moment.

On my fourth pass through produce, I tossed some bananas in the cart. An old white woman whose face powder made her look peach-colored smiled at me, and I smiled back. I stared into the middle distance like a historian on a battlefield in a documentary. I stopped again at the booze just to look at the Jack Daniel's bottles like so many idols for sale at some sacred shrine for pilgrims to buy and take home. All hail the holy whiskey. Let us drink to the dead and those who will be. Drinking was forbidden in the halfway house, so it became one more thing they could write us up for if we had a taste. Just because I hadn't had a drink in a year and a half didn't mean I didn't tremble at the thought of having one.

I got some cereal and milk and a Pepsi as I hadn't had a Pepsi for a long time. As soon as I put one thing in the cart, I wanted to buy everything. I'd come from scarcity and now faced the market might of modern America. I could buy ice cream and top it with blueberries, sprinkles, and kitty kibble and no one would stop me. I could get five different brands of peanut butter for each day of the workweek. I could buy a case of candy bars. I could indeed thump all the melons and decide not to buy one and go for a pomegranate instead. Notebook paper, pens, shoe polish, cookware, spices, produce, steaks, chicken, chops, treats of all types and configurations in a few languages. Mexican snacks, Chinese snacks, American snacks, and snacks both healthy and so laden with fat and sugar that they'd waste the enamel on my teeth and stop my sinful heart. All the smells clouded the aisles like seas shifting around continents. The possibilities kept me pushing.

In the meat section, I stopped at the chicken. I remembered my mom and grandma saying you can always tell the quality of a cook by how good their baked chicken turns out. I picked out a whole chicken. It was cheap too. A bonus considering my financial situation. Funny to break it down by the hours I worked to buy a whole chicken as opposed to steak. Prison wages ain't steak wages. I could get more than one meal out of this bird and start feeling like I was trying make a life again. I'd never cooked very much before my arrest, and this seemed a good way to mark the old me from the new me. A prison therapist said I needed to realize the boy I was is dead and grieve for him and move on, find a new way of being in the world. I put the chicken in the basket and swung back to produce to get a lemon and some potatoes to roast with it. My mom and grandma used to say a little butter and salt and pepper and I'd have a delicious dinner. *Oh, butter.* I headed back to dairy.

I arrived at the cashier. A black-haired woman, deeply tanned and lined, with the voice of a late-night prank caller asked me, "How's your day, hon?" A sweet, displaced Southern woman smacking her vivid cotton candy-colored lips as she blinked turquoise hooded eyes.

"Fine. It's a nice day out." What else to say on the first day of quasi-freedom and all the hope of a supermarket?

"It is at that. I hope the weather holds," she said.

I saw the *Las Vegas Review Journal*, so grabbed one and tossed it on the conveyor belt.

She added it to the tally. I counted out the money to her. I only had about 300 bucks saved from my 17-cent-an-hour prison job, so I only bought a few things to get through a couple of days.

At the halfway house, Mrs. Gutiérrez searched my grocery bag for contraband booze, dope, and porn magazines. "Look at this," she said to Ms. Randall. They eyeballed the chicken and then me.

Mrs. Gutiérrez said, "Under cooked chicken will kill you in a bad way."

"It's a backup. Frozen pizza can be tricky." I smiled as they looked to each other and grinned knowing grins of cooks who knew.

Ms. Randall said, "You got any questions about cooking that hen, let me know."

I smiled. "Thanks. I will."

Mrs. Gutiérrez waved me through with a flip of her hair, and on the desk, her nails clacked and flashed.

Back in the apartment, I pre-heated the oven to 550 degrees as I knew chicken must be cooked to a high temperature. It was still the afternoon, but I was hungry, so might as well cook an early dinner. There was no one telling me when I could and couldn't eat. After cutting up the potatoes and putting them in a beat-up roasting pan, I put the chicken on top. I rubbed butter, salt, and pepper on the outside and then quartered the lemon and stuffed it into the chest cavity. Carefully, I slid the pan into the oven. I looked at the clock and wondered how long I needed but remembered my mom saying it took a long time, so an hour felt right.

I started looking through the classifieds for jobs. I was qualified to be an EMT, a security guard, an armor crewman, a fast-food cook, and a construction worker. Only two of those jobs would possibly hire me at this moment in my life. After my arrest, the feds and the news media made me out to be a worse guy than I really was, but the crime needed an arch-villain. It was the mid-1980s, and it was all about looking like *Miami Vice*, even in Vegas, and putting away super bad guys even if the real bad guys slipped through. Appearances were exaggerated for dramatic effect on the news and in court just like television, and who cared? I wanted to put it behind me, move on from the eternal present prisoners live in, and make something of my life. Right now, I needed a job.

I planned to go to the union hall for electricians tomorrow morning to see if I could get on as an apprentice. At Boron, I worked as an electrician, so thought I had a shot at it.

I circled a few warehouse jobs, some ads for construction laborers, and as I contemplated how tomorrow would play out, the smoke detector startled me with its high-pitched alarm. Smoke rolled out of the oven. I opened the oven door. I grabbed a dish towel and the only oven mitt to lift the pan out and set it on the stove. I burned my fingers.

The front door opened, and Ms. Randall waved the smoke out of her face. She saw me standing over the stove, staring at the smoldering chicken. "I said you could ask for help."

"I thought I had it dialed in."

She grinned. She noticed me shaking my burnt hand. "Run those under some cold water."

She opened the freezer and got an ice tray and knocked some cubes onto a dish towel. She folded it up and handed it to me.

"Thanks."

"Mmmhmmm," she said.

When I sliced the chicken open, the inside still had ice crystals. How did I manage to make the outside charcoal, while the inside remained glacial? My mom and grandma might've had a remark or two about this.

Ms. Randall said with a smile, "You didn't already ruin the frozen pizza, did you?"

"Got me with my own joke."

With a box fan, most of the smoke was sucked out of the apartment. Ms. Randall headed back to the office as I prepped the pizza. No one else had come in. My roommate might've still been working or hanging out as he didn't have to be in until later. I wondered who he was. Living with strangers exhausted me. At least I didn't think my new roomie would stab me in my sleep. The timer dinged, and I got the pizza. A little doughy, but it wouldn't kill me.

Still daylight, I could leave and go out and walk around the neighborhood, but I sat on the couch, staring at the cracked wall. Where was there to go in this fucking city that wouldn't get me into trouble with a hooker and cheap drinks? It was a simple thing to say, Don't cave into your desires, but quite another when faced with a woman in a low-cut top and miniskirt as your hard-on jumped to attention. It was something I didn't want to test. No, not today, this evening, my first day out.

I didn't even bother to turn on the TV. The noise of the city remained muffled outside the wall, distant like someone watching a movie in the back room. Canned noise for all I knew. Exhaustion crept over me. My body felt it had traveled from the Mountains of the Moon. Gone from the present into the deep past through the deserts of my youth and back into the present. My future was out there, and I'd traveled there in my mind, trying to see what may come, but, like death, could not see past the room. I needed to find someone to hire me. I needed to defend myself in front of a court-martial from the Guard. One of my hopes was not to be discharged, to be given the chance to show I wasn't a criminal, that covering up for a friend stealing an automatic weapon and getting rid of it was only an error in judgment. I could be trusted. I was not crazy like the judge thought when he sentenced me to get psychological counseling.

Hours passed, and darkness filled the neighborhood as I sat and stared at the crack in the wall. A car engine revved, and tires squealed, and I realized I was waiting to be told to go to bed. Lights out, fuckers. Go to sleep.

Most of the smoke had dissipated, but I still smelled it along with the dish soap I squirted onto a sponge to wash the plate and knife. I didn't want to be a bad roommate. Funny, this morning I wasn't trusted with a knife. Somewhere down the street, I heard tires squeal and laughter. It was the kind of laughter kids make where you can't tell if they're happy or terrified. Maybe they were both.

I looked out the window. A porch light burned over each door like lights from watchtowers. The curtains on some windows glowed and flickered with the light of televisions. The big poplar trees loomed into the darkness. The wall with the wrought iron gates blocked the view to the street. The administrative office had the lights on, and no doubt someone was doing the paperwork of punishment. A stray dog appeared as it slivered through the wrought iron bars. It sniffed around the closest tree and lifted its leg and pissed. I let the curtain drop and sat on the couch.

For a long time, people and guards had surrounded me. I'd grown up in a big family and, after, had roommates and friends, went to basic training and lived in barracks, then married. Lynne and I always had someone over or were always over at someone else's place or out doing something in the Vegas thrum and hum of rock concerts and wandering the bells and hoots of carnival barkers calling from the entrances of casinos.

I hadn't been physically alone for a long time. Not, it seemed, since being a boy hiking by myself in the deserts where we lived at whatever mine where my dad had found a job or when we lived in tents for over a year as we tried to build a house from mud and rock in the southeast Arizona desert. I climbed for the tops of wind-whistling ridges or switch-backed down into ravines, looking for water and meaning. Sometimes I wandered in hopes of discovering something new to science or an archeological find, and other times, I hoped to uncover the sacred and divine. There was one place in the shadow of the Chiricahua Mountains where I'd hike to a particular mesquite bush around sunrise to see if a desert tortoise always used a specific path. It did. Had I, alone in the squinting sun, seen the divine in science and science in the divine?

In my childhood deserts, I discovered a meaning in nature. I was a conduit feeling the energy of the universe course through me, and I felt like a piece of the big puzzle and not a meaningless speck. Through my teen years, I struggled with the despair of my own uselessness on and off again, but I always managed to make it back to that feeling of being alive in the world. In the desert prison, though, I sank further into a darkness and lost sight of any sun. The Buddhist heroin smuggler who was teaching some of us to meditate told us the parable of a man seeking enlightenment who was sent up a mountain by a monk.

> 'Climb to the top and back down. You must not kill anything on the slopes of the mountain.' On his journey, a powerful storm beset and trapped him. He resisted his growing hunger and kept climbing, but another storm delayed him. Ravenous, he spied an old and feeble rat, which he killed and ate. The man made it to the top of the mountain and back down to the valley. Upon his return, he was surprised to find the village washed away from a landslide. As he made his way through the wreckage, he came upon the monk. 'You killed a rat on the mountain,' the monk said. The man looked surprised. 'Yes, I was starving, and it was only one old and feeble rat.' The monk shook his head. 'The rat was digging under a tree, slow and steady. The tree would've fallen and caught the first stones of the landslide, stopping it from gathering force and washing away the village. There is no insignificant life.'

But I felt parables were stories to make people feel their convictions are true. People are suckers for a story that gives meaning to their beliefs, even if it proves nothing.

Later, as I pondered the smuggler's Mount Futility story, I understood that if all life is significant, then the man's life was also significant, even as he spread death on his quest of best intentions. I might not be insignificant, but that doesn't mean I'm a good person. It doesn't mean I'm a bad person either.

On the couch in the halfway house, I thought about starting over, creating a new me at twenty-three that didn't carry the scar tissue of a felon or the scent of madness I felt clinging to me. Could I convince others to give me a chance? I got up and looked out the window again.

I wondered at the city out there I used to know, wondered who might be wandering the streets beyond the gate and what stranger might be coming in the door. I was already in the company of one stranger. Me. For this moment, I was as alone as I'd never been, even in the solitude of the wilderness with the wind through arroyos like the muted traffic beyond the apartment walls. That wasn't a bad way to feel. I started to feel a little of that old desert magic in the air.

I went to the kitchen for a glass of water. The oven still gave off heat. I looked at the charred carcass in the garbage and wondered if I'd ever master the art of baking a whole chicken.

In the morning of my first full day at the halfway house, I woke up early and got ready for the count before I realized where I was. I laughed at myself and went to get ready for the day.

Hair scabbed the bathroom sink. It wasn't mine, but I cleaned it and the bathtub. I showered, shaved, and combed my hair, hoping I looked hirable. In the mirror, I noticed a patch of hair on my neck and scraped it with the razor.

I regarded the mirror. My too tight US Army T-shirt made me feel uncomfortable and self-conscious. At least my pants weren't high-water, making me look like a total hick. I thought about what I wanted to say. How was I going to tell my story so I didn't sound like an unrepentant criminal or someone claiming false innocence? I'd see how it went. My plan was not to volunteer too much information, just what they asked.

I walked from the apartment across the courtyard to the office by the wrought iron gate. Mrs. Gutiérrez sat clacking her fingernails on the desk. Behind her, Mr. Lopez sorted through files at the cabinet. As I signed out, Mrs. Gutiérrez said, "Remember: no drinking or drugs, stay out of bars and casinos, and don't think you can just leave town to visit a brothel. You will be drug tested if I think you've been visiting those boys up the street dealing dope. You will be written up and sent back to the penitentiary, and you will serve out your full sentence. I will personally make sure additional charges will be brought if I catch you with illegal contraband."

Mr. Lopez rolled his eyes with a mocking grin of solidarity.

She continued. "Do you understand me?"

"Yes, ma'am," I said. She nodded and turned to her paperwork.

Without transportation, I walked out of the run-down neighborhood to a busy street and hitchhiked. An old guy in a big Buick stopped, and I got in. He asked, "Where to?" and I told him I was headed to the electricians' union hall. He pulled into traffic and asked if I'd rather get some beer and watch pornos at his place. I said no thanks. He nodded as if he understood and offered me a hundred dollars. I said no. He pulled the car over and told me, "Get the fuck out." My first morning in Vegas and I was already mistaken for a prostitute.

It was midmorning when I finally walked into the hall. It looked like a community center with a counter and desks. I walked up to a receptionist. The nameplate on her desk read Penelope. She had spiked dark hair and a round body swathed in a brown dress, so she looked like a pineapple. "Hi, I was wondering what I needed to do to become an apprentice?"

"Who do you work for?"

"I don't. I'm looking for a job."

"Do you have a referral from someone in the union?"

"I don't know anybody."

"What kind of electrical work have you done before?"

"I was an assistant electrician at a federal prison. I helped rewire old barracks, did routine maintenance, and helped with new electric projects."

"What company was that for?"

"For the prison itself." I looked away and back to her.

She sat back in her chair, eyes narrowing. It squeaked as her weight shifted. The sharp noise cut through the background chatter like when somebody next to you at a party drops a glass and everyone looks in your direction.

"What do you mean *for* the prison?"

I felt like I sat in front of a detective who knew everything and was waiting for me to lie so she could pummel the shit out of me with perjury.

"I was an inmate."

She tapped her foot as she measured me with her gaze, reconciling the all-American boy in his too tight shirt across from her with what might be a hardened criminal poised to attack her and take her valuables and virtue. "For what?" she asked.

"Possession of an unregistered firearm."

A smile crept across her face, then, perplexed, she asked, "That's not a crime, is it?"

I managed a weak smile. "It is," I said but didn't volunteer more.

She laughed as she said, "A bunch of us here could get arrested for that."

I nodded in a small way as if she was right, and she probably was. I'd known several survivalists I'd worked with before my arrest who had weapons that might not have passed legal muster.

She handed me a form. "Fill this out and turn it in, and if something comes up, we'll call."

I took the forms and got up to go to a table.

"Hey," she said as I began to turn away.

I stopped.

"You were that guy on TV a couple of years ago. That soldier who got busted with a machine gun."

The air left me through the soles of my feet. "Yeah."

"I thought I recognized that T-shirt. I'd never seen one with an eagle like that before. That was a big to do. Well, you're back now."

"Trying." I tried to measure the timbre of her words, figuring I'd be the subject of a bit of light gossip later.

I filled out the forms. I rushed, and my penmanship worsened the harder I tried to make it neat. Sweat formed on my brow, and it seemed all the body heat in the room swirled around me. I breathed in through my nose into my abdomen to steady my nerves. I felt like everyone was staring at me, and I wanted to get out of there. I finished and gave them to her. She smiled and told me to have a good day.

I smiled back.

By the time I got to my next stop, the unemployment office, on the bus, it was after lunch. The clock ticked as I stood in the long lines waiting on a number to be called, and then I sat in a plastic chair at the edge of a desk. A big Black woman in a flower print dress typed my information. I worried about how late it was getting and the distance I needed to travel to get back to the halfway house.

The nameplate on her desk read Mrs. Williams. I was ineligible for unemployment as I hadn't worked outside of the prison system in a couple of years and because I was fired from my jobs for no call-no show when I was arrested. "No worries. I just want to be able to access the list and apply for jobs," I told her.

"Not much call for gun-running electrician's assistants," she said.

I sat up straighter, not sure what to say. I flashed back to another wooden chair in another government building. Fucking-shit-yourself surreal, like being on a television show you'd seen a hundred times, but not. No script of dialogue came close to teaching you the finer points of law that will be used against you. Nothing in my experience had prepared me for it, so my mind went into survival mode and started fixing on the physical sensations. The shuffling of feet and papers and desk drawers opening and closing. The smell of cigarettes, aftershave, and floor wax. The steel of cuffs and a hard wood chair I was chained to as the agents hovered around me in their department store suits like minor demons bathed in those damned fluorescent lights, waiting for me to exhale my last breath.

The BATF agents reminded me I had the right to remain silent, but not the right to make shit up. This wasn't story-fucking-time. "You want an attorney, fine, but you need to remember, boy, you're on tape and an attorney can't erase a tape. Ask Nixon, asshole. Those friends, ha, those friends of friends. Wires, asshole. Wires. Keep it up. We got enough on you for 80 years, and what do you have to bargain with? Theft, possession, interstate transport, and selling a fucking automatic weapon, dipshit. You're not even old enough to drink. What are you going to do with your life now? Send him to fucking county." I tried to wipe my brow, but my hands were cuffed to my waist. All I did was clink against the wooden chair, feeling as if I were sitting in the principal's office about to be expelled from life.

Mrs. Williams smiled. "I'm just messing with you. You need to loosen up. Part of your problem is you're too tense. Just relax. You can't be talking with people and acting like you already didn't get the job or acting like you're so ashamed you can barely talk." She sipped from a can of Dr. Pepper and set the can back on a stack of official-looking papers. "I can't get you money. But I will help to get you a job if there's one out there for you."

I smiled. "I just want a chance to prove I'm a good worker and can be trusted."

"I know." She patted my hand.

This hadn't taken as long as I'd feared. I checked my time and tried to figure out how far it was to the DMV. I needed to renew my license even if my motorcycle didn't run and I didn't own a car. I walked out to the street and stuck my thumb out. I thought I could get there and done before midafternoon.

As I waited in the longest line I'd been in since the last time I went to the DMV, my stomach started growling. The curse of institutional life was scheduled mealtimes. Eat now or starve, even if you aren't hungry. Some guys bought snacks and cups of soup and kept them in their cells to eat during the afternoon or after dinner. I didn't have the money for it, so abided by the feeding schedule of the State. Hunger, though, felt like freedom even as I was imprisoned in the DMV line for another fifty minutes.

My license renewal didn't require a test or anything except a new photo and address update. I used my cousin Binder's as he lived not too far from the halfway house. When I became eligible for weekend passes, I hoped to use his place as well as Mike and Joan's, some friends of my parents who were closer to the middle of the city and had a camper I could crash in. At Binder's, I'd have a room in his double-wide trailer, but it was a long way from anything.

I thanked the lady behind the counter after they snapped my photo. She smiled back as if relieved for a change. I looked back at the people in the maze winding behind me and back to her. "Good luck with the rest of your day."

She gave me an eyeroll and said, "Thanks."

A cluster of fast-food joints weren't too far from the DMV, so I walked to the closest one and got a cheeseburger and fries. I felt odd sitting in the place, with its plastic chairs and tables and garish colors designed to get you out of there. Hurry up and eat and get the fuck out; you're interfering with our profit margin. There was also a kind of loneliness about this generic anywhere place and me alone watching others who turned in on themselves to eat even if they were with others. But for the lone diner, sitting with an assembly line meal made the same here as anywhere in the world, it felt especially weird. Last night, I'd eaten alone in an apartment that wasn't mine. Yesterday's lunch was with my remarried ex-wife, waited on by a displaced Southern woman, and yesterday's breakfast was in a prison dining hall with the clatter and noise of men chatting and getting ready for their day that was just like the day before unless they were being released, and then they were looking into the unknown—a day like no other.

Some old men sat together drinking coffee out of throwaway cups and smoking cigarettes. During those years, Vegas was a great place to be old, better than Florida or Arizona and especially California. No other place offers the dry heat, cheap drinks and food, and the miles of casinos and shows going on every night. Plus, they can get lost among the gamblers joined in the cause of losing to the house, hoping they were the outlier, the winner. In later years, we watched it become a garish, immoral theme park in its bid to be kid-friendly and attract families to burn through college funds. It became expensive. A buffet that used to cost five bucks shot up to fifty. 50-cent imports and dollar well drinks became more expensive than a California beachside resort. Old Vegas ghosts still say things were better when the Mob ran the town. They understood how hospitality worked and made people feel like they were getting a deal while fleecing them.

Even so, the old men reminded me of other old men in cafes in all the small towns I'd been around growing up. Old men gathered at corner tables with actual coffee cups that a waitress would swing by and refill instead of having to go to the counter to get topped off by someone in a polyester uniform color-coordinated to the restaurant. They'd disparage politicians and environmentalists and hippies and talk about how things ought to be and how great things were back in their day.

At the cafe in Desert Center, I got to know some of the old guys—now I realize they were anywhere between 30 and 80. They all seemed stuck in a loop of pat answers to any news story. One guy they called the Philosopher. I never heard him say anything profound, so chalked it up to my own ignorance. His catch phrase was, "What most people don't understand is..." Then he'd launch off into some opinion that didn't seem secret enough that most people wouldn't understand. Later, I'd wonder if he was like the knight in *Monty Python and the Holy Grail* whose wisdom was talking with confidence and using questions to lead the others to false answers, no matter how absurd, but feel they'd arrived at them on their own. My dad always argued with people or spun stories that made his point. He had an easy-going manner, and it wasn't hard to understand why his CB handle was Storyteller.

Eating in the fast-food place, I thought about dishwashing and looking for something in a casino/restaurant or at a cafe. I'd worked in fast-food places before basic training and right after until I started working construction and then night security. I knew I couldn't get a security guard job, but maybe something else in construction if the electrician's union didn't work out. I'd been a hod carrier the summer before my arrest for a company owned by the father of a friend in my unit I'd gone to basic training with. The hod was a V-shaped trough, like a wheelbarrow, except this was mounted on a pole. I carried the wet plaster in the hod on my shoulder from the mixer to where the plasterers were spreading it on lathe or cement blocks. When it dried, it became the stucco sides of the building. It paid well enough, but the intense heat and lime that burned my skin made it a trial every day to climb up and down the scaffolding carrying the 94-pound hod over my shoulder. I trotted all day as the boss didn't want to hear the plasterers calling out for "mud" because I was too slow. I rolled my shoulders at the thought of it.

I stared at the plastic tray with the wadded-up food wrappers and paper cup. My hunger was gone, but my stomach felt upset. The air-conditioning had cooled me and evaporated my sweat. I looked outside as I contemplated heading back into the afternoon furnace. The air on the sidewalk and street swirled with heat and exhaust. If I didn't catch a ride, it'd take almost two hours to walk back to the halfway house.

Fatigue crept over me. I wanted to lay down like I did when I was boy after hiking. At several places we lived, I'd stumble onto old homesteads that had been built on flat stretches of ground close to creeks. Always, the houses, barns, and outbuildings were collapsing, leaning hard with the wind or just falling apart by slow degrees.

One place, down by where we tried to make our homestead, had a huge barn of wood that had grayed under the sun and sand and monsoon rains that howled up from Mexico out of the South Pacific during the summer. Once in a while, an owl flew out from where the hay door under the barn's gable had been. I'd always wondered what had happened to the people who'd settled here and then left. Maybe too many disease deaths of children or a drought that killed the cattle or marauders slipping through with murderous intent? Johnny Ringo, the famous outlaw, had been buried not too far from there, and Geronimo had surrendered just over the mountains. Most likely, though, it was something as prosaic as a banker with the sheriff and a foreclosure notice—the great destroyers of homesteads and lives in America. To me, the land held both melancholy and hope. I wondered how much sweat the earth had absorbed before the tears came and the abandonment of the place once a home.

Now all I wanted was to be under those white oak trees and cottonwoods along a desert creek where the breeze clattered the branches in time to the sound of shallow water over stones, but I got up and made my way into the sweltering street.

Ms. Randall watched as I signed in, trying not to drip sweat on the paper. "Tough day?" she asked.

I nodded. "At least I got things rolling."

In the apartment, I stood in front of the fan, letting the blown air dry me and thinking about boiling some noodles and heating canned spaghetti sauce. Nothing so difficult as a baked chicken. Late sunlight streamed in between the gaps of the curtain. Motes of dust swirled in the light, pushed by air currents. I closed my eyes and watched the orange-reddish screen of my eyelids and the static of corpuscles tracing around not so unlike the motes of dust. I breathed deep the scent of worn carpeting, old furniture fabric, the trace odors of thousands of meals past, and the traces of cleanser and the fake lemon of disinfectant. The fan swept up everything in the air and washed it over me.

Lost for a moment in this place, I blended into space as if nothing existed beyond the walls or even beyond my sensations. Just me and my fatigue in a stream of air. In basic training, sometimes some of us would fall asleep while in formation. The drill sergeants had us formed up under the lights on the parade deck before dawn. The darkness of the forest beyond our barracks repelled the light as we waited for our next command. The power of fatigue. The struggle to keep my eyes open. The fading in and out of consciousness while alert. One recruit fell to the deck and scrambled to his feet as the drill sergeants yelled at him, their voices all the blunt force trauma needed to break us of our lazy, civilian ways. Sometimes, on the edge of sleep, I heard voices far off, like people talking or my mom calling me in from the desert. Even now in front of the fan, under the motor's whir, I thought I heard my dad's voice calling me with unintelligible words. I swayed like I did in formations, keeping my feet in the trance. The voice of my dad called out again. Closer, not so far away, but the name was not my given name. My nickname from prison. A name my dad wouldn't know. The weight of it snapped my eyes open. I realized someone was calling me from the courtyard outside. I turned away from the rush of wind in my face and looked out the window.

Out in the courtyard, Captain struck the very image of a fighter pilot on leave—aviator sunglasses, blue jeans, loose button-up denim shirt, and a harlequin Great Dane at his side. I first met Captain at Boron. He had misappropriated some military supplies in the name of freedom and the free market economy. "Hell," he'd say, "my tax dollars have been wasted by the Pentagon. I should be allowed to see some kind of return." A dashing former jet aviator, he knew the ins and outs of street life on four continents.

Together, we'd pulled off the great guacamole escapade. There was no stress like waiting for the avocados to ripen so you could make and eat guacamole before other inmates found out, much less the guards. Not that it was especially illegal, except for smuggled avocados, but cons would have wanted some to keep quiet and the guards because they were in charge. Captain had said, "That's not a fair bribe by any standards of human conduct."

His voice boomed as if talking over jet noise on the flight line. He called out, "I have it on good authority you are here, New Guy."

He saw me in the window and pointed at me. I dropped the curtain and opened the door. A smile lit his face as he walked across the halfway house courtyard.

Someone had a television blaring away.

"Get on over here, you flown felon, and let me see you in better light."

I had no idea what he had planned. He'd already been out a couple of months and had a month left in the halfway house, but he spent most of his time out on jobs, and his weekends were occupied with a showgirl he sort of lived with and, as he liked to say, "tousled with."

He grabbed my shoulders and squared me up. "You still looking fit, friend."

His dog sniffed around a patch of grass, circling, and then took a huge dump on the lawn. He looked. "Ah, hell, I don't know whether to clean it up or put cones around it."

He turned back to me and said, "Been working out?"

I laughed.

"Got a line on work yet?"

"The whole prison thing seems to be hindering me."

"Oh, hell, New Guy. Just tell people you lived and worked in a gated community."

I laughed and petted the dog.

"Now go to your room and wait," he said.

"For what?" I asked.

"You're a bright boy, son. I got a hunch you'll figure it out."

I went off to my room, and the next thing I knew, someone tapped at the window of my bedroom. A woman circled her face with her hands against the window, peering in to see. I opened the window.

"Help me in," she said. I held out my hands and helped her as she scrambled into my room. She scraped her arm on the windowsill and knocked over a lamp, but I caught it before it hit the floor. "You New Guy?"

"Yeah?"

She pulled off her top, exposing sunburned breasts, and started sliding off her jeans. "Careful. I'm a little tender." Her jeans hit the floor. I wondered for a moment if this was some prank. Captain had a way of getting people on the wrong side of funny so everyone else could get a laugh, but my brain shorted out in the presence of the now naked woman.

She put her hands on her hips like a surly server aggravated with a customer who couldn't figure out what to order. "What are you waiting for? Get them off."

I looked over my shoulder at the open bedroom door, wondering if Ms. Randall or Mrs. Gutiérrez were in the office or just out front or if Captain and a bunch of cons were about to rush in to snap my photo for posterity.

She climbed onto the bed.

I stood stunned.

"Now," she demanded.

I looked at her, and I was hard and couldn't think of anything else but her.

Still the good soldier, I did as I was ordered. I started to think I'd hallucinated this beautiful, sunburned woman into my room, still standing in the wash of the fan. But there she was, stretched out like some Parisian odalisque. I climbed onto her, and in seconds, it felt like, she'd dressed and asked to sneak out the front instead of going back out the window.

"What? You can't go out the front. They'll see you."

"Come on, man. I already scraped up my arm." She held up her arm and it was hard to tell the sunburn from the scrape. "Shit, I might fall on my head on the way out."

I looked out the bedroom door. "I could get busted and sent back."

"No, you won't. I'll be fast. Like a cat."

I relented, still flush and dizzy in her presence. How could I say no? "Let me double check the front. Be ready."

I peered out of the apartment door. Captain and some of the others grinned at me from the courtyard. I waved him over. When I told him what she wanted, he nodded and motioned to wait a moment. "Get her to the front door."

I went back in and told her to wait until Captain gave us the go ahead.

Captain looked to the office, then signaled. The woman looked out. Captain said, "Time to go, Bridgette." She smiled and gave him a quick kiss on the cheek as she fast-walked past him and out the gate.

Like a magic act, Mrs. Gutiérrez materialized in front of the office door just as Bridgette exited the gate. Angry, Mrs. Gutiérrez rushed to the gate and onto the street, but Bridgette had already vanished. She canvassed all of us with threats of sending us all back to prison, but none of us admitted to even seeing another woman. Her face flushed, and she pinched her lips together to stop the trembling. Her eyes squinted when she was finally able to speak, and she said, "Where did that woman come from?" She placed her hands on her hips, and I thought of nesting dolls. "I saw a woman leave here."

Captain looked perplexed and motioned around as he said, "What woman, Mrs. Gutiérrez? I didn't see no woman. Did any of you boys see a woman?"

"Only you, ma'am," someone said.

Once, a Hell's Angel joked to me in prison, "Three can keep a secret if two are dead." Turned out, more than one person can keep a secret.

After returning to the halfway house before curfew, I made my dinner of mac and cheese and hotdogs. It'd been another futile day of job searches, so I went through that day's newspaper's classified ads, circling some prospects at a warehouse and some construction companies. I folded the paper and put it in my daypack, ready for tomorrow, and sat on the couch. The Vegas summer heat left me beat. Outside, a single gunshot echoed. Some cars sped down the street and a helicopter slow-thumped over the neighborhood.

Not allowed to leave before morning, I thought about watching television. I hadn't watched much in prison, choosing to avoid the television rooms and the crowded darkness most demanded as they booed Crocket and Tubbs on *Miami Vice* or oohed and aahed the *Dynasty* divas. I didn't care for sitting in common rooms in military barracks either. I stared at the blank tube. I didn't know what to watch now and didn't care.

I grew up without a lot of television for months and months when we lived on the road between layoffs or in the desert for a year and a half when my parents decided to make the homestead in the desert. I spent most of my time reading or out in the desert.

My mom taught me to read when my dad was away at the Vietnam War. She always took us to the library no matter where we lived. I had a photo taken of me in the library for a local paper when I was a little kid, maybe the second grade. We always had books around, and my dad had once converted the front room into a study that he lined with bookcases, a gun case he'd built himself, and an enormous desk with his CB radio. Most of the books were novels about spy stories, mysteries, thrillers, westerns like the movies we watched, science fiction, adventures, and war. But when I was in the fourth grade, books on geology and gold chasing and legends of the Old West appeared.

About that time, we started camping in Oak Creek Canyon, where we sluiced the hell out of a stretch of creek and swirled gold pans like potters sitting over their spinning clay. Dad drove my mom, two little brothers, sister, and me up to the mountains. We were joined by my mom and dad's friends, Tom and Emily, and their four-year-old daughter who was the same age as my sister. The cars were rigged for camping American style. We dug and sweated and waded in the stinging cold water of the mountain creek. We kids believed we knew the weight of adult work. We lived beautiful, hazy days of wearing our bodies out in work and playing and sleeping on the ground with the sharp tang of night in our mouths. We weren't just reading stories; we were inhabiting them.

But this changed. One dark morning in the late summer before I started the fifth grade, my dad woke me. I got dressed and gathered my gear while my younger brothers and sister slept. We left the quiet house and met Tom in his driveway. We climbed into his pickup truck and rattled out of Gilbert, Arizona for the Superstition Mountains. I sat between the men and nodded off and snapped awake as we rolled through the dark.

At some turnout along a gravel road in the foothills of the Superstitions, we parked. My dad gave me a bear claw pastry and a half-pint carton of milk. I ate quickly, then clipped on a USMC web utility belt with an old metal Army canteen and a newer plastic one. I shouldered an old USMC surplus pack holding a camp knife the size of a model train car with a fork and spoon on each side, a folding shovel, cans of fruit cocktail and Vienna sausages, rope, a compass, plus the tools of the prospector: rock hammer, magnifying glass, gold pan, magnet, and whatever extra gear my dad wanted to stuff in there.

Each of the men had on a Stetson, wore a pack and a canteen, had strapped on revolvers and knives, and carried shotguns. I carried my single-pump BB gun rifle. More for appearances, I supposed. What good would it be in a gunfight with armed bandits? Shoot for the eyes? We began hiking in the dark. It felt cool and silent like a cathedral my friend Pablo had taken me into. The sound of kicked stones seemed to break the holy silence with a crack. I hustled to keep up. We needed to be at a specific spot at sunrise to watch for a beam of sunlight to shine through a stone arch and light a spot on the side of Weaver's Needle, marking a mine entrance—bright and fleeting in a dry land like cactus blossoms.

We were on the hunt for lost gold. Several different stories seemed to come to a point in those mountains. We had read of Álvar Núñez Cabeza de Vaca's shipwreck in 1527 and his escape from enslavement by the Native American tribes in the area around what is now Galveston, Texas until he finally made it back to Spanish-controlled Mexico in 1536. During his travels among the Native American tribes, he became a healer and a shaman as well as a trader as he traversed the American Southwest. Among the stories he told when he returned to Mexico City, one was about seven fabulous cities made of gold.

A few years later in 1539, on an expedition, Fray Marcos de Niza reported seeing one of the Seven Cities of Gold called Cíbola. This prompted Francisco Vázquez de Coronado to lead an expedition in search of all this fantastic treasure. There was also the legend about Portuguese bishops who founded the Seven Cities of Gold after fleeing their lost war with the Moors. It was said they retreated west across the Atlantic with sacred treasures to keep them from the Muslims who'd conquered most of the Iberian Peninsula. Somehow, they hid the treasure around the American Southwest, including the Superstition Mountains. They had left secret markings, like Catholic hieroglyphs, revealing trails leading to sacred artifacts, gem-encrusted gold crosses, goblets, jewelry, coins, idols, utensils, plates, and ingots molded in ancient gold smithies. Some of the men my dad knew said the Spanish had missed something in that wilderness. The dates seemed a little incredulous, but who wanted to be the buzz kill on a great adventure story? Certainly not the fifth grader.

My dad was most intrigued by the Lost Dutchman's Mine. When Spain still controlled the region, Don Miguel Peralta found a gold vein sometime after 1748 on the northern edge of his Church Grant lands. The Apache said the Thunder God had put the gold in the mountains for the tribe to use only in times of need and massacred the Peralta family. In the 19th century, Jacob "The Dutchman" Walz arrived in the area and took an Apache wife. She led him to the gold mine, and her tribe killed her for revealing the secret. When Walz died in 1891, no one knew for certain where the mine was, but he told the woman taking care of him some vague directions involving Weaver's Needle.

Enough gold dust had turned up on burros wandering ownerless out of the wilderness to make my dad confident that some twisted arroyo hid the Lost Dutchman Mine. Rumors of maps and hoaxes of stones showing the way filled the legend, but some claimed they could find it. But wasn't that the hope of all treasure seekers? To chase the clues like salvation and discover the trail to riches others had missed? I marveled at how a range of mountains we could see from our backyard held so much mystery. My dad often said, "The desert's so full of legends. Something's bound to be out there."

We three hiked just below ridgelines so as not to skyline ourselves against the bright stars. My dad had a map and set the course. We spread out in a line with me bringing up the rear. I was charged with looking back every so often to make sure no one followed us. I had not yet heard the myth that rattlesnakes strike the third person passing on the trail.

Both experienced woodsmen, hunters, and veterans of Vietnam, they moved with purpose. I did my best to keep up. Dressed as they were, they looked as if they'd ridden off the range in the westerns we'd watched or in the books we'd read. My dad had the tanned, rugged face of a working-class man, with hands as big as my head. He loomed over everything in my childhood. I saw him ride a bucking bronc in my uncle's backyard, and he'd taken me dove and quail hunting with Tom. Put a cowboy hat on him and guns in his hands and I believed he'd be the last man standing at a besieged outpost or pursue you across the plains until you'd dig your own grave just to get some relief.

After a couple of hours, we laid up behind a rock cairn. False dawn crept over the horizon, erasing the stars from the sky. My sweat cooled, and I shivered. We waited in the gray land as small animals rustled in the brush down the slope from us. This was the first time I'd been awake out in the wild, waiting for the sun, and not asleep in a tent with my brothers. Sitting out there struck some primitive pulse in me. This was how, for centuries, fathers introduced their sons into the world of men, teaching them how to survive and be in the wild.

I yawned on the hillside. I felt a little more grown-up. I had gone to sleep a kid, and now I was a partner, trusted with the secret of a fortune. I also had this sense of danger I hadn't known before. The anticipation beat in my chest. I scanned the arroyos and ridgelines as I watched Weaver's Needle for others who might be watching us. I wanted someone to be out there so I could spot them and alert the men. It felt like we were three desperados hunkered down in the brush, waiting for the sun to reveal a fortune.

I'd read that before us, the Mexicans ruled here, and they had fought and defeated Spain. The Spanish had marched north to claim the place and overlapped with the nomadic Apache who fell upon the Pima, the

Sinagua, and Hohokam. The Comanches migrated from the northern plains, looking for new homelands in the Southwest in the 18th and 19th centuries. They waged war and pushed out the Mescalero, Jicarilla, and Lipan Apaches and other tribes from the southern plains until they created the Comancheria. From there, they raided Anglo settlers, Tejanos, the Spanish, and other Native tribes, taking thousands of captives for slaves to be traded or kept. Then came the push of American settlers streaming into the West with their armies to wrench the land from anyone who lived on it. My head swam with the stories of all these peoples, all this violence spread over the deserts. Whoever won the last war claimed everything within the range of their warriors and armies. For us, we all believed lost treasure belonged to whoever found its location.

I'd read that during the California Gold Rush, men streamed westward or sailed around the Cape, lured by the fantasy of nuggets as big as your fist or some other tale of easily-grabbed riches. In the stories I learned, most of the fortune seekers arrived too late. All the good claims were gone. The only diggings left were harder to reach in harder to work areas with deposits so scant of gold that they were measured in how many fractions of ounces you could get per ton of rock crushed. It didn't register with me that what we sought had already been found and spirited off or was just some drunk's barroom story. The stories of sudden wealth, of lost claims, and maps of hidden stashes of gold got our blood pumping. More than the adventure and wealth, though, we would write our names into the epic tale. We would be the last chapter.

I was told a story about the Spanish conquest. For years, I'd believed it'd taken place in North America but was a tale from South America. How myths change with the retelling. The Spanish heard about the golden man. They believed him to be made of actual gold. But as stories go, yes and no… Priests prepared a mixture of gold dust. After the ritual prayers and offerings, they painted the new chief with the holy mixture. Gold flakes glittered even in the shadows and shimmered a halo around his body in the sun, a divine flame. The legend was that he dove from a raft, but I heard once that he walked to a bluff above the edge of a sacred lake. How long did he stand there, and who else stood with him? What eyes from the surrounding forests spied the strange apparition of another world? Did the man tremble with anticipation before his holy dive? Did the wind ruffle the water's surface as he arced through the air before slicing his reflection? For a few seconds, he occupied two worlds as the concentric circles rippled for the shore. He journeyed from one world to the other. In that fraction of a held breath, the gold dust washed away, leaving an ordinary man to emerge cleansed.

Coronado found the Zuni village of Hawikuh that Fray Marcos de Niza had believed was Cíbola. Fray Marcos's scout, Estevanico, had been killed there, forcing Fray Marcos to retreat to New Spain without ever coming close to the village. When the Spanish saw the pueblos were made of earth and stone and not the precious metal, they became enraged. The conquistadors razed the village and murdered the people in their anger. After the bloodletting, they regrouped and continued their search for the riches de Vaca had reported.

During the years-long expedition, they stumbled into the Grand Canyon, the Painted Desert, and marched over to Baja California and the Pacific. They traversed the sky islands of conifer forests across the deserts and threaded the canyon lands and Monument Valley out onto the western edge of the Great Plains when Coronado heard of Quivira, another city of gold only a little further on. They struck out across the plain's grassy sea and found a collection of mud huts shored up along a river and no gold.

I imagined the conquistadors before the expedition, listening to de Vaca's stories and later Fray Marcos de Niza's claim of having seen the Seven Cities of Cíbola like a bunch of out-of-towners listening to some old cowboy's tale in a bar. A guy telling a story he knows they want to hear, hoping they'll stand him a beer when it's done.

I thought of de Vaca traveling from East Texas overland to Mexico after living for years among the Natives around Galveston. He talked and bartered with people who brought stories from the deep interior of the continent. The Natives considered him a shaman when he healed tribal members by using the sign of the cross. He must have sat alongside people in their last moments of life as European diseases slouched their way across the countryside, strangling and burning up the indigenous populations. Along his journey back to New Spain, how many other healers did he exchange stories with to help ease the dying? Did he share objects, like the rosary or crucifix, and rituals and signs to confront the mystery? How many times? No one can tell. But who is to say de Vaca didn't pass on his myths, and his stories didn't spread along the trade routes of the continent before the first Spanish missions were built? The words like the seeds of grains, the stories bread to nourish the dying and make gentle that transformation of their life to death. Isn't part of a healer's job to reassure a person heaven awaited so he or she can die peaceful in spirit? The ritual of dying. Maybe de Vaca whispered to the dead and, even as he adopted native habits and customs, remained Catholic enough to coax confessions and perform last rites for those about to die. Didn't his heaven have streets of gold? A paradise? Didn't some Native Americans believe the spirit world existed alongside the world of the living and shamans could travel between them, and, in the right conditions, could this other world be visible?

So the story goes, and so it also changes. How many times have we heard it? Far over the horizon, beyond the sky where the dead go, is a city. The spires gleam even in starlight. Your thirst will be slaked like a desert filled with monsoon rains. You will not want. The city of the dead is golden, and you will finally reach it after your long journey through the wilderness. What would it be like to realize you'd been chasing a metaphor for an afterlife and not the worldly metal?

We three watched as the sunlight struck the highest peaks. I looked toward the sunrise and could make out the arch, a black ring with the gray light filling it like an eye in the mountain. We all scanned the far side of the canyon. Each of us sat up as if waiting for a starting gun to go off. I looked back again at the arch in the distance. I wondered if the light coming through it would look like a laser beam or like the sun focused through a magnifying glass. It continued to rise. Sunlight flooded the canyons. No sign. At first, I wondered if I'd missed it by looking back at the arch, but by the looks of my dad, it hadn't worked out.

The men consulted the map and pointed in different directions. They debated if the date was accurate. They decided to explore the area. As we did, we looked for tracks and signs of people in the trails and methodically scouted the terrain ahead and behind for human movement. We hiked dried arroyos tumbled with boulders up to knife-edged ridges glittering with mica, quartz, and what dad called leaverite. "Leave it right there" rocks. All the thorned scrub brush and trees stabbed and pulled at our clothes and punctured our flesh.

We found springs and refilled our canteens. I soaked the canteen covers to cool the water as I hiked. The water ran down from my belt and soaked my butt as we hiked higher into the dry mountains. I'd get down on my belly and drink the cold water before continuing. I felt like one of those big cats on nature shows lapping up the water from a pond.

The world at once collapsed into itself amongst the ravines and peaks and expanded with my sense of place within time. We found opal in the rock, so I busted them free with my rock hammer. Milky white, they weren't what I expected. I'd always seen iridescent opal. My dad explained there were different kinds of opal but to keep on the lookout as I could come across the flashier kind. We moved in geologic history. We hiked up layers of sandstone telling those who knew how to read the land how far back in time they walked. You, friend, just scampered up a cliff formed when dinosaurs roamed the earth 65 million years ago. Some of the rocks formed out of the first fires belching up out of the earth's guts some two billion years ago. Opals and agates, peridot and amethyst molded and crystallized in the pressure and heat. You, kid, cracked the ancient face of the world with your hammer.

At midday, we stopped in the shade of a large rock for an afternoon snack: Vienna sausages, some canned nuts, water, and leftover pastries from breakfast. The wind came up from the Valley of the Sun. Phoenix, the city named after the mythic bird, which after being destroyed in flames, arose reborn. It was only a couple of air miles away from us, but billions of years into the past. That place had been the center of my universe, and it was exhilarating to look over it from the mountain heights.

I looked around the landscape and imagined the conquistadors marching through this very desert, looking for Cíbola. We were separated by time, but not space. I wondered if I could feel some trace of their energy in the land, some fourth dimensional footprint of their passing, the clatter of their arms, the creak of leather, the cuffs of horses, or the screams of their victims like smoke from a long-gone fire.

My dad had told me about legends based on tricks of the senses and natural phenomena. The Flying Dutchman, the ghost ship, was an optical illusion, a trick of light called a superior mirage—*Fata Morgana.* It was easy to imagine a mirage, with the wavy lines and the translucence of the vapor, being confused as a ghost if your worldview allowed for that possibility. Perhaps Fray Marcos wasn't the Liar Friar he was called after no cities of gold were found. Maybe he truly believed he saw Cíbola. Maybe the city of gold was really the walls of a cliff dwelling glowing in the golden sunlight when viewed from a distance. That's no city of gold, but mud or rock buildings in golden light, the story of streets of gold a myth of heaven. The man painted in gold dust was no god, no golden idol, just a man.

We went back weekend after weekend, hiking and searching. When we came to fissures too narrow for them, I'd shimmy my way in and explore. Once, they boosted me up a cliff face, and I scrambled into a small ravine that wound back into another escarpment. I hungered to find the mine entrance or some treasure and return with my own story—"It's just beyond the second bend at the foot of a bluff."

Sometimes I'd crouch in the brush and keep lookout to warn them if someone was coming as they searched a box canyon so they wouldn't be trapped. My hands became scratched and then calloused climbing over granite, and my feet toughened in my boots. I began to learn what my body could do against the mountains and desert and what it couldn't do. I learned the strength of men and how dad and Tom's physical power not only overwhelmed mine, but could without much effort. I realized fighting with them against other men was a fantasy.

Toward the beginning of fall, my dad and Tom met another man who had a small claim. He said he had a map to the Lost Dutchman's Mine, or at least, a strike so rich they'd never work again. He needed help because he was too broke and too old to get it by himself. It would be a hard hike up into the highest part of the Superstitions, so they decided to get mules and lay up provisions for an extended foray. I'd been bragging to the neighborhood kids about my adventures and showed off the opals and other stones I'd brought back. They listened intently to my Old West-style story, and when the two mules appeared in our suburban backyard, my brothers and I became the coolest kids around.

My dad worked as a cop then. One night, he came home early, and all I knew was the old man out at his claim had called to say some people had bushwhacked him and he needed help. My father changed his uniform for his Stetson, jeans, shirt, and cowboy boots but kept the gun belt, carrying his .357 revolver. I started to get my gear to go with him when he pointed at me and said to mind my mother. No other words were needed. It stung my pride. When the going got tough, I was only a kid again.

Mother packed him some sandwiches and a thermos of coffee for the hour plus drive and kissed him at the door as if he were leaving for work. This was what men did: go to the aid of their family or partners in need, even strapping on their guns to do so.

The call turned out to be a false alarm. The old-timer said it was a test. The old-timer kept saying he needed another week and then another month to be sure about our loyalty before giving us the final information. "Oh, and by the way, could you spot me some money to eat on?" Dad had come from an honor system where a man's handshake and word didn't need testing and became furious.

By the time fall ended, my dad abandoned going into the mountains. Forced to face the wasted time, the disappointment was cure enough to take the fever out of his body. A dreamer who believed in his place in the story so much he couldn't see any other possible end to the tale. What was it to be a man who wanted a way out of the daily timecard, a chance to break the working-class cycle of the same dull repeated days, to break with the poor kid past and rewrite the future and escape the one he was born into? What was it to believe you'd be a part of the history, the narrative of frontiersmen and adventurers, only to discover your map was fabricated by a man who never set foot in the mountains? How does such betrayal shape a kid's worldview? How does a kid make sense of going armed and standing by a guy, like so many had done in the old family stories, only to discover that man was betraying you? What could a boy do when he no longer trusted the stories he read?

At first, my dad gave me the thrill and challenge of the search—to venture into the unknown, to chase the mystery and, even if I couldn't name it, the feeling that came from becoming a part of a story centuries in the telling. He taught me to pick up the strands of the story and realize we don't exist in a vacuum. We existed in the history of other people's stories, and many of our stories we tell to make ourselves seem heroic. My dad also taught me about carrying the burden when the quest comes to an end. It's not bad to have a father who's a dreamer; it's just hard when the dream becomes unwound.

My dad led the mules out of the backyard and down the side yard for the last time. Their hooves clomping along the concrete driveway so out of place in the suburb. Clusters of kids stood along the block, watching, talking amongst themselves. I knew some were snickering. He loaded the mules onto a trailer, and as soon as the gate was secure, the truck rumbled to life, jerked, and pulled away with a puff of smoke that faded like a mirage. Dad stood in the street for a few minutes, watching the truck. With the late afternoon sun at his back, his shadow fell in a long pool past our yard. It was as if he stood on the bank of a great lake, cleansed of gold. We'd never go into the Superstitions again.

The next summer, he boxed up what books he didn't sell or give away when we moved down to homestead the desert. He kept them in a six-person tent with some of our other possessions. The small school at Ash Creek had a library, and it was where I first read about Jane Goodall, how to make model rockets, and desert survival, among other things. In that library, I read about the Natives who'd inhabited the region for thousands of years and how they lived. I loved reading about the lives of others to discover how they lived, their trials and joys, and the places and times I'd never see but longed to learn about. Long desert days I spent in the shade of a bush in a light breeze with a library book or a book my dad had brought to the camp. I read less of the fictional westerns and turned to science, science fiction, and history. Also, in the desert, I read firsthand accounts about the Vietnam War, like Philip Caputo's *A Rumor of War*, and World War II, like *Guadalcanal Diary* by Richard Tregaskis. With these books, I'd begin learning the horrors of war, but also the magnetic attraction it held.

In the halfway house, I sat on the couch as cars went by on the streets. The sound of tires on the asphalt like sand slipping down a dune. It made me think. I was in a story I didn't want to inhabit. Tomorrow, if I had time, I'd go to the library. I'd had a card for the Clark County Library, one for the University of Nevada, and for the community college. I loved the card catalogue, pulling open the skinny drawers and thumbing through the cards, then wandering the maze-like stacks through the world and history.

I looked in my wallet, and there they were in a slot behind my old food handler card. *Cool*, I thought. Tomorrow, after I was done job hunting, I'd make a point to go to the county library, find a book, and sink into a story not my own.

The day stretched into a week of swinging by to see Penelope first thing in the morning with her sweet smile of rejection. From there, I spent the day going to the employment office to check the job board, then going to any of the leads. After that, I'd go to places I'd found listed in the newspaper. No casino would hire me, not for dishwashing or carrying out trash. The nonunion construction foremen said they had enough laborers who worked cheap, so I should move along. They all suggested I get some skills in one of the trades by becoming an assistant someplace else and then come back with experience. When I said I'd worked as an electrician, they didn't act as if it counted because it had been in prison. The deadly trap of we'd hire you if you had experience, only free world experience, but you'll get no experience with us.

On Friday, before I headed back to the halfway house, I hitched a ride to my parents' friends, Mike and Joan. My dad had been one of Joan's brother's best friends growing up back in Kentucky. They used to race their cars and drink moonshine while avoiding the police until my dad dropped out of high school to join the Air Force at seventeen.

Mike was a big wheel in a casino on the Strip who wore a suit and tie and kept tabs on millions of dollars, hundreds of dealers and croupiers, and gamblers. He was a quiet, even-headed guy, but powerfully built. He looked like he could handle a rowdy gambler if security couldn't. To me, he was like the uncle who loved to collect gadgets and work on stuff in the garage.

Their two daughters, Becky and Gina, were wild. They smoked and got high. One was a year older than me and the other a year younger. I took the youngest one, Gina, to see Blue Oyster Cult at the Aladdin when I was a senior. We'd spent vacations together, going camping and panning for gold. Or we'd go spend the weekend at their house in Vegas, hanging out and watching television while the adults went out gambling. I never drank or got high with them. They were both beautiful and cool city girls, and I was an awkward, non-drinking dork from a mining town. They'd help me get my first job at the fast-food joint they worked at when I'd moved to town after I'd left LA.

When I went over, both he and Joan were home. I hadn't even seen my folks yet. They'd always been good people, and I looked up to them. When I rang the doorbell, I felt like I was disturbing them and I should just go back to the halfway house. I'd been sweating and had a thirst working. Heat like that can make a person haze over and feel gauzy. Before I could turn away, the door opened, and cold air rushed over me. Joan stood there.

"Hey, how're things? Can I get you some iced tea?"

"Doing okay," I said. "I'd love some tea."

"Get on in here before the heat keels you over."

I stepped over the threshold. She told me to go on into the living room while she went to fetch some tea for me.

I went into a house I'd been in dozens, if not hundreds, of times, and it was as if I were a teenager again, visiting, and everyone was about to show up or walk around the corner or come in from the back room or the backyard where we'd all be grilling burgers and hot dogs and eating deviled eggs and ambrosia. Joan was one of those old country women who didn't give two fucks about your feelings when she told you what she thought and would say as much in the same breath. I half expected her to tell me what a fuckup I'd been by hanging around with fools and I shoulda known better given the fuckups in my family. She didn't, though. I figured she didn't feel the need considering I'd only been out less than a week.

Mike came in. "Oh, hey, you're here. Did you want some tea?"

A clatter of ice into glass came from the kitchen. "I'm getting it," Joan called from the kitchen. She came in with a glass of tea and a plate with a ham sandwich. She set it on the coffee table and motioned for me to sit down. I did.

We made small talk. They asked how the job hunt was going. I asked how their girls were. The oldest was getting married, and the youngest was living with her guy and working. No grandkids yet. They asked about where I was staying, and when I told them, they looked concerned, knowing it was a neighborhood of low-flying police helicopters and drive-by shootings.

They asked how my family was doing. When I said I hadn't had a chance to visit them yet, they nodded. Joan said, "We haven't seen them since what happened. You mother just closed herself up."

It was then, mid-bite of a ham sandwich, a chill flowed through my heart I knew I'd never warm from. While I'd worried about my mom and knew what had happened hurt her, hearing Joan's witness testimony of her closest friend made it real and breathing in the world.

We talked in the cool living room. I finished the sandwich and drank the tea, which Joan refilled. I was glad I'd come. It wasn't as bad as I'd feared. In fact, it was reassuring. I'd been stressed about meeting friends and family and the awkwardness of talking with them and the inevitable questions about prison or the 'I told you not to hang around bad people' lectures. But this was mostly, "Gosh, we haven't seen you in so long. How are things now in the present moment for you? We know you had it hard, so hard. Can we help?" And they did.

Mike and I went out to the garage. He had an old ten-speed bike with the swoop down handlebars. The paint had faded with age, and the chain needed some oil, which Mike applied. It had a headlight and a taillight that were both powered by an electric generator the size of an electric toothbrush handle. It was attached to the front fork, and a spring kept the small wheel at the end pressed against the rim of the tire. The big wheel turned the little wheel, and voila, electricity for the lights. It also had a rack on the back to strap things on.

In those days, you could bike back and forth across Vegas fairly quickly. I'd done it quite a bit before my arrest. In fact, I owned a bike still, but I was sure it had either been impounded or stolen. I'd ridden to the armory and locked it to a bike rack when I'd gone to see the battalion commander. He'd requested a meeting, so I went. Inside his office were two agents of the BAFT who read me my rights and cuffed me. They led me across the assembly hall and out into the bright April light in front of waiting cameras and reporters from local television stations, the same footage Penelope would remember as I stood in the electricians' hall. People love a perp walk now that we don't have the public ridicule of pillory and public flogging. Looking back, I'm sure the agents called ahead and arranged for the made-for-TV moment and the drama of arresting me at the armory. My bike, though, remained there. I didn't feel the need to go back now to see if they kept it safe for me. As the military saying goes, "Gear left adrift is a gift." I knew someone had bolt cutters and removed it, and my bike probably found its way into a garage not unlike Mike's.

Before leaving, I asked for Gina's number so I could give her a call. We'd been closer in age—her sister just old enough in the teenage span of life to set her apart from us—and had spent more time together. It'd be good to hang out and catch up. I felt as if I were turning a corner now. I felt I was able to start seeing people I'd known from when I was free.

The streets of Vegas lacked bike lanes and respect for people on bikes. A town built for the sole purpose of gambling and drinking and, even if illegal, prostitution, anything getting in the way of that was extraneous to the infrastructure and attitude of get them in the casino or bed. In a strange way, biking in Vegas was Vegas at its core. One of someone who risked it all. They bet their life they wouldn't get their asses ran over by a driver in a hurry to get to a drink or play nickel slots. I both hated and loved biking, but at least I didn't have to hitchhike anymore.

Twice I'd been mistaken for a prostitute, which had happened when I was free too, but twice in as many days was a record. The desperation in their faces for sex when they asked if I was sure I didn't want to party with them bordered on the resignation of someone in a breadline when they'd run out. I'm sure it was the same look I gave when denied by the parole for the second time. The same look women get every night of the year from men full of longing and cum. You have the power to give me this one thing, and you won't. Bitch.

Once, a Holy Roller picked me up thinking I needed salvation. She rolled up to the curb in a beater Chevy Chevette. I bent down to look into the passenger window. She sat behind the wheel like a stick figure in a tank top and cutoff shorts that were baggy on her. Her unwashed blonde hair framed her waxy and sallow face. She had the air of a recovering junkie. I told her I needed a ride to the unemployment office. "I can make that happen," she said. She crushed out a cigarette in the full ashtray as I got in.

The Chevette reeked of cigarette smoke and unwashed clothes. A string of pooka shells and a rosary hung from the rearview mirror, and a crack ran diagonally across the windshield. Religious pamphlets were strewn all over the backseat with fast-food trash, rumpled clothes, and other detritus of someone living moment to moment and unsure of a plan beyond the coming night. She shifted into drive and got back on the road.

Once merged into traffic, she asked if I'd been saved. I told her I had not, but it wasn't for a lack of others trying. I didn't tell her I'd left the church in the fourth grade and wasn't looking back at it fondly. She went on about how the Lord had rescued her from the streets and Jesus could help me find a job if only I asked for His help.

She licked her cracked lips a lot, which I knew from being inside with a bunch of medicated convicts meant that she was now on, or had been on, a lot of mood-altering drugs. Her eyes flicked from the road to me and back like a nervous tick. It was both her wanting to engage me in conversation with eye contact and her defense mechanism from the streets and probably her growing up in an abusive place of shadows and strange men. Keep your awareness. Don't make eye contact. You're only an arm's reach away from a beating and rape.

I didn't debate her theology. She clearly needed it, and it kept her sober. Even if her convictions weren't raising her out of poverty and living in her Chevette, it gave her a rope to hang on to in the dark sea. Who was I to try and rob her of that? Not like she was using her religion to murder or to oppress and persecute people or to look down on others with moral superiority. The desperation in her voice to convert me wasn't unlike the desperation of the men who wanted me to blow them. But in her case, it was to save her life and help find solidarity with others for her beliefs. She could be sure her convictions were true if she could get others to believe along with her. But I still couldn't go along with it for her any more than I would make a few extra dollars with those men. But I wouldn't try to dismantle her beliefs with my skepticism and reason like I did with so many other self-righteous assholes and doorknockers. They kept her alive, and I was no killer.

At Boron, waiting for my second parole board, I went to see my counselor, Ms. Smith. She always acted like a high school guidance counselor trying to figure out how she can save the failing kid. When we first met, I tried to guess her age. We could've been high school classmates.

I went into her office. The a/c whirred. After the heat outside, I shivered. Her nipples pressed against the fabric of her blouse, or maybe I just imagined the ripple in the crest of fabric as her nipple, but still, desire had its own vision of the world. I was surprised to be alone in a room with her. No doubt she had a panic button and a camera trained on me, with guards poised to goon the fuck out of me if I so much as raised my voice. I strained to listen for the heavy breathing and shifting men weighted with body armor and riot helmets beyond the wall. The slide of batons through gloved hands. I imagined the smell of sweat pooling under the Kevlar and ballistic nylon.

She asked me if I'd asked for letters this time. The parole board was going to convene soon. I'd been denied at my first parole hearing. The warden, I was told, hated gun offenses, and considering my crime involved a machine gun, he didn't exactly put in a good word for me. It didn't help that I refused to get letters from my family and friends and didn't take the counselor's advice on going to church services. I wouldn't be caught dead in church just to get time off my sentence. I was just a guy who wanted a fair chance, to learn to play music, and to not be hassled for what I didn't believe. I worked hard. I'd started as an electrician's assistant before moving over to the emergency crew. Two guys were teaching me how to play the blues guitar. We met after dinner or during the afternoon on weekends and played on the edge of the bluff with the desert stretched out below us. Some days, the sound filled the arroyos, and other days, the air sucked up the music like water spilled on dried earth. The first guy we called Flat-Five, an older Black man whose fro had slipped to the back of his head. He'd smuggled weed by the van load until a dog didn't like what it smelled at a Border Patrol checkpoint, and he played a killer Delta blues. Which, when you think about it, was legit. We called the other guy Brew, as in Hebrew—and he had the Jewfro to prove it. He was inside for a cocaine rap and also played a wicked blues about oppression, imprisonment, and mass executions in the name of state security. Which, when you think about it, was legit.

I thought of this as self-improvement. I worked my job, kept out of trouble, and didn't make hassles for the guards. That should have been enough.

After I told her yes, she told me to write a statement about how I'd changed, my life of crime was behind me, and I'd worked hard to be a model inmate, so I'd be a model citizen. Include all the stuff I'd done to that end, and "Be humble, but not begging or desperate. You look desperate, they'll deny you parole out of spite."

"I never had a life of crime. I made a stupid mistake, and everyone thinks I'm some sort of gangster."

"It's not about what is, but their perception of you. That's what you have to overcome. Have you signed up for college classes?"

When I said I couldn't afford them, she asked if my parents could pay for them. I said, "They've paid enough already."

The whole thing felt like I was trying to make a long-distance call on a payphone, but all I heard were the clicks of switches and the buzz of electricity through space.

Ms. Smith looked like she was sketching instead of taking notes on her legal pad. In the lull, I listened for the goon squad. They had to be there, poised like a drawn bow. Just beyond the a/c whir, beyond the soft fabric of air filled with perfume between me and Ms. Smith. The smell and feeling on the skin triggering not a memory, but a daydream of an unreachable future, like being on a sinking ship with land on the horizon, where your mind thinks clearly and you can focus and sleep and wake up next to the woman you love on some Sunday and you linger in bed together and make love and don't get up until driven by another hunger and you meet friends for brunch and hope you can say no to too many mimosas or switching to shots and becoming obliterated by midafternoon. You daydream of staying tipsy, in the splendid beauty that feels like enlightenment, and not becoming the full raging drunk you know you are but want to avoid. That savage is wired in you like the full moon waiting to rise. What you want is to go home with your woman in a delicious haze and eat a late dinner like the Spaniards do and hold on to her lightly until you fall asleep with the television on while she softly snores with her blonde hair lighting the pillow. I touched my chest pocket.

Ms. Smith looked up. "You can't smoke in here."

"I don't smoke," I said.

She watched me a moment as if I might produce a cigarette anyway, then asked, "Did you decide to go to church services?"

"Pretending to be something I'm not? I didn't go to church before."

"They love jailhouse conversions. 'I was blind, now I see' type of thing."

Leave it to the prison system to want you to parade around your faith like a pile of poker chips. Poker chips are useless outside the holy sepulcher of the casino. They want the faithful to commit the sin of vanity or, in my case, bearing false witness so they could feel good about themselves. What about private spirituality? What about those who have seen the corruption of churches and religious leaders and have withdrawn into themselves to embrace the mystic, the mystery? People say they lose religion, but really, what they mean is they discovered a different way of doing their metaphysical business. But what of us who are agnostic and atheists? Do we get points for sticking by our convictions? Or do convictions only count if it's what the party in power wants? Maybe the State should mind its own fucking spiritual business.

I didn't lose religion; religion lost me. But also, God lost me as the inevitable next step. Even though reading Bertrand Russell and others had given me the rational reason to leave the church, and my father gave me the emotional reckoning to do so, it was Carl Sagan who gave me balance. I didn't need to be a dick about it and be condescending toward the faithful if they minded their own business. On *Cosmos*, Carl Sagan said, "Extraordinary claims require extraordinary evidence." He said it in relation to extraterrestrials, but what is more extraterrestrial than an all-knowing and all-powerful overseer? I agreed with Sagan that if you find comfort in religion, then who am I to deny that solace? I had no problem with Brew's regaining Judaism or Flat-Five finding his heart filled with the spirit of the Lord, and they sure weren't trying to murder me just because I had no faith in men or gods. And that made a difference.

When I was first asked to write letters, I considered the option of doing another year here instead of having to write my parents and friends. We used to torture and kill the accused by breaking them on the wheel. Now we've figured out a way to bind prisoners and their families to the wheel of hope and break everyone on it. Write letters and get your family's hopes up so some asshole can pass judgement on you and deny you? It's just good business and not the business of rehabilitation.

This time, I weighed six more months by not going to church and participating in the theater of religion just to kiss their asses. No mercy for the sinner. Some mountain ranges have no pass to the Promised Land. You just have to go the long way around and hope you survive.

When I pushed the bike through the gate at the halfway house, Ms. Randall came out. She gave it a look like, "This antique thing still works?"

She said, "It's got some miles. But it'll make things easier for getting around."

I agreed.

She asked if I had any plans for the weekend. I could go out during the day but had to be back for curfew.

I told her Lynne had invited me over for lunch on Saturday and I was going to visit my uncle. I thought about trying to call Gina or maybe just wandering about with no particular place to go. Just wander about to see what was new, what had changed, and just stay out of the enclosed room.

Mrs. Gutiérrez came out of the office, ready to go home. She looked at the bike as if I was smuggling in contraband. She gave me the once over. "Have a good weekend and stay out of trouble. It's your first one back."

She left, and I went into the office with Ms. Randall to sign in.

Friday night, I sat on the couch reading a library book about the Vietnam War. Outside, the rotor slap of police helicopters, sirens, and occasional gunshots punctured the night. I stopped on a page with a photograph showing a stick of Huey UH-1B helicopter gunships flying low over a rice paddy. Machine guns stuck out from the sides like curb feelers on a big Buick. My dad had ridden right there in that space. That might have been him in one of those low-flying birds, scanning the tree line for the backblast of a rocket-propelled grenade.

In photo albums growing up, I saw the photos mom sent him that he brought back from Vietnam, and I saw the photos he sent my mom. There is a black and white of him, 19, on a beach in the Philippines, athletic in swim trunks, on R&R before flying over to Vietnam. In the photo album, there was a similar photo of him in swimming trunks, but this one was at an Arizona reservoir with my mom in a bikini before he left. A series of photos in the album show me growing over the year he was gone. It's a strange quantum continuity. In prison, most of us had photos sent from the outside. Most of us didn't get to see family that much because we were incarcerated so far from home.

At Boron, I parked my things on the top bunk next to a window, and a small old Mexican guy called One with gray-flecked black hair was below me. He'd been a bank robber who was only going to do one more and quit when he got caught in the last one. Across the room was Punch, a fat Mexican on skinny legs with a Poncho Villa mustache who wore his button-down shirt only buttoned at the neck over a white T-shirt. His pompadour was a marvel of hair engineering. He'd been busted trafficking heroin in the northern part of California's Central Valley. He had the single bed across from One and I, and an empty single bed was flush to one of the narrow ends of the room.

I liked the top bunk. On the second floor, I looked out the window across the dried lake to the mountains beyond. A two-lane road cut north and south, and another cut east and west. From my bunk, I could see the crossroads some six miles away. At night, the lights from the gas station and cafe looked like they were anchored in a dark bay with shadowed mountain range rising behind them.

One afternoon after work, One sat on the edge of his bunk looking at some photographs. He showed me his wife, daughters, and grandkids. "Been a long damn time, mijo. So long. I can't wait to retire from this place."

Earlier photos showed his wife with black hair, smooth skin, and a smile broad and bright. They progressed through her graying hair and gravity and grime's long war on her complexion, and her mouth became the tight smile of someone who doesn't want to show their teeth. The same for all the members of his family. Kids who grew into teens into adults into parents and grandkids who grew from infants to toddlers with all the continuity of a flip book on aging.

I had a few photos of my family and Lynne, but we were not apart so long yet as to create a new person before our eyes.

I said to One, "You have a good-looking family."

"Thanks. The worst part is all my memories are compressed into cells and bunks and prison yards with snapshots of my family. It's like time has not passed until I look in the mirror. Don't get me wrong. I have felt time dragging, but in looking back… They've gone through all these changes. Grandkids I've never seen for real, you know, mijo."

When he got back home, he'd know everyone's name by sight and sports or hobbies everyone liked, and he'd know the flavor of birthday cakes or ice cream everyone wanted on their birthday. But they'd see him as a familiar stranger from photos over twenty years ago and a mugshot that resembles one of the grandson's school pictures.

Walter Benjamin wrote that photographs don't possess the "aura" of a handmade work of art, meaning its unique presence in time and space. The photograph removes a work of art from its essence, its traditional space, and diminishes its presence and meaning. A photograph of da Vinci's *The Last Supper* has none of the power of standing in front of it in the Basilica di Santa Maria delle Grazie. Benjamin talked about how art originally had a cult value—the religious, magic, and ritual value. As we entered the modern age, it developed an exhibition value. This is political in nature, and the works are meant to be removed from sacred spaces and displayed in public spaces, like in museums and galleries, to the masses. Although, during his life, most people didn't consider photography an art form. It was documentary in nature, as in documenting events, landscapes, life and death.

Early family photos were taken of the dead, especially infants, as memorials to be kept in the home. Benjamin believed photographs had only exhibition value except for the ritual and spiritual value that existed around photographic portraits of the dead. It isn't just a display. These photographs are like religious icons connecting people with the spirit world. Benjamin could not have anticipated prisoners with snapshots of the living, who change and essentially die before their eyes like in One's stack of photos. Those kids don't exist anymore, but they are still living as adults. In this case, it is the dead who might be said to be looking at remembrance photos of the living. Time passes, and people die you never got the chance to apologize to or just say I love you to one last time if at all. Every photo in prison has an aura, an aura of absence and the hope of a life after prison. Benjamin also could not have anticipated the context of the public and private space that is the prison cell. Both the spiritual and exhibition values collide with prison photos. The personal-spiritual and the public-political cannot be separated. It is some sacrilege when guards toss a cell and tear personal photos from the wall in a political act of violence.

Photos transform our memories, and photos taken for one purpose change when looked at out of time. The images of me sent to my father during the war had the purpose of showing him how his son was doing, growing. My mom couldn't have foreseen me looking at them over the next twenty years and having a new experience or thought about them each time. Is that my grandmother in the background, an aunt? My mother and father were younger in their photos with me before he flew off to Vietnam than I was at that moment sitting next to One. Now both of my daughters, older than my parents were when they were on the beach of the reservoir, look at the photographs of their grandparents and me during that time and draw different feelings and meanings from the images no one then foresaw.

Old photos show where my daughters' smiles come from or the way they stand with a hand on the hip and the ways they will age in family photos—My, you are the spitting image of your grandmother at your age… They can see possible futures or predict where kids and grandkids will end up, like college or living on the road bouncing from job to job or military service. A photo of a parent becomes the photo of a son or daughter. As a kid, I looked at a photo of my father in his uniform next to my mother in a wedding gown and didn't know I'd be in a photo standing in my own uniform as I got married. There are no photos of me in prison, and that makes me happy.

Photographs are not only a reminder of absence, but a reason to persist, to go on. My father said when he was in Vietnam, the photos my mom sent him during the year he was gone gave him faith in the future, a reason not to despair. Simple snapshots of me crawling on the floor, me with my mom reading to me, me at Thanksgiving, at Christmas with a tinseled tree in the background, my cake-smeared face holding two fingers like a peace sign. Returning veterans get home and suddenly appear in the stream of photographs. A prisoner's photos are pregnant with the same hope. In another strange way, photographs become memories. My dad has a photo of us next to his hot rod at the drag races. He holds a trophy, one of several that were in our home. I don't recall the drag races, but I have the impression of being there. It is as if I do remember, or did it only trigger a recollection of burnt rubber and exhaust that flood my mind from later drag races I recall? A surrogate memory we all have in the age of photographs.

One shuffled through his photos like trading cards of athletes he'd never meet.

I said to him, "Getting close to getting out, though."

He considered a photograph and looked out the window. "This ain't like no other prison you ever known, but it's still a prison."

Lynne called and left a message for me that lunch was at 1:00. She gave me the address, and I looked it up on the map and figured out how long I'd need to bike over there. On the way, I shifted gears, and the chain hopped the sprocket and bound up, causing the bike to come to a dramatic stop. I almost got bucked off in front of a Cadillac. I lifted the bike onto the sidewalk. The sun blazed down on me as I flipped the bike upside down. The derailleur was out of adjustment. I moved the shift lever and unbound the chain. I aligned the sprocket teeth onto the chain and turned the pedals as I threaded the chain through the derailleur guides. I'd have to be careful about how far I pushed the lever so as not to repeat this performance. I spun the pedals and let the chain clatter and settle into place. My eyes stung from sweat. I went to wipe it out of my eyes and off my forehead but saw my hands were covered in chain oil. *Fuck*, I thought. I looked around. A gas station where I could get some paper towels was up the road.

I lifted the bike to put it back on its wheels. A car horn honked. I looked toward it. Two white trash, long-haired dudes in an old Firebird grinned at me. The passenger yelled, "Get a car, faggot."

I flipped him off.

"You did not!" he yelled.

The car burned rubber and pulled around into a parking lot, cutting off two other cars. The passenger got out and stormed toward me.

Great, I thought. "Look, I've had a bad week and don't need this drama," I said as he slowed his pace.

"Fuck you, faggot."

I shook my head. "This is ridiculous."

He took a step toward me, and something clicked in my brain. Rage. It burned hard and felt like my nerves all fired at once, focused on nothing but the overwhelming anger at this asshole. Before basic training, before prison, I'd been mad or angry, but not like the intensity that filled me afterward. I thought too of my dad and his sudden rages when we kids fucked up and the rage at the car breaking down and the layoffs and fucking December. His rage was my rage now. I don't know if he had his father's rage or if it was a war souvenir he brought home from the jungles of Vietnam. Maybe both. All I knew was that it had been unlocked in me. I wondered if the drill sergeants had given me the key and the prison system had thrown away the lock.

I hoisted the bike over my head and threw it at the asshole. He put his arms up, and it nailed him. He staggered back, his arms gouged and his T-shirt torn across the chest. Blood started to ooze from the scrapes.

"What the fuck, man!" He started to backpedal.

"Run, coward," I said. "Run!" I yelled. He did as I walked after him. I yelled, "Coward!" as he climbed back into the Firebird. The driver popped the clutch, and the tires smoked and squealed as they sped away, flipping me off.

My hands started to shake. I felt my heart in my throat. I turned back to inspect the bike. *What the fuck was I thinking?* ran through my mind.

I wasn't, was the answer. One front fork was scuffed from hitting the asphalt, and the seat had a small tear at the edge. Fuck, how was I going to explain this to Mike?

Traffic was going by like normal, with the sun bearing down on me. I looked up and down the block. No one waited up ahead, no cops, no Firebird, no concerned citizens. No one to call Mrs. Gutiérrez to inform her of my violence and how I needed to be locked away to protect the decent people of Las Vegas. After a few deep breaths, I mounted the bike and headed for the gas station.

I arrived at Lynne's ranch-style house sweaty and in need of cool air. Lynne laughed. "Like you fell into a pool."

"Damn feels like it too."

I locked the bike to the front post and stepped in. She headed for the kitchen, and I followed her. Still hot, sweaty, and aggravated from the asshole. She opened the fridge to get a salad she'd prepped for us. The door stood open as she set the bowl on the counter. Inside, I saw a six-pack of beer. The cans glowed and glistened under the fridge light. With the day I'd had, I felt the tidal pull of having a drink. Riding in traffic was stressful enough, but I was also feeling tense about having to explain to Mike how I'd messed the bike up.

"Earth to Major Tom."

Lynne's voice broke my trance. "What?"

"Soda or tea?"

"Tea, please. Thanks. Sorry, just zoning out. Long week."

We ate some salad and grilled cheese sandwiches she made. I cooled off both physically and emotionally.

Her husband was at work, and for a moment, it was like how we were before all the chaos that we'd brought on our marriage. Sometimes I forget that at that moment, I was only twenty-two and she was twenty-one. It felt like years had passed between us, and we were eating and visiting decades in a future where we had just managed to age well. Maybe that just spoke to the closeness we shared and finding forgiveness after my long absence into the penal system that created this bubble of eternity we existed in when we were in each other's presence. We cleared the dishes, and when Lynne put the salad bowl back in the fridge, I caught a glimpse of the beer again. I wished I knew why I felt so compelled to have one. The feeling, both mental and physical, rose out of nowhere. I turned away.

Sunlight filled the living room where we sat and talked. Three incense sticks smoked from where they'd been stuck in the soil of a potted tree by the fireplace. A bong sat by the coffee table, and her record collection took up ten or so feet on either side of the stereo. I pointed to the acoustic guitars on stands by the stereo and asked if she'd started playing.

"No," she said. Her husband played, and I should come over and hear him when I got a free evening. They often had parties, and he jammed with his friends. It was a good time.

I told her I'd love to do that. I'd started learning to play the blues when I was at Boron. "When I start getting weekend passes," I told her, "I'll for sure come as long as it's cool with your husband."

She shooed at me. "Get out. Of course he's cool with it."

The afternoon drifted by. She said she was going to go back to college and study bookkeeping like her mother.

"Cool," I said. "Steady work." The thing most of us in our class of kids worried about, although it hadn't quite caught up to me yet. I didn't know yet what I could see myself doing the rest of my life anymore. I saw nothing for me, and the things I really wanted to do were off limits either because I was broke or a felon, but mostly both.

My dad arrived at the halfway house ten minutes early. A lifetime of habit. If you're on time, you're late. Mom didn't come. I took the things and stashed them in my room. It was an odd feeling to look into the box and see the clothes from two years ago. I tried on a shirt, and it was tight. The pants fit as my waist hadn't changed and I'd never worn tight pants to begin with. I'd have to get some new shirts when I could afford them. I was going to look like I did when I'd had a growth spurt growing up and my clothes didn't fit until we could drive to a store sixty miles away after payday to buy some.

Dad looked okay. I'd never forget him in the courtroom. There is a special kind of defeat that comes over a person in the court amid the trappings of power and justice. For all the ritual, robes, suits, and decorum, it is the place in society that enacts the greatest violence on the human psyche. You have no hope, and while there are those who smirk and mock the court as judgement is passed on them, they are just acting out the role. I'm tough, and this means nothing to me. Except that it does. Unless, of course, they are completely off-the-rails crazy. And for those of us with family in the court, their powerlessness sucks the blood from our hearts until it collapses like a dying star.

On my arraignment day, the marshals led me over in shackles and a waist chain hooked to handcuffs on each side of my hips as if my skinny ass could overcome two armed marshals. Maybe they'd worried a bunch of mercenaries would bust me out. One marshal was a shorter guy with a military mustache and the other a six-foot two-inch Valkyrie with tight blonde hair and wide hips I wanted to hold on to. In the holding cell next to the courtroom, they'd give me clothes to change into that my dad had brought. I had no real nice clothes as I didn't know how to dress like that. My uniform was the nicest thing I had, and I didn't have it. Maybe I should have worn it. I changed with some other sorry fucks looking on. No shortage of federal felons in Vegas. The marshals laughed and joked as I changed but became stone-faced as they led me into the courtroom, ready to beat me dead at any sign of a wrong move.

They led me in and sat me next to an attorney. He was a family friend of Mike and Joan's. I'd glimpsed my dad sitting in the front row and nodded to him. What else to do? The prosecuting attorney's skin looked like a Kabuki actor's, and his permed hair looked like the porn star Ron Jeremy's. When the judge, an old white man, came in, we all rose at the bailiff's command and then sat. Someone read the charges. What stuck with me as I stood before the man was wondering, *Who in the hell do you think you are?* Even with the tinnitus in my ears, I heard the people of the United States of America versus Me. The whole fucking country was all I could think about, every citizen. From guys sleeping in cardboard boxes to Ronald Reagan, the very man I thought I might help in his covert war to spread freedom and democracy to the peasants and save them from the communists. I thought about how G. Gordon Liddy became a hero and darling of the right. I would not.

The prosecutor and my attorney said some things, then the judge said some things and then read the charges, asking what my plea was after each one. I replied not guilty to each one of the four. I was guilty as fuck, but admitting guilt, so I was told, makes it harder on you. Plead not guilty, I'd been advised in a meeting with the attorney. Then he'd get a chance to see the evidence and see if he could swing a deal to plead guilty to reduced charges and lessen the threat of jail time. If you ask for your right to trial, they will punish you for it. How dare you. It was the American way. He said he knew that much, but he was a civil attorney and had never worked a criminal case before. But as a favor to Mike and Joan, here he was. My family couldn't afford an attorney at the going rate, and they felt he was better than a public defender. I had no idea. I was still coping with being in jail and trying to survive, so anything outside of not getting fucked up became a lesser concern even as I faced forty years. None of it mattered if someone stabbed me to death between visiting times.

The BATF agents told the prosecutor I was a flight risk and a menace to society. They told him I would seek retribution, come after them, because I told them that if anyone crossed me, they'd better watch their six—the old fighter pilot saying to not let the enemy get behind you, your six o'clock. I never said that exactly, but would they expect any less of themselves? No, they wouldn't, but context is a cocksucker. I stood at attention listening to this. I was clean shaven. My attorney objected. I didn't even have a passport and was very close to my family. I'd been such a hard charger, exemplary student, soldier of the year, General George S. Patton Jr. award winner, an honor graduate from basic and advanced training, State Medal of Merit winner, battalion top gunner, someone who always volunteered for extra duty—just a good kid gone astray. He motioned to my dad sitting in the front row. A good, hardworking man. A veteran of Vietnam, and someone who had been a police officer and a municipal judge in a small town. He made the case that if I was released into my parents' custody, all would be well; I'd show up to court and not create any disturbances in the community.

The prosecutor countered that my military and martial arts training and my adeptness at each made me a greater danger and was not something to be considered as an argument for my release. Indeed, the very opposite. My exemplary record as a soldier was what the citizens of America had to fear the most. I was trained to kill and create mayhem and had been recognized as exemplary in doing just that with all manner of weapons and my bare hands.

My dad had offered to put up the family home as collateral for my bail. The attorney thought it more than enough. When the judge ruled that I was a menace to society and would be denied bail, it felt as if I'd stepped into a dark room and tripped on something on the floor. It seemed prosecutors had taken and twisted Nadar when he said juries should not ask, "Is he guilty?" but rather, "Is he dangerous?"

What a shame, I thought, to be told your worldly possessions weren't enough to release your first son.

The marshals marched me back and forth to court over the next couple of weeks. I tried to be stoic each time. Sat and then stood at attention when called on to rise. Said nothing unless asked and responded like I did when talking to a commanding officer. Stoic to the system meant unrepentant. Every evening, my march into and out of the courthouse made the nightly news. The other inmates in the pod jeered at the marshals as they unloaded me from the van and flanked me as we made our way into the building. Some reporters wanted to interview me, but the attorney thought it a bad idea. I might say something incriminating or look bad in the public eye. More incriminating than what they already had because of my rat best friend, or worse than I already looked to the public being marched back and forth by the marshals and the endless trash talking of the prosecutor and BATF agents? Later, I'd come to understand what he was really concerned about was saying something that would piss off the prosecutor or the judge. They'd be less inclined to give me a plea bargain or less inclined to give me probation or, as it turned out, add more time to my sentence just to show me who the boss was and why fucking with people in black robes was always a loser's gambit.

I stood tall before the man. The prosecutor offered a plea deal, and my attorney urged me to take it. If we went to trial, I faced forty years behind bars and fines in the hundreds of thousands of dollars. Save them the hassle. Save myself. He said I'd get probation as they understood it was someone else who had stolen the weapon and I acted to cover it up for him, a friend, and then acted to get rid of it for him. Misplaced loyalty. This was what he said.

The judge pronounced sentence. It was cold in the court. He asked me a series of questions about what I knew I was losing and giving up as a consequence of my plea. I had said yes, but I had not one fucking clue as to what any of it meant. I shivered. I sensed all the eyes on my back as I stood there, like swells you can sense coming as you stand in the ocean, and even as you anticipate them, they catch you off kilter as they roll by you. The same elemental force I felt walking in jail or sitting and eating or waiting to use the phone, especially after I'd been attacked from behind and had my skin split at the edge of my eye with blood and pain blurring my vision. The staggering loss of control and any sense that things were going to be "okay." Nothing was going to be okay, and at any moment, some douche bag trying to prove something to others could make it not okay forever.

I felt the eyes of malice. I felt the harm others wished to inflict upon me, whether by brute force or the force of the justice system to lock me away. The judge, though, had no malice. He looked down on me from his bench, puzzled and uncomprehending as he regarded me but business as usual. I was but another name on the docket, but one that seemed to give him pause. The judge had the power to hand down the lightest to the harshest sentence, and I had no idea what it'd be. The attorney was confident it would be probation. I hoped so, but always, a kid of layoffs and lost jobs and wandering the American West with his family as his father searched for work knew not to expect anything. We were owed nothing.

As I was taught on the parade deck, I stood ramrod straight. No crack in my face belied the crack running the length of my spirit. I knew exactly what it was like to let everyone who ever believed in me down. It was there. It was deep. Tectonic plate deep. But I would not show it. I'd hold it in. I wondered in later years if I looked like a psychopath trying so hard not to show any emotion, to not show the terror that made me tremble in the night as I lay awake in my jail cell bunk listening to the machinery of incarceration drone. The biting sting of shame and the disgrace I'd brought on myself, my family, and my unit. But most of all, it was facing the dread of prison, like hanging on to a precipice after slipping from the trail. It burned and pitted my stomach. I knew to go was to never return the same person, and the horrors of what could happen to me loomed in my imagination and nightmares.

I kept thinking about how the attorney said I'd get probation. Been such a hard charger. A good kid at heart who had learned his lesson. You had so much and were fucking stupid. I promised if given the chance, I would never cross the law again. I'd be more than a model citizen. I'd be a citizen who worked for the good of society. I just wanted a chance.

The judge pronounced the sentence much like a high school counselor giving a kid the news, You're not getting a scholarship. The gavel came down, and the sharp clack made me flinch even as I stood stunned, not sure I'd heard him right. My attorney shook my hand and said, "Sorry." Two years in prison and not probation. The judge ordered I be sent to an institution where I could receive psychological treatment. I didn't know what that meant. I was filled with fear from *One Flew Over the Cuckoo's Nest* and Nurse Ratched and a system designed to drug you and keep you shuffling in a haze or sitting in a chair drooling, waiting to be spoon fed apple sauce as people screamed at a world no one else saw. What did they hope to do to me? Was it because the judge wondered how such a good kid went so wrong? What madness consumed him to make him criminal and ruin his military career that was looking up even as he was arrested? An acing all the tests kind of guy who wasted his potential. The guy who had it all until he covered up for a friend and then lost his steel-trap mind. How did that happen? The marshals led me out. I can't remember my father's face.

I dropped from the newscasts. I disappeared from the newspapers. I found myself chained and shackled in a van speeding down the highway south out of Las Vegas and into my home state of Arizona. In the marshal's van, the landscape flew by like I was strapped into a chair, stuck staring into a zoetrope as the images of the past spun by. The bright sun made me squint. The bodies of the other men, none of whom had been in my pod and none of whom I'd seen on the news, generated more heat than the air-conditioning could overcome. I sweated. We sweated. No one talked as the marshals in the front seats kept their eyes on us in the rearview mirrors, with their mirrored sunglasses reflecting us back and back and back again in diminishing images, ever smaller until we disappeared into ourselves.

I'd traveled miles of desert roads, and even the most desolate of them see a lot of accidents happen along those two lanes. Some drunk crossing the center line or a trailer fishtailing behind a car that swims out like a scythe or someone rolling too fast into a turn and swerving, overcorrecting out of the turn faster than the car or driver can handle and suddenly becoming airborne like an acrobat tossed into the air, released from the bonds of the road but for a moment before the fall back to earth. I hoped the van didn't turn into a fiery crash where the chains and shackles would keep my charring body secured like a heretic tied to the stake. I hoped it didn't swerve off the road into a reservoir where we'd sink like the lost crew of a submarine. Hoped I didn't die in a van chained to a bunch of men I didn't know reeking of sweat. I hoped I wouldn't die in prison. Hoped I didn't wind up bloody and ass-fucked in a shower where the guards would find me a long way from home while they made their dull daily rounds. At least I still hoped. That was something, no matter how slim.

Sunday morning, I got up and signed out with Mr. Lopez. He was listening to sports radio. "Dodgers gonna make it," he said.

"They might. They cost me a pint of ice cream losing to the Cards last season," I said.

He laughed a wheezy laugh. "Burned me too." He laughed again.

"A hard lesson it was."

I started out for Uncle Binder's when, down the street, I saw a dark-haired woman in front of one of the apartment complexes with the hood up on her car. She wore a black skirt and white blouse with a vest with a name tag with Barbara engraved on it. *She must be a dealer in one of the casinos*, I thought. I coasted to a stop on the street behind the '76 Mustang.

"Need a hand?"

She peered from around the hood. "You know anything about cars?"

I introduced myself. "I know a little. What's it not doing?"

"It won't start. It just turns over and over."

"Well, that means fire, fuel, or air. I can look if you want?"

She looked up and down the street as if a tow truck might be on the way. "Sure. I got some tools my old man left behind." She stepped out from in front of the car.

"Blackjack?" I asked.

"Poker."

I took off the air filter. It looked clean enough. I set it aside and worked the carburetor spring. Gas sprayed.

"Climb in, and when I ask, turn the key for a few cranks." She got in the car. I took off the coil wire and held the metal lead against the manifold. I used my hand to shade it from the sun. "Alright."

She turned over the engine, and there wasn't a spark. "That's good. You need a coil. You're not getting fire to the cylinders."

Leaning out of the car, she asked, "Is that hard?"

"Nope. I'll show you." She climbed out and came around to see. I pointed out the coil and how it was wired and the bolt that kept it attached to the engine block. "Just loosen this one, slide out the old and put in the new one, and tighten it down. Then replace the wires exactly the way they come off the old one."

"Where can I get one?"

I pointed up the block. "Parts store by the 7-Eleven. I can do it for you if you want."

"No, that's cool. If I have a problem, I'll call you. How about that?"

"Sure. You'll have to leave a message. I'm at the halfway house there."

She nodded, then asked, half joking, "You're not a rapist or murderer, are you?"

"Nothing like that. Just a misunderstanding about a machine gun."

"I got a friend coming to get me for work, so I'll get to this later. Thanks."

"My pleasure. See you around."

She waved as I pedaled off.

At Uncle Binder's trailer park, I coasted over speed bumps past trailers with strips of grass and lawn ornaments, like grazing deer, gnomes, and pinwheels. Some wind chimes chimed with the light breeze, and the sounds of televisions came from most places. Sports or the televangelists seemed the two common Sunday morning soundtracks, but also some cartoons and one porno on a little loud. On a bike, like walking, you get to know the roads, with their slight uphill and downhill grades that go unnoticed in cars and the ragged edges lined with broken bottles and beer cans, fast-food wrappers, and lost clothing, like bras and socks, and where there always seems to be an inordinate number of dead dogs and cats. You can hear things like kids playing or what people watch on TV or the radio or the arguments they have when they've run out of patience. You can smell cut grass or dirt and weeds, food being cooked, cigarettes and cannabis smoke, motor oil and spilled fuel, weed killer and pesticides, and other toxic waste. You learn where all the chained and unchained dogs live and which ones will come rushing out to bite your leg. You get to feel the vibe in the air.

Binder had a double-wide with a deck built onto it. In the driveway sat his factory green '64 Dodge Dart, and his Mazda Miata, that on a night in the not-too-distant future would be wrapped around a power pole north of town on a two-lane road, was parked in front along the street.

I locked the bike to the front step hand railing. I wiped the sweat from my face with a hand towel I'd brought from the halfway house. His wife, Jennifer, opened the front door. She might've been five-two and had jet-black hair and a pale complexion and piercing eyes made more so by her glasses. My uncle and she had been high school sweethearts back in Michigan. He and a couple of other uncles had originally come west looking for the promise of a job in the mine my dad worked at in Eagle Mountain. Binder was only a couple of years older than me, more like the age of an older cousin, and that's how we related to each other. Before I started kindergarten, we had gone back east to live in Kentucky from Arizona. We'd stayed with my dad's parents, and he and one of my cousins the same age as him would tease me, knock me about, and scribble all over my comic books by drawing huge stitches on any of the figures. But after he'd come out to look for work when I was in high school, we became pals. We played golf at the small nine-hole course by the lake and went shooting guns out in the desert.

When the layoffs came to Eagle Mountain, he traveled north to Mountain Pass eventually and arrived when we still lived in the travel trailer that first winter before we got the single-wide set up. Things were tight. Another of my dad's brothers showed up not too long afterward to find work, bringing his son who was about the age of my next youngest brother.

Jen gave me a hug and declared I must've gained "a hundred pounds lifting weights."

She asked if I'd eaten and if I wanted a pop or iced tea. My uncle was still asleep as he was on the night rotation at the mine. Her two brothers, who had also come west to work at Mountain Pass, were going to be by later and wanted to visit.

I told her I had a curfew, so couldn't be around very late.

She understood and asked how looking for a job had been going.

"Nothing yet, but I know where not to go back to look." I hadn't even gotten a check back with us later except at the union hall, and then I thought she was just being polite. I wanted to believe she really meant it but also knew it was never going to happen. No one wanted to hire a recently released felon living in a halfway house. The bitterness of it was collecting in me like sewage.

After a few minutes, she led me to where my motorcycle, Bad Bob, had been parked between a rickety metal storage shed and the back of the double-wide. A tattered blue tarp hung off it like a sail on a ghost ship. I asked if I could use the water hose and if they had a bucket and some soap to wash the bike and a towel to dry it off.

She slid open the shed door, the metallic rasp like scratching a chalkboard. In it were the things I could use. I ran the hose from in front, then started to take the tarp off. It tore, and pieces of it flaked off and drifted in the air. Jen said to ask if I needed anything as she was going to get some food ready for my uncle. He was due to wake in an hour or so and get ready for another ten-hour night of grinding ore-bearing rocks to dust.

I bought the KZ650 the spring before I went to Fort Knox. "Bob" had been painted in gold letters on the black gas tank. The guy I bought it from didn't know who Bob was, and neither did the guy he bought it from. Bob wasn't even a memory, but his name lived on. I called my bike Bad Bob because it reminded me of the albino outlaw, the fastest gun in Texas, who wore all black in the western, *The Life and Times of the Judge Roy Bean.*

Bad Bob's tires had dry rotted and flattened. I'd need new tires mounted and balanced. Almost two years of desert blown in and the grime of smog made me feel like an archeologist uncovering some fossilized machine of an ancient civilization. I lifted Bad Bob off its stand and felt the old urge to ride off. Old gas sloshed in the tank. Dried weeds snapped and popped, and dust swirled as I pushed it. I caught sight of a black widow nest between the tank and the carburetors. The spider moved its long legs as the web trembled. Light caught the red hourglass gleaming against its minor-piano-key body. I patted the seat, and dust exploded in a cloud that hung in the air. The tank had been dented high on the right side from where it must have fallen. I ran my finger into the dent, rubbing out the dust, checking to see if the metal had been punctured. Luckily, it hadn't, but rust had started.

With a towel, I wiped the water off.

Along the street, a woman who wasn't more than four feet tall rode by on a BMX racing bike. Her curly platinum hair like a spotlight tracing the street. Behind her, a thin man with raggedy hair and a two-week beard jogged after her. His wallet chain jangled against a key fob. "Hold on, honey," he called. "I can't keep up." He wheezed and coughed and spat in the street.

Some of the shine on the tank started to come back. The trim had flaked off and glittered in the water on the ground, but the rest looked fine. I smiled. I had very little money, no job, no wife, no prospects of any kind. In the moment as the sun filled the tank's surface and reflected the sky back black, I felt like prison hadn't crushed everything out of me. I pressed on the seat, and brown water squished out and left sandy streaks down the side covers and frame. It'd take a lot of work, but I was determined to get the old bike up and running.

Well, at least no one wrecked it. I wondered why no one had taken the time to start it and take it for a cruise to make sure it stayed ridable. Out of sight behind the trailer, other things to do, or maybe the fear of breaking it and having to spend money? Maybe the unconscious sense that they'd be moving on soon and would try to start it up then. Get laid off enough and that feeling of why bother with this today when I'll have to do it tomorrow sieges the psyche. I figured that's why my dad never really fixed some things but patched things together so that they existed in a state of temporary fixes. It made me think of all the houses and shacks I'd seen withering into the land as people existed with the decay. Why bother? We'll be out of here soon anyway.

I sprayed off Bad Bob. The spider sailed out on the stream as its legs flailed. It washed into the dirt, and before it could right itself, I crushed it with the toe of my boot. I fished the key out of my pocket and put it in the ignition. I turned it slowly like a nuclear missile launch officer. No light came on. I figured the battery was deader than cut flowers, but I had to hope. A battery was more money than I could afford. I knew I could refill the dried-out battery cells, get the charger, and see if the motor would turn over and fire, but it'd need a new battery.

Looking over Bad Bob, I began to make a list of things I needed to get. The chain was coated in dirt and had rust, so some solvent and lubricant. I'd need carb cleaner because no doubt the evaporated fuel had clogged the jets and stuck the floats. I'd need to give it a new oil filter and oil change, and I'd better purge and replace the brake fluid. I'd need to check all the vacuum lines for dry rot and leaks. The old gas needed draining, and the fuel lines needed to be inspected. All the wiring and the electrical connections needed to be gone over and cleaned and refitted.

I squeezed the clutch and brake levers and rolled the throttle. A little gummy, the cables would need to be cleaned and lubed. I knew my uncle would let me use his tools, so at least I had that. Mine were probably up at my parents. Not like I had a way to carry them around at the moment.

I looked over the motorcycle again. It always amazed me the amount of damage that happened to something just sitting around.

Picking the ratty tarp up, I then stuffed it into a garbage can. I stood a moment in the sun. The heat was already pooling. The sound of whirring air conditioners and swamp coolers hung over the trailer park.

Binder was at the kitchen table eating bacon and eggs with a cup of coffee when I came inside. A ball game played on the television that he half paid attention to as he ate. He looked groggy, and his eyes were red-rimmed and bloodshot. The dust from the mine had irritated them. I went and sat at the table with him.

"Hey," he said. He lit a cigarette and coughed.

I said, "Hey," back.

"You looking fit," he said.

"Thanks."

"Any line on work?"

"Not yet. Been stopping by the electricians' hall."

That's how it was with us. Not much in the way of catching up, and no dwelling on the past or excuses of why no one wrote or came out to visit. Just the underlying understanding that everyone was too busy, had work and a life, and had family in the free world to visit with. We'll see you when we see you.

Jennifer set a Corelle plate with a ham sandwich and some potato chips on the table next to the iced tea in front of me. I said thanks.

"Hope you still like mustard."

Although I couldn't see them, I knew in the refrigerator were cans of Miller High Life, maybe bottles, as sure as there were empties in the trash. Like yesterday, I felt the urge to drink. It wasn't just the frustration of cleaning and inspecting the motorcycle in the sun and coming in from outside to the cool whir of fans pushing a/c around with a baseball game playing as I sat down for lunch on a Sunday afternoon. Most times, I'd been good at quashing the desire for a drink, but in the right spot, it welled up in my body like the heat off the asphalt. A beer could cool all that and smooth it over.

"If you can stay for dinner, I have some leftover spaghetti."

"I'd love that, but I need to get back."

I asked them if I could use their place to stay on weekend passes when I finally got one. I told them I just needed to give them the address with the understanding that when I stayed there, the halfway house administrators could pop by on a surprise visit to make sure I was staying there and not off smuggling guns across the border or off in Pahrump at a whore house or something. They agreed, and I was relieved. *It'd be nice*, I thought. Now that I had two addresses to give Mrs. Gutiérrez, I felt like I was making headway in transitioning back into the free world. I just needed a job.

My alarm buzzed. I shut it off and stared at the ceiling for a few minutes. Monday and looking into a short-term future. I got up. After shaving, I ate a bowl of Cheerios. I heard an apartment door slam. Someone else off into the morning. A car started. The engine revved a couple of times before it backed out into the street and took off with a roar. I looked at the classified ads from the Sunday newspaper I'd circled last night after getting back from Binder and Jen's place. At least I had some leads to chase for the day.

I put on shorts and stowed a shirt and pants in my daypack. The heat made me sweat like crazy as I pedaled, and I didn't like arriving sweaty. I'd thought about it after coming back from my uncle's place the day before. My plan was to ride to a fast-food joint or restaurant that was close and change in the bathroom, then go talk with a potential employer without looking like I'd been in a water fight. Coming in dripping with sweat with soaked through clothes was almost as bad as having to tell them I was a felon in a halfway house hoping to make good on the promise of my potential.

As I signed out, Ms. Randall asked if I had any interviews lined up.

"None yet."

"Just keep after it. Something will come of it."

I smiled and went off into the day.

On the way over, a guy honked at me and rolled down his window. I slowed down, thinking something was wrong with the bike.

He shouted, "Hey, want to party?" I shook my head and started off again. I supposed biking in a pair of nylon running shorts and no shirt might be sending the wrong vibe in this part of town where no one bikes along a row of off-the-Strip, dingy casinos, but whatever. Later that afternoon, I felt better when a couple of smoking hot women in a convertible T-Bird honked and hooted at me. I waved at them as they sped off, hooting, arms in the air.

At a place close to the union hall, I locked my bike outside and changed in the bathroom before going the rest of the way. At the hall, Penelope looked happy to see me. "Hey, how you doing? Monday, am I right?"

"Off to a good start, I hope."

Her business side kicked in. "Thanks for coming by, but not anything as of yet."

I sighed and smiled and said, "Thanks. See you tomorrow."

She waved as if I were an old friend. "See you then." She went back to her paperwork and answering the phone.

I didn't change to ride to the unemployment office. I figured I'd dry out while going through the job postings. Why make a long day longer?

In the unemployment office, there was a posting for a janitor at the school district. I wrote down the address and biked over to put in an application. Good pay and benefits would suit me right now. All I had to do was sweep, mop, take out the garbage, clean bathrooms, and whatever else they needed done. I wasn't thinking I'd do it forever, but it'd be a good start.

At the office, I talked to the receptionist at the desk, and she gave me an application. I sat at the table and filled it out. It always made my stomach sink filling in the job history and the inevitable questions about the address.

One hiring boss asked me, "What exactly is an FPC?"

When I told him Federal Prison Camp, he asked, "Like Club Fed?"

"More like French Foreign Legion outpost in the Sahara," I answered.

He laughed and said he'd call me if anything opened up.

On the last page of the janitor application, like most, was the question asking if I'd ever been convicted of a crime, excluding minor traffic violations. And if so, was it a felony, and what were the exact charges? I stared at it a long time. So long, in fact, that the receptionist asked if everything was alright. I said no, I wasn't, but there wasn't much could be done about it. I finished the application and took it to her. In the overhead lights, the counter reflected the underside of the application. The mirrored words on the page were almost legible in the reflection as I set the application down. The box with the felon question gleamed blank. I chose not to answer. They could make of that what they would.

When I signed in, Mrs. Gutiérrez handed me an official-looking letter. The return address read the Nevada Army National Guard. I faced a court-martial. I used to receive accolades in the mail, now this disgrace. My, how the high-flown had fallen. I carried it to the apartment and set it on the dining table. I didn't want to open it. I turned on the fan and stood in front of it. I leaned down and said, "Ahhhhhh," into the airstream to make my voice quaver like we did when we were kids. Silly, but it somehow made me feel good. Face in the wind and the fan blades whirling to invisibility almost, just a blur I could see through. We kids would pretend we were on motorcycles or on the deck of a PT boat like JFK's skimming over waves in the Pacific or in the open cockpits of biplanes barnstorming our way across the Great Plains or with the Lafayette Escadrille over the Western Front. Anyplace the wind washed over our faces without anything between us and the horizon and something to be risked.

I thought about the first time I drove a M60A3 tank at Fort Knox. We learned to drive with the hatch open and our heads above the tank's hull—always dangerous if the commander swung the turret—and with the hatch sealed. Enclosed in the driver's compartment, though, we looked out of three periscopes. At night, we swapped them out for night vision scopes. The effect was the exact opposite of having your face in the open wind. The loss of depth perception played havoc, and I ended up driving off a twenty-foot embankment. It rocked the hell out of us. I never let off the accelerator. Later, I learned the commander almost got bucked off. Inside the hull, the heat built up, and the sweat running into my eyes didn't help my driving. There was a fan for cooling, but it just blew hot air around. I still loved it. I loved everything about being a tanker, especially when I became a gunner.

I didn't intend to be a tanker. It just happened to me.

I'd been driving or riding my bike by the armory on the way to classes at the community college. Then one day, I pulled up on the street in front of a single-wide trailer situated next to the armory. The National Guard would help me pay for college, and the six years would be ticking off at the same time, so after four years in college, I'd only have two more left but be free to keep pursuing whatever it was I wanted to pursue. I don't know why I stopped and climbed the steps. Was it all the stories my dad had told us or the allure of tanks and soldiers I'd seen rumbling across so many television and theater screens or read about in books? The strange sense of power it embodied? The uniform every boy imagined made women swoon? I don't know why the short, blocky staff sergeant who had a Ranger Tab, a Pathfinder Badge, paratrooper wings, a scuba pin, and a wicked sense of humor captivated me. He was a dude's dude. He wasn't a braggart or one of those guys who always had to talk about how tough he was, but a regular guy who everyone knew was a badass. Just look at the uniform.

"Here you go, friend. You too can amass all these cool patches, tabs, and pins while having adventures, paying for school, and serving your country. Not a bad way to be. When others are dicking off during the summer, you'll get to drive a tank and blow shit up. Seriously, blow shit up and shoot machine guns. Get a ribbon to be a fully qualified badass."

I told him I needed to finish the semester, and he said no problem. They'd send me to Fort Knox during the summer. They do that thing all the time. "Yes," I said, and I took the ASVAB and impressed all the recruiters. Then I took the physical where I flunked the ear test. Sergeant Von called me with the disappointing results. My guts sank. I'd worked myself up to do this, and now it had been snatched away. Apparently, a childhood of shooting high caliber rifles and pistols while driving around the desert and going to rock concerts had destroyed the high frequency range of my hearing. Mom had been right all along—you don't get that back.

"Don't worry," he said. "We might be able to get a waiver, but that's a long shot. Just try and pass the test."

I heard the static on the phone line and became acutely aware of the ringing in my ears that never left the background of my day-to-day life. "Okay," I said.

"Can you head on back down there and do it again this afternoon?" Sergeant Von asked.

I said, "Yes."

"Good. Now remember, these things are on a timer. You think you should hear a beep after a pause, just press the button. It's all timing, friend. Take it from a ranger. It's all timing."

After rushing back to the medical center, I sat in the soundproof box and strained into the background fuzz and the slight ringing that was physically in my head. The earphones squeezed my ears. Just me and the joystick with the tiny red button. I tried to imagine being John Glenn in Freedom 7 alone in a dark capsule. This one test would change the course of my life. I'd already been bragging to friends and family about joining and now faced the prospect of being a miserable reject. The beeps came out of the void. They gained in volume and moved through the headphones from one ear to the other, the buzz of a hummingbird flying by. I pressed the button like it triggered the ejection seat of a burning jet. Then the pauses lengthened, and I pressed. I worried glory was about to be snatched from me. I wanted it badly. Odd how before I'd stopped off at the armory and talked to Sergeant Von, I could've taken it or left it. But now it meant everything. I sat in the dark soundproof box alone with the ringing in my ears. How does one overcome failing a hearing test? No studying or exercise or listening to special music or affirmation tapes or anything. You had what you had, and all was hopeless and out of your hands. I pressed again at what felt like a good enough space of time. Sweat rolled down my forehead, and my hand cramped from holding on to the stick. I pressed. Was I really hearing the beeps, or was it my imagination? I didn't know anymore. What was real or not? I trembled and pressed. Did he say something about a waiver?

In the dark, it reminded me of when we'd camped out at the homestead on the Arizona/Mexico border. I'd awoken in the tent I shared with my two brothers, needing to pee. I worked my way out so as not to wake them. I slipped my sneakers on and crept out under a starry new moon sky. My dad had always told us to piss as far away from camp as possible. I couldn't see the ground even though the sky blazed with the Milky Way, so I shuffled carefully until I thought I'd gone far enough. I relieved myself and turned to walk back and paused. Only the blackness. I stopped. I wasn't sure anymore if I was pointed in the right direction. No one wanders across the desert in a straight line during the day, much less at night, groggy from sleep. I strained to see the eaves of a tent, the slope of a car windshield, but it was all blackness. Could I smell the remnants of the campfire, or was it all cold ash and stone filled with dinner's cracked bones of a rabbit my dad had shot? Even the air had hushed.

I walked forward and paused, hoping to catch a sound of my sleeping family. My dad snored, and I couldn't believe that of all the nights he wasn't, it'd be one I wandered blind. I crept and waited, crept and waited for a sound. I wanted to yell out, but in me was the shame of sounding like a scared child. Out in the dark, I heard, or thought I heard, other sounds: paws over sand, a rustle of brush, a click of stones turned up by claws digging into earth. My heart thumped faster at the thought of being savaged by coyotes. I held still, cocking my head. How close were they? Were the coyotes passing by on their way north, like the migrants I sometimes saw skirting the foothills, or stalking me, a lost boy? Could I accidentally step on a sidewinder? A shooting star bounced and sparked the length of the sky. I couldn't see a few feet in front of me, but looking up, I saw billions of light years into space and into the past, and it comforted me.

The tinkle of dog tags broke through the darkness. My sister's mutt shifting around. I called out her name softly, and I heard the sweeping of the dog's tail against nylon. As if a fairy spell had been broken, the low chorus of my brothers breathing and someone shifting in their sleep from the tent of my parents and sister rose out of the darkness. I saw starlight glinting on the car's windshield and felt I'd traveled out of deep space to this time, this place, by chance, like the starlight catching in my eye.

The hearing tech opened the booth and told me I was finished. I could go on home. They'd be in touch. I took off the headset. My ears hurt from the pressure of pressing one hand against one of the cups. Later that day, Sergeant Von called and said I'd passed. "Barely's good enough. I barely survived Vietnam and that made all the difference. Let's sign the contract."

The armory wasn't far from the halfway house. In fact, the shortest route to most places I needed to be was to pedal past it, but I went two blocks out of the way. I didn't want to see it. I didn't want others there to see me on my bike with a daypack out to beg for work, to recognize me even as I tried to keep my eyes front, pedaling fast as if trying to outrun my darkness, and feel them shake their heads and avert their eyes like so many betrayed brothers—He is lost. Look away.

I remembered swearing in, taking the oath. Sergeant Von administered it to me with another recruiter looking on as a witness. It was one of those moments that went by in a span of seconds, yet the power of words meant it lasted a lifetime. The weight of it didn't hit me at the time. I'd never had to take an oath before. To my young mind, the life changing implications didn't register. It was no more than agreeing to do a job. I've thought about how many times my dad had given his word to do a job or to take part in a business venture only to have the corporate rats or backstabbing partners fuck him over. It was only as good as you gave, but raised under the Vietnam veterans' mantras of being fucked over by politicians and military leadership in the war and the liberal press's constant undermining of them, it was hard to think of the oath as more than yeah, I'll do this thing until you show me I can't trust you. That never happened. As it turned out, it was me who couldn't be trusted, but it still lay like a stone on my chest. The oath, the words, was as powerful as the judge's sentence and my life now as a felon doomed to always search for redemption in the wrong places for decades.

One thing I never understood was why I wasn't tried in a military court under the Uniform Code of Military Justice (UCMJ) and was instead sent through the civilian federal court system and incarcerated in the Federal Bureau of Prisons. It's just like I don't know why I was transferred between so many places. I thought, like most people, once convicted, a prisoner is sent from the county jail to a prison where they stayed for the rest of their sentence. I went from the Clark County jail to the Federal Correctional Institution in Tucson and was surprised when they transferred me to spend one night in Phoenix before sending me off to the prison in Lompoc. I was there less than two weeks when I was loaded into a bus to be taken to Terminal Island for a couple of weeks before ending up in Boron. Some inmates said they shuffled some of us around to keep us off kilter, and others said it was to make us invisible. If we were in transit, we didn't count in the population and were therefore invisible to the statisticians, the public view, and the grim accountants of incarceration.

To go by the armory and invite more derision was something I'd chosen to avoid. I knew, soon, I'd have to dress in my Class A uniform and face my court-martial. I didn't know if they could sentence me to more prison time in Leavenworth or fine me or if it was only to discharge me under the glare of the public eye, to stand in disgrace again and feel the heat of humiliation. I planned to fight my discharge. To be charged and sentenced under the UCMJ for the same crime was not unconstitutional. So always in the long nights in prison and now in the halfway house, I worried that I'd struggle to find work, make friends, get my motorcycle fixed, and maybe start seeing a girlfriend only to discover after my release from the halfway house that the military police were waiting on the street to take me into custody to begin the nightmare again.

Even now, I waited to be swept off the street every time I saw a cop. Would I invite someone from the armory to call the police if they saw me riding by, afraid of some unknown crime that I might be casing the armory for? What underlying fears did they have at my return? Do they think I might want to seek revenge because they let the thief escape justice? I didn't think so. It was more that I didn't want to face them before I had to, even if it was only passing by on the street.

Like the parole board, I needed to secure letters of reference from those I'd served with, and I planned to ask Sergeant Von. He knew I'd made a tragic mistake and only wanted to prove myself honorable and worthy to die in the service of my country—*Dulce et decorum est pro patria mori.* Would they listen to me? I knew that the officers who would sit in judgement would be officers from my unit. They knew me and all the things I'd accomplished and my value as a soldier. The downside was that they were officers from my unit and had suffered the disgrace and humiliation of my crime. They knew I didn't do the right thing and come forward to rat out my friend and fellow soldier. The sting of shame they felt might only be assuaged by punishing me further. Drum him out, strike his name from the unit roll, and let no one ever speak of him again. Let him rot.

The system had given me no illusions that, even if I did all that they required or expected, they would do anything other than keep punching me in the head. I had hoped not. But until then, I'd go the long way around and avoid the armory altogether as I headed south of the halfway house.

On Wednesday, I left the halfway house. As I passed the apartment complex, the poker dealer stood next to her Mustang. She waved, and I waved back as I pedaled.

"Hey," she called. "The coil worked! Thanks!"

I braked to a stop. "You're welcome."

"Let me fix you dinner. Friday?"

"It'll have to be an early dinner."

"Five work?"

"It does. What's your apartment number?"

"Twenty-six. See you then."

We waved, and I rode off feeling like things might be looking up.

After swinging by to talk with Penelope, I went to a garage that had an advertisement in the paper looking for a mechanic. I got there, and the supervisor asked where I'd gone to school. I hadn't, I told him. But I'd worked on cars growing up. We'd lived out in the deserts in remote mining camps or small farms, so had to know how to keep things going or be stranded. In high school, my friends and uncle worked on muscle cars or trucks and raced them on the frontage road. We worked on motorcycles, ATVs, lawnmowers, tractors, whatever fired and turned.

He laughed. "A shade tree mechanic." He said it like he was calling me shit. "Thanks, but we need certified mechanics and not some guy with a toolbox, duct tape, and baling wire."

He told me to go to mechanic school and then come back. I couldn't afford mechanic school, so I left the smog-filled shop. The worse job I ever had, someone said once, was no job at all. We knew we were no more than cogs in the rich people's money machine, but to be without work was not to even be part of society. Bums, goldbrickers, frauds, and trust fund babies didn't care how useless they were. But to folks like me, this notion of work ethic and loyalty to the job, even as we knew they'd fuck us without hesitation, held value. Somehow, the Puritan work ethic was hijacked by robber barons and industrialists. They'd put themselves in place of God. Do good works for salvation from the unemployment line. We had to play by the rules of make a wage in a system designed to keep us from getting above our raising and excluding those they looked down on, like me, a kid who came from *The Grapes of Wrath* struggle and then went on to be a felon. Because of that helplessness, we carried ourselves with the pride of those who endured, even as we spat with bitterness.

No one cared if you were out of work, and there was always some asshole to remind you that you didn't belong. You stupid Okie white trash piece of shit. Go on back to your Dust Bowl. You may have fixed cars a hundred miles away from any auto shop under a desert sun that'd leave you and your girlfriend roasted and delirious, but you don't have a piece of paper. You don't belong. I could set the ignition timing on a car without a timing light and set point gap without the feeler gauge and make a car start with the starter fried. Once, I used baling wire and pliers to create enough belt tension on the alternator when a mounting bolt cracked loose and drove out of the desert and sixty miles to a parts store to replace the bolt.

The anger I felt from all the rejection made me want to burn the garage to the ground. But that was another splinter that worried the wound. I was helpless to do anything but keep walking.

A whole week and nothing but condescending assholes or those who wanted to act like they were hip with helping the downtrodden and pretended they were sympathetic to my situation but still, with lowered voices, said they couldn't hire me on to work even the most menial of tasks. Along with good behavior time in the halfway house, I also needed a job to be considered for a weekend pass. It wasn't enough the State wanted to restrain my freedom, but the social prejudice against me as a newly-released-from-prison ex-con constrained my freedom. They too, small clerks and shop keepers and administrators, acted as moral judges, passing judgment out of the juggernaut of fear and loathing. Everyone talked forgiveness and rehabilitation, but no one lived it. Suck it up, dickhead, you brought this on yourself. Did I? This was how it felt on a bad day, and today was a bad day.

As I peddled back to the halfway house, I started to pump harder. The blood rushing through me. The tension in my thighs that made them feel electrified. I dodged ragged edges of asphalt, potholes, and bottles between the street and its edge, sometimes a sidewalk, sometimes the creeping weeds of vacant lots. I swerved to avoid cars turning ahead of me. Someone behind me honked, but I didn't look back. My focus remained forward, concentrating on what other cars ahead of me might do and the traffic lights. I had the right of way, although the right of way on a bike in traffic is academic if the driver runs into you because their desire to reach a place five seconds earlier was more important than good manners on the road or human life. I thought, *You're in a car. Don't worry. You'll make it and not even break a sweat unless your a/c is out.*

Here in the city, I rode as hard as I could. I rode all out all the time, and even as I wore down and slowed my pace, it was still as fast as I could go between the lights, stop signs, and drivers pulling out in front of me from side streets or parking lots. But it was mostly unsatisfying. Just to get from here to there as I looked for work or did the business required of me by the State.

I wanted to leave this city and ride along a desert road without cars for as long as I could. To ride out the anger and frustration pressurizing my chest. I wanted to climb up to a summit and then coast down a long hill with the wind rippling over me as a hawk might feel as it dives for its prey far below on the ground. Freedom with gravity at your back, sailing right at the edge of control, at the edge of oblivion and life. The speed was relative. Someone running full tilt, a bicyclist at top speed, and a motorcyclist at over a hundred all had the same divine feeling wash over them when they reached that barrier between falling apart or maintaining the road. It was about the speed itself in the conditions that allowed you to push as fast as you dared without a place to be, just a moment when the speed peaked and you still held on, still kept upright, and sailed through it with nowhere else to go.

No one was around the halfway house other than the three who guarded the entrance. It amazed me that I never saw anyone else except the time Captain called me out. My roommate still hadn't appeared while I was there. I heard people come and go, heard televisions, smelled dinners, but never caught sight of anyone.

On Friday, after signing in, I went and showered for my dinner date. Although I knew it was a gesture of thanks, I couldn't help but hope it might take a romantic turn. Sure, I was a horny guy just out of prison, but I was also a lonely guy just out of prison. I just wanted to be with someone to be intimate with, to share inside jokes, look forward to our weekend plans, and lie around naked in bed as a fan blew cooling air over our sweaty, sex-sated bodies. I'd had that with Lynne before our marriage came crashing into the ground at the bottom of a cliff that we had both driven over while fighting to steer our own way.

Out of the shower and drying off in my room, I looked at my pile of laundry. Small domestic things irritated me. It reminded me that every day, we decay a little more. It seemed we had been sentenced this never-ending series of chores to do every day until we died, and then someone else would have to tidy up for us because there was no way any of us died with a clean place. Kind of like when they arrest you and someone else has to come in and see what damage was done and put things in order before they could attend to the grief of your departure. At least, in darkness, I could kid myself that all was clean and tidied up if I disappeared again.

I combed my hair and looked at myself in the mirror. For a second, I marveled at the glass. My face had changed in small ways. The scar on the outside of my right eye socket was perhaps the most striking. The small lines like I'd been squinting into the darkness and mist. The long wearing nights of insomnia. The thickening of my face from lifting weights. And although I still had boyish looks, I saw how age and stress had tarnished my wonder, and dread had drawn a cloud over my face. Now I wondered how this new grind of felon-looking-for-work beat on me. Even as a boy, I'd find myself sucked into vast, flat depressions that seemed to stretch out like darkened plains without horizons. But more than darkness, the sense of pointlessness. Life as a joke and meaningless, even before I'd read the existentialists, like Camus or Sartre or *Notes from the Underground* by Dostoevsky.

Once, at night, as I sat in the tank gunner's seat looking downrange through the scope, I watched the tracers from the cannon rounds fly into the darkness, hit the target, and, as they passed through it, skip and sail almost straight up before disappearing into the background of stars. I fired three more rounds as fast as the loader slid rounds into the breech, but they didn't ricochet after they all plowed into the targets and blackness after that, just gone. That night, I didn't miss any of the targets and set record times for acquiring and hitting targets. In me stirred both the rush and sense of accomplishment, especially with the soul-rupturing firing of the big guns, but also the sense of brief tracers burning hard against the night sky and how it was only death that mattered. It was only power and the threat of violence and death that created societies and civilizations and enabled them to thrive. I felt it then, and prison reinforced it—being subject to violence and the constant threat of violence from society, the courts, the guards, the parole board, the warden, all the administrators, other convicts, and the violence I too engaged in to keep people from fucking with me. The threat of violence always under the skin that shivered when death passed close.

I closed my eyes and shook my head. *Enough of this negativity*, I thought. Yeah, the last two weeks sucked, but the worst week semi-free was better than any week locked up. Besides, this evening, I was going to go have dinner with a pretty poker dealer, and it was going to be fun. Who knew, I might even get laid, and that would make it a banner year.

On the walk over, the teens hung out up the block, passing baggies through car windows and taking money. I watched a second before turning away. They were too preoccupied with looking tough and watching out for rivals or cops to worry about me.

Her Mustang sat parked where it had been the other morning. I walked up to the complex, looking for how the apartments were numbered. Some kids were playing tag in the courtyard where all the grass had been worn off. Heat still hovered around the concrete walkway. The whir of window-mounted a/c units created an underlying drone for the mix of television shows and kids yelling and laughing. I stood in front of the door with the number 26 on it. I prepared myself to knock by taking a couple of deep breaths. I felt a little dry-mouthed and shaky. From inside, I could hear the Texas blues rock of Stevie Ray Vaughan: "All the telephone lines are down." Cooking smells wafted around the apartment complex, so I couldn't tell what was coming from her place. Some car doors slammed, and the sound of men talking inaudibly echoed in the complex. I knocked.

She opened the door. Her bloodshot eyes glistened, and she smiled when she saw me. She wore a blue crop top with a unicorn that looked warped from her breasts and a short brown, flared skirt. In one hand, she had a glass of red wine.

"Come on in," she said.

I stepped through the door and saw, on the dining table, a bottle of wine, a pipe for smoking weed, and a couple of *Vogues* and a *Cosmo.*

"Thanks," I said.

"Dinner will be ready in a moment. Wine?"

I explained that I wasn't allowed to have wine as part of the conditions of my stay at the halfway house. She made a pouty face and said it was unfair. Whiskey she could understand, but dinner without wine was uncivilized. She giggled. "Oh well."

I had to laugh. Wine, as far as I knew, was something classy people or winos drank. I didn't know anyone who drank it except some of the high school teachers.

She led me to the living room area—it was all one giant room with the bedroom in the back, I supposed. We sat on the couch.

"Did you have a good day?" She leaned in as if going in for a kiss. I readied myself, not believing what was going on, but she swerved away. In her tipsiness, she might have been swaying oblivious to her orbit.

"It was a day," I said.

"You play poker?" she asked. She scooted over a little closer to me.

"No."

"I could teach you."

"I know how to play. I just don't. I'm a bad bluffer."

A timer dinged.

She jumped up, and her skirt flipped up enough to see the lace of her underwear. "I can help you with that. I can see all the tells."

With some potholders, she took out two TV dinners from the oven and set them on the table. From a drawer, she got two forks. "All I got is wine, water, and beer. I suppose beer is off the menu too."

I went to the sink to take the water glass from her. She leaned in as if she was going to kiss me, but as she rubbed her breasts against my chest, she slipped by me. The front of her shirt hung over her flat stomach like a theater curtain half raised above the stage.

"I want a beer, but I can't." I wanted one bad, almost as bad as I wanted to fuck. Her sexuality filled the room. Her movements and gestures, the way her eyes locked on mine as she came close as if she wanted to devour me. But then her moving past me made me ache.

"I hope you like Salisbury steak."

I nodded. "It's good stuff."

Sitting back, she smiled.

The room warmed. Electricity coursed through the air. I hadn't been alone with a woman in an apartment for dinner in so long I couldn't remember the last time. Much less with a woman so alluring and full of sexual energy. The last time I'd planned to have dinner with a woman, I was arrested on my way there. What I wouldn't give to run my hands over her body and pull her close to me. But I played it cool. I didn't want to come off as some sex-starved ex-convict. I wanted to develop some sort of relationship even if it didn't work out in the long run. At least I'd get a taste of a normal life and sex on a regular basis anyway. Desire as an illusion felt more absurd to me as she leaned forward with her breasts pushed out as if about pull up her top.

"It was cool helping me with the car."

"Where I come from, we see a hood up, we offer to help."

We finished eating and took the trays into the kitchen to throw away. At the sink, she washed her hands. I stood there, not sure what to do. She grabbed a towel to dry off her hands, and I waited. I followed her toward the couch, but she stopped short, and I nearly ran into her. She stretched her arms up. She brought her arms down, looked over her shoulder, and smiled. I was so taken by her I reached and caressed her cheek. She pushed her cheek into it. I started getting hard and pulled her closer to me. She swayed her hips against me.

She whispered, "I get a little drunk and a little high and I get a little flirty." She smiled, and I felt like I was going to explode.

"But…"

I leaned back to look into her face. "Boyfriend?"

"No, I have Hepatitis B. We can't do anything, even though I really want you."

"Oh." At that moment, with my hard-on, her so close the wine on her breath filled my head, and her heart beating so fast I felt it across the short distance between us, I'd have risked it with her. She stood there in her short skirt and crop top like she had stepped out of a porn flick. Damn the odds. "I see."

"Believe me, I got a Texas flood going on, but you know."

I did.

We went back to the couch. She turned on the television. I didn't pay attention to the game show that filled the screen with overly dramatic contestants. Instead, I breathed in slowly and out like I was taught by the heroin-smuggling Buddhist to try and banish desire, to remain in the sexless present. My hard-on started to recede. The evening was still free for me for a couple of hours, and I was still with a woman and not alone in the halfway house reading about the fall of the French in Indochina. I settled back into the couch, and she snuggled into my side. We watched television until it was time for me to go.

In the 3 am darkness of Saturday morning, I woke with a start, sucking in breath as if coming up from nearly drowning. My heart thumped hard, and I sweated.

In prison, I started having dark nightmares where I wasn't sure if I'd awakened or was trapped in some dark place. My body stretched out on the bunk, seized up, and was rigid like glacial ice. Those nights, I struggled to move so hard I thought muscles would tear from my bones. I was conscious of being pinned down, felt a crushing force on my chest, but no matter how I tried, I couldn't even quiver. In my rigor mortis, I became aware of two perceptions. One was me trapped on the bed, and the other was me floating and looking at my body, hovering between two worlds. And the smell wasn't me pissing myself from fear, but my corruptible flesh. Screams filled my head, and I understood they were the wails of all the damned. Those souls swirling into nothingness. My soul, my spirit, my life force, or whatever you called it, floated between that nothingness and my body paralyzed on the bed. The screaming might've been me in my head, like the screams in dreams. But it sounded as if it came out of the air. No matter how the saved wanted you to believe in salvation, in Heaven, there was nothing, and just before your soul was extinguished, it wailed against that big void just as you'd wail if you were pushed out of an aircraft at night. You knew it was over, and nothing was going to save you from the blackness now no matter how hard you tried to fly.

I stared at the ceiling, exhausted. I didn't have to get out of bed, but I did. It felt like a crypt and no place of comfort. My teeth hurt, and my muscles were sore. It was too early to ride over to Binder and Jen's, too early to go anywhere that wouldn't get me in trouble. I wondered if it was too early to sign out even. What if I wanted to go to a diner for breakfast? To just walk about and get out of this glorified jail cell?

After I ate some cereal, I sat at the table reading *Hell in a Very Small Place* by Bernard B. Fall. The quiet outside—not even cars in the distance—made for good reading and helped clear my mind. I thought about how many former German and Italian soldiers from the Nazi and Fascist armies died in Indochina. Ten percent of the garrison at Dien Bien Phu were German, and the Foreign Legion lost 3,000 German legionnaires who were killed between World War II and the end of that siege. No questions asked. Enlist, take a nom de guerre, go to their training, and for the next six years minimum, wherever the French empire needed soldiers, the Legion sent them. In a world of conflict, it seemed a great place to go if you needed to outrun the law or your Waffen SS past. Sure, many died, but in their minds, I could see a soldier saying, at least I died fighting in the time-honored tradition of mercenary soldiers going back to the March of the Ten Thousand. At least dying on the battlefield wasn't at the end of the rope or wasting away in a jail cell or living out their days terrified they'd be discovered and denounced and tried as old men, humiliated finally as they knew they should be. What of felons rejected from society and doomed to live along the margins of their community, never forgiven and never allowed back in? I thought about the ex-Ranger at Boron who went to Vietnam when he got crossways to the law instead of sitting in prison. We had no war I could've been sent to in a foreign land. My life stagnated and steeped like hemlock tea.

When it got late enough, I got up and stretched. I'd had my dad bring my motorcycle repair manual, so I tucked it inside the daypack with my pants and shirt. The morning was bright and the air eerily clear and still. No one was hanging out along the street.

The ride over to Binder's wasn't so bad. No honking assholes and hardly anyone else racing up and down the streets. Inside the park, though, an old man in big dark glasses and a bucket hat driving a huge Caddy nearly took me out. I dodged out of his way, hitting a garbage can.

"Fuck you!" I yelled as I flipped him off. A little yap dog barked from inside the double-wide. An old woman in curlers parted the curtains and looked out as I righted the garbage can I'd knocked over. I waved and mouthed sorry. She looked aggravated and disgusted as she dropped the curtain. I shrugged. She probably thought I was drunk.

I got to Binder and Jen's. As I locked my bike to the porch, Jen opened the door and invited me in for a few minutes to make sure I didn't need a sandwich and offered me a glass of tea. I took the tea out with me to look at Bad Bob.

Binder had a nice set of tools and stuff like cleaners and lubricants and shop towels. I planned to take off the carburetors and start cleaning out the fuel that had dried into them. The jets would be clogged, floats gummed up, and a thin layer like varnish in the bowls. I started to pull off the vacuum lines, and they all cracked. Black dust came off on my fingers when I touched them. The rubber from the air filter also cracked and broke as I struggled to loosen rusted and gritted clamps. Bolts seemed welded tight, and small nuts started to round off. I applied WD-40 and let them soak before giving it another try. I busted my knuckles when a wrench slipped. The sharp pain of bone against steel made me wince. I clenched my fist, ready to punch, but breathed in and out to relieve the frustration. Blood eased through the scraped flesh like through gauze. I wiped the blood away with a shop towel and went back to work. I finally got the carbs out and set them on the ground. The gaskets had deteriorated and tore. I saw the intakes had discolorations and looked grimy. I sprayed some carb cleaner into it and covered it with some plastic to keep any other dust and dirt from getting inside the cylinders.

I took the four carbs and went to a worktable. The manual gave me step-by-step instructions on disassembling and reassembling them. All the screws and nuts were as stuck tight as everything else had been. I could feel screws starting to strip out at the screwdriver, so held up. *Fuck*, I thought. It was going to fight me at every step. I sprayed the whole thing down with carb cleaner and let it set. After a spell, I started at it again. By small turns, I got each one apart. All the gaskets tore or crumbled as I tried to remove them. The O-rings were shot. The insides were worse than I thought they'd be, but now I was expecting nothing but struggle. The float springs and jets were inoperable, so I soaked them in solvent. The 1/8" detent ball for the choke was stuck on the spring. I tried to work it loose between my thumbnail and index finger. It popped out and bounced off the table, falling between it and the trailer. Gritting my teeth, I set everything down and looked for it.

First, I moved the table away looking for it, then got on my hands and knees into the dirt and patchy grass, catching a cobweb in the mouth. In the dirt between the trailer skirt and concrete pad, I found black widow webs and roly-polies, a couple of marbles, several old-school pull tabs from beer cans, a plastic soldier, and a rubber band that was in better shape than all the O-rings and vacuum lines on Bad Bob, but no detent ball.

The scrape on my knuckles stung. I brushed my hands together to knock loose the dirt and pea gravel. I regarded the dimples in my palms, then the congealing blood and grime as I clenched my fists so hard my fingers hurt. Sweat ran down my face, burning my eyes. Heat waves rose from the street. My breath flowed toward it. *Funny*, I thought, *how at times you can feel the heat drawing your life away, suffocating you by pulling your breath into the atmosphere, leaving a void in your chest.*

I paused, a moment away from taking a hammer and smashing the carbs to pieces. I felt the rage in my guts building like a wind picking up dust in the distance and moving over a playa. Sitting back on my heels, I breathed deep. My mind blanked with anger directed at nothing but the meaninglessness of this moment. A blank rage where all my awareness constricted, and I sensed nothing but rage and the overwhelming desire to destroy. The sweat made me feel coated in plastic. Dust and dirt clung to my face and hung on the hair of my forearms.

I crawled out from under the table, stood, walked over to the motorcycle, and kicked it over hard. It crashed against the concrete. Fuck all the work and the cost of all the parts I couldn't afford. For what? This relic? This machine that would need everything replaced or taken apart and scoured to get rid of the two years of rot and disuse?

Binder came out of the trailer. "You okay, man?"

"No. I'm not okay."

He looked at the carbs on the bench and to Bad Bob on its side. "Let me give you a hand."

"I don't need a hand. You can have it. Whatever you can make off it to cover the cost of keeping it. I'm through."

"Hey, now. Give it some time. I know it's got to be frustrating, but we can get her running tip-top again."

I looked at him. "Nah. I'm finished. I'll sign the title."

After lunch, I'd calmed down. Binder needed to get ready for work, so I got my backpack and started to head out. I said my goodbyes and thanked them for lunch. The sun crossed midday. My shadow, thin and narrow, trailed next to me on the street as I pedaled, not sure where to go.

My third week back in the city fared no better than the last. The riding to the union hall to be told nothing yet by Penelope, going to the unemployment office, and pedaling to as many leads as I could before heading back to the halfway house. The tone in Mrs. Gutiérrez's, "Oh, really," when I said I hadn't found anything yet made me feel like a deadbeat, and my dwindling cash made me uptight and worried what I'd do if I didn't get work soon. I'd seen Barb, and she waved but looked away as if she didn't want to see me, or maybe she was just in a hurry to get to work. I'd seen Bridgette too, but she was hustling up the street with some guy in a black Benz with tinted windows and a fresh wax job. The teenagers were idling along the curb, on the lookout, waiting to make sales or run from the cops. The afternoon rush was on in the neighborhood.

I thought of the long supply chain. In the county jail, I'd known small time dealers like them, guys who ran the local organizations, and those who flew drug-filled aircraft from Central and South American jungle airstrips or ran cigarette boats up the coast or island-hopped loads to the mainland. A billion-dollar enterprise pointed like a cannon at the US streets and homes, and the US government's billion-dollar War on Drugs pointed back at it. We laughed about it in prison. Rehab would do more to shut down drug trafficking, but where's the glory in that? Addiction treatment, though, is a tough sell to voters who see it as a moral failing.

One of my dad's brothers, like many in his family, struggled with alcoholism that led to crime and being sunk in a system that didn't treat the root cause problem. He died alone in prison surrounded by employees of the State, without any kin to sing him back home. What satisfaction does a society get from forever punishing people like my uncle for not being able to overcome addiction alone? They die feeling like it was their own moral weakness and lack of will power, not a hitch in their biology and genetics and poverty and social institutions, that led them to this miserable end. Fyodor Dostoevsky wrote in *The House of the Dead*, "The degree of civilization in a society can be judged by entering its prisons." To which I might add, the moral caliber of that society.

After going to the union hall for the fifteenth time, I'd applied for a telemarketing position with the *Las Vegas Review Journal* in their customer service department. All I would have to do was call subscribers and ask a series of questions about their satisfaction with the newspaper and upsell them. I hated phone work, and this was minimum wage, no benefits, and no future, but no one else would give me a break, so I gritted my teeth and showed up to the newspaper boiler room to fill out the application.

The room was full of small desks, like school, where each one had a phone and a stack of papers. People were talking on the phones and marking responses on their lists. If this was the best I could hope for at the moment, then I felt dismal. The supervisor had read my application and set it down as if it was headed for the shredder while saying, "If something comes up, we'll call you." They had an ad for help in their morning paper, so I knew this was yet another brush off. I fucking hated the disinterested we'll call you. I told him I'd follow up with him on Monday, and he shrugged like, "Whatever."

After leaving, I went and scarfed down a fast-food burger. It settled into my gut like wet plaster. It was just after one o'clock. I was so beat from another long week of riding all over town collecting rejections I didn't want to go anyplace else. I wanted to sit and just think in the a/c, drink some iced tea, pretend things were going to be okay. A kid in his polyester uniform pushed a mop bucket from the backroom and started slinging water that reeked of bleach or ammonia. Fuck, it made my sinuses hurt.

When I'd first arrived in Vegas after high school, I'd been having a hard time finding and keeping work. Most places didn't want to hire a kid out of high school, and I was always perplexed by entry level jobs that required experience that you couldn't get because no one would hire a person without experience. In the classifieds, telemarketing jobs promised thousands of dollars a month. Desperate for a job and the promise of easy money, I fell for the ad.

I rolled in before 5:00 am. I was kind of overwhelmed by all the people talking into headsets trying to close a deal by getting a credit card number. People wore all sorts of clothes from suits with vests to guys like me in a T-shirt and jeans. The fluorescent lights made me feel as if I were in a surreal science fiction movie where we were all locked inside a test station for observation. My first morning, I sat with a guy in a suit. He had the script memorized, so he liked to stand and pace wearing a headset. First thing he told me was to follow along on the script and save any questions for when he was done. Never interrupt a pitch. The next day, I was on my own and unsuccessful. Good thing as it happened. My third morning, the FBI shut us down in a predawn raid for fraud and a list of interstate crimes. I was questioned, had a Polaroid picture taken against a wall, and was released. My first Vegas job ended in Vegas style. At least I knew the FBI wouldn't be raiding the newspaper boiler room if they hired me.

My second job was at a gas station, which lasted three days when I told an asshole in a Cadillac he couldn't talk to me like I was some fucking peasant. When he said he could because I was a fucking peasant, I tossed the squeegee on the hood of his car and walked off.

Mike and Joan asked their daughters to help get me work at their fast-food joint, and they did. I showed up and started working the closing shift and going to classes in the morning at the community college. I was taking intro to journalism, philosophy, psychology, chemistry, and sociology. About a week into the job, the assistant manager invited me to a party. When I said I didn't drink, he grinned. "You are so exiled." I paused, not sure if he meant that I was to be exiled like some bad villager or that I was already living in exile like Grendel. He said, "We got to solve this problem."

I smiled, thinking, *Sure, whatever*. I didn't need booze to have a good time. My dad had always promised to kill me if I started drinking in high school. I believed him. He rarely drank, but alcoholism burned people to death on his side of the family. My mom's family was "liquor never passed their lips" Methodists except for that one black sheep who had the good taste never to mention it in front of grandmother. It was some testament to the willpower of my mother to help my dad overcome all that genetic and environmental dependency and weather the nickname of "Bible thumping bitch," which she wasn't, to keep him from descending into the pit. I often thought of the quiet power she wielded.

I'd drank twice before the weekend of the work party. The first time was some beer with a couple of guys I'd just met before my freshman year started. We floated on inner tubes on Lake Tamarisk. It was an artificial lake out in the middle of the desert with houses on one side and a trailer park on the other and a nine-hole golf course slung below one end. My dad had found a job at the iron mine in Eagle Mountain, California, and moved us into the single-wide trailer on the desert edge of the trailer park. I felt so guilty and terrified, especially out on the lake where anyone driving by could see us. I drank one beer and then slowly dumped another two into the lake while pretending to drink. My dad, when enraged, could hoist me over his head and throw me about twenty feet. You ever been hit so hard you pissed yourself because there wasn't any room left in your body from the force of it?

My second drink was in the middle of my junior year. My dad gave me some gin-inspired thing on a blustery New Year's Eve in the mountains on the California state line above Las Vegas. He'd been laid off from Eagle Mountain that fall but landed a new job during the holidays. We were celebrating our good fortune, so I suppose he thought a drink was in order. Maybe he also sensed my unhappiness and thought the camaraderie of a father-son drink would buck me up. I'd had to leave my two high school pals, Adam and Jane, behind. They were over three and a half hours away now. We were a family of six in a ten-foot travel trailer huddled against the mountain winds, but we weren't living on open ground in the weather again. We could eat now—and not jackrabbits and pinto beans or Spam and fried potatoes cooked over a campfire. We could save some money before the next disaster. But after that, I didn't drink until the night of the manager's party.

I felt this want to be accepted. I was in the city without friends. In high school, the older guys I hung out with drank, but I didn't because we all feared my father's wrath. They knew him and wanted nothing to do with being on his wrong side. But I never had the desire to drink and was kind of a little priss about not drinking or getting high. That was for losers and burnouts. Awkwardly enough, most of the others who didn't drink were self-righteous Bible thumpers. So the people I fit in with was a narrow band of people.

As I thought about the upcoming party, I figured having a beer or two to fit in wouldn't be a big deal. My dad had a couple of beers with friends or at weekend BBQs, and nothing bad ever happened. We knew who the drunks were, and we all knew it was because they just couldn't handle the booze. They didn't know when to stop.

The weekend arrived, and I slipped into my first drunken stupor. I jumped out of a second-story window of the assistant manager's apartment on a dare. I made out with Pam, a hot brunette from morning shift. When I threw up in a rose bush, my face got scratched up. The next morning, I woke up on the floor next to Pam with my mouth feeling like old velvet. Someone had thrown a blanket over us, but we still had our clothes on. I sat up. My head hurt worse than any dirt bike accident, punch, or football hit I'd ever taken. My body felt creaky and wrung out. I made my way home, and even with sunglasses, the light stabbed my eyes.

That evening, after I'd clocked in, Becky and Gina were like, "Holy shit, man. We thought you were, like, this total straight nerd, and last night, you were, like, all craziness and dancing like it was 1999 and all that shit. Man, that was some wild shit when you went out the window and hit the ground, rolling up onto your feet. And, like, holy shit, we thought you were, like, this quiet weirdo, but no way, man, you were, like, holding in the wild man. Fucking, like, fucking cool shit. Hey, like, want to get high?" I didn't want to get high, but it was nice to be offered. After that night, I became a freight train of booze rolling through Vegas.

At the end of the week, I went to visit a friend. Jack had been a corrupt politician who not only embezzled city money, but gave fat contracts for kickbacks to friends. Those friends rolled over on him like cars speeding too fast in a sharp turn—the velocity of trouble. We'd ridden in chains together from the Clark County Jail in Las Vegas to the first prison I was laid over in outside of Tucson, Arizona. We were part of a small group of Vegas guys that included a loan shark, a bookie, a Hells Angel, a mob boss, an embezzler, and other associates you wouldn't want looking for you. When we arrived, everyone knew my story because my case of aiding and abetting the theft of a machine gun from my National Guard armory had made national news. And of course, the Vegas guys got copies of the *Las Vegas Review Journal* sent to them to keep up with what was going on in the city.

Jack had been released from the halfway house before I'd gotten there but had left a message to come visit him at the bar where he worked the afternoon shift. I decided to pedal over I'd been avoiding going but wanted to make good on his invite. Besides, he might've had a line on work. Bartenders got to know what was going on in the area.

When the door creaked open, I couldn't see into the darkness. Just the blur of dim lights. I entered and let my eyes adjust. The only white guy there, some of the men looked me up and down as I walked in.

"New Guy!" His smile reminded me of when he laid down gin on a cardsharp, stunning the common room to silence. He won fourteen cartons of smokes. Not a smoker, he traded them for ice cream. It made me happy. His afro was a little grayer, but his skin glowed, so he looked younger than when I last saw him over a year ago. The freedom health plan was working for him. He wiped the counter down. At the taps, he drew a lager and set it in front of me. I looked at it, unsure. I'd been dreaming of a beer. In the supermarket, I'd walk through the liquor aisles and beer coolers as if at a shrine at the end of a pilgrimage.

He smiled. "Go on. Just have a couple, and after, eat some of these." He pulled a pack of peanut butter and crackers off a rack.

Laughing, I said, "I had an uncle who advised us teens that if we wanted to hide our drinking, to eat a spoonful of peanut butter."

"There you go."

"He always smelled like whiskey and peanut butter."

Jack laughed. "I bet he drank his whiskey mixed into a Coke bottle to hide his drinking."

"He did."

"Mine did too."

"I don't have to be back for a few hours, so a couple won't hurt."

"A brother has got to pace himself."

As I sat on the stool, I felt outside, staring at a life going on without me. Time was broken. Here in this bar, with my fellow felon friend, I was again not wanting to say no. For camaraderie, but also the last three weeks of rejection. Riding around all over that miserably hot city and frustration played havoc on my self-esteem and body. The power of thirst I had for a drink right then overshadowed any thirst I'd ever had for water. At least now I wasn't underaged.

I looked at the glass. The bubbles rose to the foam. Some beer had slopped over and created a puddle. I smelled it. My mouth felt the want of it. I figured a couple of drinks couldn't hurt. It'd make me feel as if I'm coming closer to being free.

Other guys came in and walked past me as I sat chatting with Jack. It was like a working-class bar in any working-class neighborhood where folks went to knock the edge off sore muscles and hard knocks. They said hi to him and gave me the 'what's up' nod after Jack introduced me as one of his friends from prison and asked if they knew of any work about. No one did. I stared at the beer as Jack served other guys. Like a blackjack player, I weighed the odds of taking a hit and beating the house or busting.

After a moment, I sipped it. The beer sent a shiver through my body as it flowed down. *Holy smokes*, I thought. The edge melted away and a warmth spread through me as I took another drink. The glow of the lights warmed. The barstool squeaked as I shifted my weight. The background noise and chatter comforted me like the steady hum of tires on a long road going nowhere. In here, I belonged for a few minutes. I had an old friend who knew what I'd been through, and what we didn't say was as meaningful as what others say in an hour of conversation. I remembered the dreamy Sundays with my ex-wife, Lynne, as we listened to records and lounged about drinking tequila sunrises. A bubble of sound and hazy light where a palpable vibration wrapped around us. It was better than I remembered. Things would be okay.

The time slipped away. I felt caught on a sandbar in a slipstream. It swept along, and I was helpless to wade into it. Three weeks of semi-freedom and I felt myself hurtling toward nothing. And now time and memory started to blur, collapsing in on themselves. It was like when I first entered the county jail. After the initial shock, the days blended like muddy water with only blips on the days I went to court or had a visitor, and then the stasis returned after going back to the pod. It became worse in prison, where nothing broke up the days except random violence, and then that too became collapsed into one long day where every day was like the next, and we lived in our eternal present where nothing changed. All our days were debris spinning in society's back eddy.

Jack refilled my glass twice more. Warmth filled me. The blurred edges of neon light, the cigarette smoke, the jukebox playing a soul song, and the flashing lights and clatter and dings of video poker and slot machines. A haze rose around me, like being inside a mirage. I laughed and joked with Jack and a couple of guys around me but felt like I was watching a show, watching a guy trying to fit in someplace without fitting in anywhere.

After two more beers, I scarfed two packs of peanut butter crackers, washing them down with soda. I said bye to Jack. He said to come on back if I got the time. I said thanks. I enjoyed visiting with him, but what would we ever talk about other than prison? Out front, I unlocked my bike. The treeless streets shimmered in the heat. Lightheaded, I steadied myself against a light post. So much beer after so much time affected me differently than before. An uneasiness crept over me. It felt like hearing the buzz of a rattlesnake, not knowing where it lay coiled. I shook it off. Some cars tooled around, but no one was out in the heat except for some dudes in the shade of a dumpster passing a paper bag. I checked my watch. A few hours left before curfew. A restlessness filled me. I'd be damned if I'd return to that half-assed prison before it was time.

Riding west, I bent my head into the dry air as I pumped my legs. I knew if I kept going, in a few miles, I'd reach the desert on the edge of town. It might be beyond the boundary I was supposed to stay within, but I figured, fuck it. If they wanted to violate me for wanting to stand alone among the cactus and scrub brush, then let them. Not that they'd see me from their office. I didn't think they'd even drive by me by chance. What would any of them be doing out there anyway? No road signs, no mile markers, just broken bottles and trash to mark the way. None of them struck me as the "Let's go drive into the desert along a road that turns into gravel then stops miles from anywhere for no apparent reason" kind of people. I was that kind of person, and they were nothing like me.

Sweat poured out of me and evaporated in the heat and wind created from my forward motion. The water bottle mounted on the bike sloshed, about three-quarters full. The traffic became less and less. I went by a couple of under-development subdivisions where all the houses were variations on each other, with different colored stucco and Spanish tile that in a hundred years or so would be broken pottery scattered over the desert. The unfinished houses, with the exposed wooden frames and wires sticking out at odd angles, looked like shipwrecks on a beach with only the ribs left. Was it decaying or in dry dock, ready for the sides to be laid on and fixed into place? The crews working on the sites labored under the sun, and to me, flying by was like watching a movie in fast motion. The road started getting rougher, so I slowed down, not wanting to shake the bike to pieces. I coasted to a stop and looked out into the desert. Lizards scurried around in their lizard lives, waiting for a raven's sharp beak to the back.

I watched the lizards. When we were kids trying to catch them, it horrified us the first time one of their tails popped off in our hands as they escaped. We ran with the tail to our parents, in a panic we'd killed them. How the knowing smiles of our parents caused us to pause, unsure of their humanity, until they told us the tails would grow back. It was a defense mechanism. What could we sacrifice to keep living?

I breathed deeply into my abdomen, feeling the dry air in my sinuses and lungs, and it warmed my insides. This time of year, the height of summer, everything smelled of dust, dried wood, and bone. When I was a kid, I'd begin wondering if we'd ever smell rain on the wind again. Home for me had been a series of desert locations. Some in isolated outposts like frontier gold rushers, a small farm we had to leave after being lied to by the landowner, or our attempted homestead close to the border. My dad wasn't able to stitch together enough paying work to pay the bank, so they forced us off. Occasionally, cowboys rode by looking for their shit-assed cattle, looking down on us kids afoot without livestock or the good sense to wear boots and wide-brimmed hats.

I knew the look of those who thought they were better than me my whole life. Just like when I'd been shipped from prison to prison, chained in a bus or van to all the waypoints of my incarceration. I knew what we looked like to people in cars who sped past the van, staring, hoping to see what bad men rode the highway. To people who stopped in rest area parking lots where marshals let us out of the Department of Prisons van, with its darkened windows to shield the public from any obscene gestures we might inflict upon them. One at a time, we stepped onto the asphalt like steers through a chute into the killer's pen. We milled about in jumpsuits, blinking at the light, no sunglasses to cover our eyes, no hat brims to shade our faces, clinking in chains like Marley's ghost. We haunted vans and parking lots and houses of detention until release. Then we haunted society and the dreams of good people everywhere. In our empty hands, chained to our waists, we carried the burden of all we had done and all we would ever do.

But here along a rough road, no one came by to judge me or felt the need to ask my business or spit on me to prove they were a better class of people. Just me and the desert. Only the wind filled my ears. It flowed over me as if I were a wing with a void at my back. I stared into the almost white sky. A hawk cried on a thermal. I glimpsed the shadowed wings before I looked down. I blinked away the sun blindness and saw contorted and spiked Joshua trees, creosote brush, and yucca foresting the desert floor. Beyond that, gray and red mountains stood against the sun-faded horizon. Out here, I felt free and close to home. In the wind, I felt I heard my mother's voice in the distance, like when I was twelve at our attempted homestead. She'd stand on the edge of our camp, backed by the fire rising in the ring of rocks as my dad stoked it with mesquite, and call. Her voice carried through the gloaming, over the low brush and cactus, like a prophet in the Old Testament. "Night's falling. Come eat."

I turned to face the east. Las Vegas spread across the valley. The roar and hum of it flowed over the playa. In the dust, smog haze, and heat waves, it appeared as if the city floated on a silver lake. It looked like I imagined a trading city along the old Silk Road looked to the caravans coming across the steppes or out of miles of tactless dunes. All those towers with the promise of prosperity and the chance for respite in the desert. I realized my respite was the desert. I'd left it to come to the city I stare at now and, once there, slowly wrecked myself with booze, a broken marriage, and a prison sentence before I'd turned twenty-one. Cars along the highway in the distance gleamed in the sun like polished stones and gems as they disappeared into the mirage.

My beer buzz had dissipated, and I was sure the heat had sucked the booze out of my body. I needed to get back before dinner and curfew or face a write-up. My mouth was dry. I drank the water from my bottle in one long swallow. No use conserving it. Better to die with it in you than in the bottle next to your corpse, or so the old-timers told us. I turned my bike around and started pedaling down the sun-glazed road like all the other sun-glazed roads I'd been on in my short life. The way back to the halfway house wasn't as far as I'd ever ridden before, not even half as far, but felt as if I'd never make it out of this big-hearted desert.

Monday morning when I signed out, Ms. Randall handed me a pink message slip. On it, she had written the name and call back number for the supervisor at the *Las Vegas Review Journal* newspaper customer service office. She had made a smiley face at the bottom. Using the office phone,

I called, and he asked if I could start that afternoon. I said, "Yes, what time?" He asked if I could come in at 2:00 and work until 9:00.

I paused. I asked Ms. Randall if working until then would be okay. I didn't want to be late for curfew. She motioned for the phone, and I handed it to her. She identified who she was and if he was indeed the supervisor of that department. She nodded. She then asked for his supervisor's name and phone number. She wrote it down with a smile.

"It'll be fine," she said.

After telling him I'd be there, I put the receiver back in the cradle.

"Told you something would open up."

I still went by to see Penelope. She smiled but said they didn't have a position for me. I waved bye and said, "See you tomorrow," and she waved back. I biked to the newspaper boiler room. Once there, I changed out of my shorts and T-shirt into "appropriate office attire," still sweating from the heat.

The supervisor came up to about my shoulders. He wore a short-sleeved shirt with a brown tie. His thin hair had been combed over and held in place with gel. I followed him over to one of the desks with forms listing the names and numbers of subscribers and if they were daily, Sunday only, or some other combination. Next to it was a stack of forms with questions I needed to ask before recording the answers in ink. At the end of the satisfaction survey, I was supposed to upsell them if they didn't take the paper seven days a week. I sat at the desk.

"Any questions? It's easy enough."

"Easy enough," I answered.

"I'm right over there if you need something." He pointed to his office cubicle in the corner from where he oversaw all the employees. The room was an open office space with a false ceiling with fluorescent lights dangling in a grid formation. The bright lights made everyone look like we existed in an overexposed film. The erasure of the shadows flattened us and made us almost two-dimensional. If hell had a waiting room, it'd be lit with fluorescent lights.

Everyone chattered away on their phones, hung up, and redialed. That indecipherable background noise cocooned us at our desks where we sat with no time to talk with our co-workers. In front of us, the supervisor kept watch, checking his watch, making sure we didn't spend too much time talking to any one customer. We had a quota, and the big shots in marketing took every call seriously. We heard about it from the sup if we didn't get through the required number of customers and record their answers accurately to create the raw data from which they could create graphs, tables, and make recommendations to maximize readership. We were all strapped in and rowing this galley ship of commerce. I'd wanted to be a writer, and now I was the lowest cog in the business.

I looked around the room. A mix of young and old, men and women, but not one of us wore the three-piece suit of the con artists in my first telemarketing experience. We all dressed like we'd gotten up and threw on clothes to go shopping or walk about in the park. My sweaty ass was in jeans and a T-shirt. None of us looked like we were being groomed for promotion. Everyone seemed broke and worn out. Some of the men hadn't shaven, and some people hadn't combed their hair or wore frayed ponytails. We all looked animatronic with flat eyes from staring too long at pieces of paper and our repetitive motions tight to our bodies.

A wall clock hung high in the center of the wall we faced. It was hard not to keep looking at it like a kid in class waiting for the bell to ring. Except these students wouldn't be headed out to recess. This crowd might head out and hit the slot machines or head home and cook for kids after shopping for generic store brands to stretch what little money they made.

At the end of my shift, night had begun to fall. The city light kept the dark at bay. On the bike, I switched the lights on and engaged the little generator on the front fork to the rim. It made a buzzing noise as it spun, like the sound of toy car motors we kids played with on slot tracks. The heat persisted on the asphalt and concrete, but if I rode by a park, the air felt cooler as it was being sucked away from the well-watered grass and trees by the heat rising into the darkening sky. The rise in humidity enveloped me, and when I rode beyond the park's edge, it was like emerging from a shallow sea onto a beach flowing with lava.

At the halfway house, Mr. Lopez asked how it'd gone.

"It's a job," I said. The job sucked and was boring, but I needed it. I knew they wanted me to act as if it was my big break, but I knew it was a nowhere job. At least I had the opportunity to make money even if there wasn't a hope in hell to save enough for an apartment when I got out and still buy food I needed now.

Mrs. Gutiérrez came out from the back office. "What time did you get off?"

"About forty, forty-five minutes ago or so," I said.

"Glad you came straight back. Some think they can come in here making excuses that their new job kept them late."

I signed the check-in sheet and wished them goodnight.

In the apartment, I made mac and cheese and a couple of hotdogs. I sat at the table eating. Earlier, I'd called my parents and let them know I had a job. They were happy for me. Small working-class victories. We always felt that no matter how menial or pointless the job, at least it was a job and could lead to something bigger. At heart, we knew it didn't go on to something bigger. More likely, we'd keep getting knocked back until we couldn't hang on and killed ourselves or just drank ourselves to death as we slipped between the cracks, leaving those with luck, connections, and timing to make it. I thought about those guys who were laid off right before retirement and how the company didn't pay them out their retirement because they didn't have enough time in. What is it to lose a job you worked at for years as suddenly as a car accident in a downsizing, yet those that caused the downsizing kept their job? Now they were old and moved stiffly like a lizard before sunrise, and no one would hire them. That was our reality even as we acted like things would be different this time.

The room darkened. I turned on a light to keep reading more about the siege of Dien Bien Phu. As the night deepened and the helicopters began buzzing, the neighborhood and sirens created sentences between the punctuation of gunshots. I went to bed and lay awake. A long while went by, but I knew eventually sleep would come.

Every afternoon, I sweated it out and called subscribers to ask them the battery of customer service questions, hung up, and dialed again. Call after call. Dial. Read the script, branching off with the prompts of yes or no questions. Hang up. Dial again. Hello…

An old woman answered, and when I told her I was with the newspaper, she cut me off and said, "No thanks, I already get it."

I explained I was making a courtesy call to see if she had any complaints or suggestions to improve her service or if she was happy with everything.

"I don't need anything. Although, it'd be nice if you covered more on the Test Site. I mean, aliens are living out there, and that can't be safe for us. We're so close."

"Sure," I said. "I'll let the editor know your concern." I didn't know what else to say to her, so why not? I wrote it out in her comments box. I told her to have a good day and watch for upcoming news stories on the Test Site.

Before my arrest, I'd had a friend who worked for a private security firm out there. He said he spent a lot of time riding around in a truck along the perimeter, armed to hold off a battalion. All sorts of whack jobs thought there were aliens and spacecraft at Area 51 and would hike through the desert and climb the fence. "We'd pick them up, most dying of thirst and glad to see us," he said. I'd asked him if he ever took part in arresting the hippies who walked across the boundary during Easter protests, wondering if he had detained Lynne on one of her anti-nuke marches or prayer vigils.

"Fucking anti-nuke fucks. They don't know shit," he said. "But no. Law enforcement did that during those times."

He also mentioned they had orders to shoot anyone who didn't surrender. Serious business violating national security. I asked if he'd ever had to shoot someone. He shrugged. "I can neither confirm nor deny the existence of any shallow graves near or within the Test Site perimeter." We all had a laugh about it.

When we trained for riots and looters, we joked that we'd fire warning shots before commanding, "Halt or we'll shoot again." I'd thought about applying to be in the security detachment at the Test Site, but I had to be twenty-one. Instead of joining them, I turned twenty-one in jail. Later, at Tucson, when I saw prison guards driving around the prison's perimeter and all the desert beyond the fences, I thought about my friend and naturally thought they weren't only keeping people out, but keeping something in.

On another call, I had an old man yell at me as soon as I said I was with the paper. "This number is unlisted! How the goddamned hell did you get it?" He went on to rant how he'd been scammed by the likes of me before and there was no way in hell I was getting his credit card information. After telling him I was just conducting a satisfaction survey, he said, "Well, ask me." He still sounded wary. As I asked him to tell me if he was satisfied with his service, he said everything was okay, but "The goddamned phone call frosts my ass." I wrote it out in his comments section.

"I'll be sure to let management know."

"Take my goddamned number off your list."

"I'll let management know."

"Unlisted means unlisted. Get it? I'm fuc—"

I hung up on him. I tore up the comments sheet and wadded it into a tight ball and shot it into a wastebasket. A middle-aged woman with tightly curled hair at a desk next to me gave me a thumbs up as she talked on her phone.

On a new sheet, I marked him down for a follow-up next month. Fuck that guy.

I looked up at the clock. How the hell had I only been here fifteen minutes?

When I'd made about twenty calls, I stood up to stretch and drink some water. At the water cooler, I filled a paper cup and sipped from it. The supervisor came over to me. He wanted to know if everything was alright. I said, "Yeah, just needed some water after all the phone chit-chat." I cleared my throat to make a point. He looked up at the clock and informed me a break could only be taken after three hours of work. That's why some of the callers had those giant convenience store tankers of soda, or others filled cups with water and took them to their desks. I scanned the room. The woman with the tight curls picked up a coffee mug and drank from it as if demonstrating the supervisor's point. I noticed everyone staring at me. It was weird to look at all those faces fixed on me as they talked into phones. Almost like they were keeping tabs on me as they talked with a 911 operator. No, he's just drinking water, but that's against the law here when it's unscheduled. He's a known felon. Please send a squad car right away.

I looked down at him. "I see." I breathed deep like the Buddhist heroin smuggler taught me to control my rising anger. It would suck to get sent back to prison now.

I crumpled the paper cup and dropped it in the trash next to the cooler. Without another word, I went back to my desk. I sat there for fifteen minutes without calling anyone. The clock hands moved in their measured circles of our mortal time. I knew how to be still. I knew how to wait out the clock. I knew petty authoritarians who rattled their teeth like keys to let you know who was in charge and their rules were meant to be strictly observed. Fuck that guy too.

At the halfway house, I set my bag of groceries on the desk for Mrs. Gutiérrez to paw through. At the supermarket, I'd cruised the liquor section and dreamed of drunkenness. Lynne and I had such fun getting liquored up and hanging out. Sometimes things got out of hand, but mostly we had a good time until the end. If it weren't for drinking and partying, we might not have gotten together, and we might not have gotten married. We might not have gotten divorced either.

Time breaks in strange ways. I'd gone to basic and advanced training over my 19th summer, became a top gun tanker, a lean, mean killing machine, an honor graduate, a STRAC soldier with a new tattoo of a grinning death's head, and was no longer a civilian scumbag. Getting back from Fort Knox, I rented a studio apartment in the same bunker-like cinder block complex with sliding glass doors I'd moved out of in May. I didn't have much in the way of possessions, so I'd kept them at my cousin Binder's place. After getting the couple of cardboard boxes, I lined my books up along the wall and taped up my Bruce Lee poster from *Enter the Dragon* onto the white cinder block.

Just sixteen and a half weeks was all. It seemed a lot longer given the drill sergeants had completely rewired my head. I started back at my job at the fast-food joint where everything was just the fucking same as I'd left it, except the women I'd been sleeping with were no longer interested. I wanted to go active duty, but the Army recruiter said I had to wait six months to fulfill my Guard obligation. I wanted to ride around in tanks all the time. I wanted to go to Germany or Korea and become a paratrooper and train on the Sheridan armored fighting vehicle. I wanted to be like one of Patton's soldiers driving for the relief of Bastogne. This life of community college, slapping together burgers, and trading fast, drunk hands with women felt empty.

Like most kids raised along the margins of civilization, I went shooting up the deserts, but that was nothing like tanks in a row with main guns erupting with fire and feeling the sudden jolt and rocking back of the Earth on its axis. Plus, there was something alluring in the life of discipline and precision. The recruiter told me to use the six months to my advantage. "Don't be a slug," he said. "Volunteer at your armory for every field exercise, extra duty, and take any classes they offer. Do the Army correspondence courses." It'd look good on my record to get the assignment I wanted. But until then, "Keep working out, and," he laughed, "don't kill yourself out of fucking boredom." I was a shoo-in.

My first week back from Fort Knox, I tuned up my motorcycle and went on a long ride. A couple of days later, I rode over to visit my buddy, Mooncat. He was one of the first friends I made at the fast-food joint. A high school senior, he only worked until midevening and on weekends, so we hung out some nights I didn't work. Mooncat played guitar in a band that sounded like a mashup of The Clash and The Rolling Stones. His mom worked a lot of hours for a casino on the Strip, and his father had long since abandoned them, so mostly it was us hanging out in an empty house.

We lay on his bed, drinking Jack Daniel's and eating quesadillas while watching Letterman or MTV. I was bitching about how the girls I'd been seeing were gone or seemed put off by me. "Oh, hi. Nice haircut. When did you get back?" they'd ask.

I ran my hand over my bristle-short hair. "It sucks."

He laughed. "What did you expect from those hippies?"

Mooncat got up and retrieved a Hi-C can he had made into a bong and loaded the bowl. "My friend, Lynne, is single again." He fired up a cook's propane torch used on crème brûlée and took a big bubbling hit. He held the smoke until his face turned red and let it out. "Come with me to the midnight movie and meet her." He handed the can to me, but I turned him down. "Shit, you gotten uptight. Maybe Lynne will be too wild for you."

On Friday, my buddy, Matt, called. He had a Honda CB750cc bike and wanted to race about like we had before I'd left for Fort Knox and he Camp Pendleton. We met in the parking lot at the fast-food joint. As always, he wore top-siders without socks, khakis, and a polo with a popped collar.

I rolled to a stop next to him. I flipped my visor up. "What's the news?" I asked.

"Got an AR-15 today."

"Spending that sweet boot camp money?"

"No, a present from my parents for not dropping out."

I nodded. "We got to spar. I learned some techniques from these Illinois guys."

He laughed. "Tankers don't need hand-to-hand. They got a tank to hide in."

"I'll still kick your jarhead ass."

"We'll see about that. I learned some things too."

I look out to the street. "Race?"

He nodded.

We flipped down our visors and pulled onto the Maryland Parkway.

At a red light, we looked to each other and nodded. When the light turned green, the motorcycle leapt away from the white line. The front wheel rose a moment before touching back down. Within seconds, I crossed the intersection. The Kerker header funneled noise from four cylinders into the street and off the buildings. Cars still sat at the light as if their engines had stalled. My KZ650's black gas tank gleamed under the streetlights, and the gold letters, 'B-O-B,' glittered below the fuel cap.

From my peripheral vision, I saw my best pal Matt's front tire. His CB750 trailed a split second behind me. The key to winning the sprint was knowing when to begin stopping. Too soon and he'd overtake me. Too late and I would end up in the cross traffic. You had to keep an eye on the light. Was it green when you started? How long has it been green? Was it red and you could hope it'd change before you got there? If I began to slow down and the light flicked green, then Matt could pull ahead. The light turned green. I threaded the line between the cars still not moving and crossed the intersection past the front cars who'd started moving. Someone honked. I flipped them off over my shoulder with my left hand, the right occupied with the throttle. The honk sounded again, but further away.

The green light ahead was stale. I felt I'd have enough time to clip part of the yellow and hoped Matt would chicken out. At nearly 100 mph, I hunkered over the gas tank. This bike wasn't a crotch rocket designed to be laid on. But for short bursts, it wasn't a big deal. The light went yellow. I was too fast and too close to brake. I hoped to sail through the intersection before the other traffic moved. Matt throttled back. On the line between the cars, the light turned red. Within a moment, the cross traffic began to turn left. I aimed for the right of the intersection. Time slowed. In those moments, dread filled me, as did the stupidity of what I was doing. The traffic lights smeared in my slow motion. Faces behind the wheels of cars looked horrified or oblivious. Someone honked, brake lights flashed, and I swore if I survived this, I'd give up racing motorcycles. My stomach contorted, sending bile into my throat. My heart pumped so fast it didn't beat but whirred like a wheel.

I flew between the cars and past the intersection. Matt stopped behind me. I pulled into a bank parking lot. The temp on the reader board read 98 degrees and the time 11:21 pm. I sat on my bike. The heat from the asphalt seeped through the soles of my boots. The hard knot of terror in my stomach began to subside, replaced with an overwhelming sense of euphoria. My body trembled in the exhilaration after the fear and danger had passed.

Matt rolled up and pulled in next to me. We shut off the engines and flipped our helmet visors up. He shook his head. We chatted about what we had done over the summer. He'd gone to Marine Corps boot camp for the reserves. I'd made friends with Matt at the fast-food joint when I was first hired. We worked the closing shift. After the place was cleaned up, we'd drink Jack Daniel's mixed into vanilla milkshakes, and Matt and I would practice martial arts. I'd learned San Soo Kung Fu in high school from a guy who worked at the mine. He put on classes for a couple of us. From my reading of Bruce Lee's books, I felt what Ben taught had real-world applications and memorized and worked on the forms and techniques. Matt and I knocked the shit out of each other until two in the morning sometimes, which made my 0700 classes an endurance test. I started taking caffeine tablets and diet supplements that were essentially speed to wire myself awake. I took them by the handful, figuring I was young and could handle it, but sometimes I crashed if I quit moving for very long. Once, I snapped awake in my psychology class, and the professor used me as an example for hypnagogic states of awareness and altered states of consciousness. Matt and I trained to fight and be tough guys in this hard-assed way that wasn't that tough, as I'd discover during my first week in the county jail.

I wanted to train in a combat-style martial art and not the kind that were more dance and gymnastics. I read books on the various styles and went to dojos and talked with the sensei but always hesitated joining, worried it wouldn't be geared to real combat situations and I'd end up wasting money. Matt did too as he wanted to join the Marines. We talked about how it'd also be cool to be part of the CIA and fight with indigenous forces to keep America safe. Like the soldiers I'd read about who helped the resistance during World War II and in Vietnam.

After a few minutes ticked off the big clock, I told him I had a blind date I needed to be off to.

He laughed and looked at the reader board. "Only in Vegas would you have a blind date at midnight."

The midnight movie was *The Rocky Horror Picture Show.* I parked. I'd never seen so many fishnet stockings, panties, garters, bustiers, and bras in public on men. Women too dressed as if they were the leads in *Chicago* or *Cabaret*, and the whole crowd buzzed. I felt the heat of the night not as oppressive, but as expanding, blooming into something exciting I couldn't name, but when Mooncat called my name, it was like the ringing of a bell calling me to church. We bought our tickets. Mooncat had his hair spiked up and wore a headband of the Japanese Rising Sun. He wasn't sporting women's underwear but instead wore tight leather pants, a torn T-shirt, and leather wrist cuffs that looked like something a sword fighter would wear. We went down to the front row. He introduced me to a bunch of people and, last of all, Lynne, with her big smile, shimmering makeup, and stoned eyes glistening in the theater lights.

Lynne played Columbia, the top-hatted dancer in short shorts covered in sequins and spangles and stripes. Her nipples slipped over the dam of her sparkling bustier as she danced heedlessly in full character in front of the audience. The audience shouted lines, throwing rice and toilet paper and toast and cards as performers sang and acted in front of the screen.

By the finale, a near riot erupted when everyone jumped up and danced the "Time Warp." Hundreds of people twirled, stepped, and thrust their hips in a whirlwind of bodies. How I fell in love with the chaos of makeup, women's lingerie, and chorus lines of unrepentant sexual desire. I saw my first transvestites in full flower and felt every bit the bumpkin that comes to the big city.

Because I was wearing a motorcycle jacket, jeans, and boots, people assumed I had dressed as Eddie, Columbia's biker love interest in the movie—the failed first creation of the mad transvestite, Dr. Frank-N-Furter. I hadn't, but I didn't refuse when Lynne grabbed me out of the front row to dance: her Columbia to my Eddie, the botched first son. The mob had me.

I'd heard about the movie, seen a couple of pictures, and heard the soundtrack in high school from my pals, Adam and Jane, who had been to the show in Orange County. But this was my first experience of *The Rocky Horror Picture Show*, and it swept me away like a flash flood destroying a rock festival. I became a "creature of the night." After the show, Lynne and I roared away on Bad Bob. By dawn, we were drunk in a gritty bed, covered in glitter and red wash-out hair dye, smelling of sex, leather, and cigarettes, with a motorcycle's engine ticking as it cooled in the kitchenette.

When she started leaving deodorant, tampons, and toothpaste at my place, Mooncat said she was slowly moving in. I'd never lived with anyone not family before. "Nah," I said. "She just needs some things for when she stays over for a night."

"Man, I'm telling you, one day she'll come over and not leave except to go visit her mom."

Me and Lynne's relationship was weird in so many ways. She with her pooka shells and moccasins, braiding feathers into her hair, dropping acid, painting peace signs on her face, and going to anti-nuke rallies at the Test Site gates, paired with my guns, martial arts, and peace through superior fire attitude. But we loved rock 'n' roll, drinking whiskey, racing around on Bad Bob, and fucking like we were the only two people who knew how. Some people might say we were superficial and wasting our lives, but they'd be wrong. We were driven by something deep in us, something primal that always bordered on chaos.

I'd volunteered for a winter field exercise with the Third Infantry Division at the National Training Center at Fort Irwin. I saw a pal from basic training. He had been an older recruit who joined for steady pay and insurance on his two kids and wife. I always thought of him in his 30s, but he was only 24. When I asked him how Army life was treating him, he rolled his eyes. "There are no shortage of dickheads. I'll tell you that. Remember, in basic, we kept saying we just need to put up with the drill sergeants for a few months and it'd get better? Fuck. All they do is fuck with us. It's like they get bonuses if they're a bunch of dicks."

I told him I was going to go active duty from the Guard. "Fucking don't do it, man. You got it good. You get to come out and train and shoot the big guns but go home where it's your own rules and these sonsabitches can't fuck with you every time you think you doing alright."

We said our goodbyes, but before he took off for his platoon, he said, "If I didn't have the kids to think about, I'd be out of this shit."

Lynne was okay with me going active duty, but anytime I talked to another soldier, they talked like I was the slow kid who just didn't get it. "Man, don't get in the van no matter how much candy the guy gots."

I came home from Fort Irwin. I opened the glass door, pushed Bad Bob into the kitchenette, and leaned it onto the kickstand. Lynne lay on the bed smoking a joint and watching *2001: A Space Odyssey* on the TV bolted to the wall. I was still dirty and reeking of sweat, cordite, and exhaust. I took the bottle of Jack Daniel's off the table and drank from it. Lynne jumped up and wrapped herself around me so hard it almost knocked me over. "Easy, baby, you nearly knocked the Jack out my hand."

"Can't have alcohol abuse."

I took another swig as she hung from my neck, kissing my face. "You taste like a salty pallet fire."

"The heat of the party."

"Let's go see our favorite bartender." Our favorite because he never carded us, and he was a hell of an old-timer with great fucking stories. The bar was walking distance through a frat neighborhood, so we didn't have to worry about driving.

A low-lit place with fake candles burning electric lights on the tables and booths of deep cushioned leather you might expect in a mob movie hit. We sat at the wooden bar on high-back stools. The poker machines inset in the bar top pulsed a bluish light that made us look bloodless and randomly made noises to attract the attention of errant drunks. The nicotine-yellow mirror ran the length of the ten-foot wall with the formations of bottles tiered in front of it. The bartender threw a couple of coasters on the bar in front of us. His gray face had the gravity and whiskey sag. The skin below his eyes drooped like how kids will use their fingers to pull their lower eyelids down to look like freaks and laugh about it.

He set a Cape Cod in front of Lynne and poured me a tumbler of Jack. "You just get back?"

I nodded. I was still in my dirty uniform. He held a Zippo lighter with an anchor on it to Lynne's cigarette and then fired one of his own. On his wrist, he had a Seiko dive watch with a metal band that had the Trident of the US Navy SEALs on each side of the watch. I took a sip and let the burn go down. Lynne clinked the ice in her drink and asked, "What's the news with you?"

"Glad you asked, darling. I drew two cards to an inside straight flush and won a thousand."

"Holy shit, man. That's great," I said.

"Then I spent three grand chasing down another." He laughed. "Fucking gambling. But it's my life's work. What can you do?"

"Any happenings?" Lynne asked.

He leaned back against the counter in front of the mirror. "We're going to have a poker tournament next weekend." He took a drag from his cigarette. "And bingo on Tuesday." The smoke came out of his mouth as he talked. "A jazz trio on Friday."

"I like bingo," Lynne said. "My grandparents play the shit out of it at Sam's Town."

"Some take it as serious as heart surgery," he said. "They say poker players are as serious gamblers as you'll find, but fucking bingo players will cut you."

"That's my grandparents for sure. My grandma would be tracking her numbers even if they were wheeling her out on a gurney."

Her grandparents were cool old people. They lived with Lynne's mom in a regular neighborhood like I'd lived in as a kid before we started living in the desert and mining towns that'd hire my dad. Her grandmother had been an auctioneer and a housewife in some backwater Minnesota town and now killed it at bingo every weekend. I imagined her at bingo with her auctioneer voice—Can I get B15, a B15, B15 once, B15 going twice. BINGO! With the B15 to the old women in the muumuu and turban with too much rouge. Lynne's grandfather had been an old-school wrestler in the Midwest in the forties and fifties after his stint in the Pacific Theater with the Marine Corps. When Lynne introduced us, he challenged me to trade blows to the gut. I was like, what in the fuck, old man? He had a potbelly, bifocal glasses, and hearing aids I imagined flying off his head. "Nah, sir. I can't hit an elder like that."

"Are you too chicken to take a punch when it's my turn?"

"Go ahead," Lynne said. "He's fucking serious."

So I punched him, but not hard. I'm not an idiot. His gut was hard as hell, but still. Then he punched me. I was braced, and it knocked me back a little, but I acted like it was a lot harder than it really was so the old man could feel good. Respect meant not being a tough guy dick to an old man, your girlfriend's grandfather. I could tell that back in the day, though, he'd have sent me to the floor like a pile of sniveling dirty laundry.

Our favorite bartender refilled us. He stole a glance down Lynne's top. She didn't give a shit about it and sometimes went topless at the lake until some uptight ass whined. I didn't care either. I knew some dudes would get fucking all hot and worked up about it, but they were her tits. "Thanks, man," she said.

He nodded and flipped open his Zippo to spark another cigarette. A couple of poker machines chimed their 'come hither' jingle. His watch reflected light as he looked at the time. He grabbed the remote to turn on the television—*Cheers*, where everybody knows your name.

We drank our way into headaches with the deliberation of a jury and staggered on home in the dark early hours. I had this crazy exhausted but wide-awake feeling. It was still weird to me how I could be so drunk and so awake. I hadn't even been drinking a year yet and was still learning its different effects and how to handle it, or, as happens, mishandle it. I stumbled into Bad Bob in the kitchenette as Lynne tugged at my belt. In a drunken heat, a military web belt can bind on a person like a noose, and it took what seemed like forever to free it. We fell into bed and fucked in a spinning haze. We ignored the upstairs neighbor pounding on the floor for us to keep it down. After we finished, we lay sweaty and smoking. I was so hungry but couldn't get up. The simple act of microwaving a quesadilla became a labor Hercules couldn't accomplish. We passed out with the television playing the National Anthem.

At 11:00 am, she shook me awake and said, "Let's go get married."

I sat up on the bed. The inside of my mouth was like cat litter. The studio apartment was as big as her bedroom in her mom's suburban home. It didn't seem like a place a married couple should live.

"Come on," Lynne said. "Let's do it. Why wait for what society expects from us? Let's be impetuous." I shrugged and found my jeans and decided today was a good day to get hitched. I still hadn't even showered yet as I'd been sucked into Hurricane Lynne since I got home.

About thirty minutes later, we stood before the Justice of the Peace. Lynne wore a leather-fringed jacket like some hippie frontier woman and a braided hemp headband with a flower in it, calf-length moccasins, and a sundress that clung to the curves of her body. I wore jeans, combat boots, a brown T-shirt, and my fatigue jacket. Both of our mothers were horrified when they found out. Mine because I didn't set a date and invite the family to a traditional marriage ceremony, and hers because she had fallen into the patriarchal trap laid for young women.

We did end up having a formal ceremony for the families with flowers, wedding cake, and decades of dance moves. I wore my dress Army uniform, the nicest clothes I owned, and she wore a white gown that could've been a strapless prom dress with baby's breath in her pinned-up hair. In the light, as she danced with her grandfather, the small flowers looked like will-o'-the wisps above a golden field. Even though we were underage, the adults looked away when we and our friends drank. Lynne wanted us to take our "friends only" wedding party photo in the men's restroom. There, we milled about in the smell of disinfectant, urinal cakes, alcohol, and the drift smoke of weed. Drunk, high, none of us twenty but filled with all the optimism our class of kids have of making our own future and ignorant of our criminal hearts.

Was it possible to be so caught up in ceremony and ritual and the idea of the event that a person missed the essential point of it? I lifted Lynne and cradled her in my arms as if about to cross the threshold of a bridal suite. She threw her arm back as if finishing her big song at *The Rocky Horror Picture Show*, our stoner, new wave, punk rocker, hippie friends disarrayed around us dressed in blacks and reds and chains and leather and studs and spikes and piercings and pooka shells with teased hair and boys wearing makeup, and then there was me with my pressed Class A uniform with its patches, ribbons, badges, name tag, and polished shoes, lifting a woman in a formal gown in front of a urinal and a sink.

Back then, I couldn't see the irony of the uniform. To which world did I belong?

Funny, I thought, how the memories washed through me looking at bottles of Jack Daniel's and cans of beer stacked in coolers like so many knickknacks brought home to remind you of vacations and weekend trips you blacked out on. The memory of it made my body shiver. An urge rose up from the basement of my consciousness. I wanted to get a tall boy beer or three and down them in the parking lot out of brown paper bags. I'd eat some peanut butter and ride my bike around for an hour, push the edge of curfew before coming back here where I knew Mrs. Gutiérrez would be staring at the sweep of her watch's second hand. The beers I'd had on Friday were still on my tongue, but I resisted. The buzz would have to wait.

On Saturday, I rode over to where Gina lived. Joan had said she'd wrecked her moped. She had lost control in the gravel on the road's shoulder and flipped it into a concrete-lined canal. She was pretty banged up and had a broken wrist.

When she opened the door, her eyes got big with surprise. "Holy fuck. Mom said you got fit but didn't say how fit."

I smiled. "Fed's Gym," I joked.

"Looks good on you." In a tank top and shorts, I could see that besides the scuff mark on her forehead, her legs and shoulders looked like she'd been sandblasted.

"Beat watching TV in a darkened room or losing at cards to gangsters."

We went back to her living room. "You need to sign my cast." She held up her right wrist.

"Your mom said you took a nasty fall."

"Yeah, trashed my moped too. Fucking asshole in a big-ass car." She eased herself onto the couch with a grimace and groan. On the side table sat an ashtray, a pack of smokes, and a lighter. After fishing a cigarette out of the pack, she lit it. To be fair to assholes in big-ass cars, she was high, riding like a stunt woman up and down the embankment before losing control like Evel Knievel jumping the fountain at Caesar's Palace and endoed herself crash test dummy style.

I sat on a recliner but didn't recline, sitting upright.

She regarded me. "You used to be so skinny." She shook her head. "And such a goody-goody. You didn't even get high at Blue Oyster Cult."

"I kind of went off the rails, didn't I?" The fact she was the bad kid growing up and I, the one who memorized *Star Trek* and *The Lord of the Rings* trivia, the one who sat in libraries across the Southwest copying science information for hours, was the one who went to prison was not lost on me.

She chuffed and coughed.

We talked about what she'd been up to, working and thinking about going to nursing school. Her boyfriend was a slot mechanic at a casino in Henderson. They shared this little two-bedroom.

I saw her record collection and asked if I could look through it. I found an old Uriah Heep album, *Sweet Freedom.* I had seen them in concert. They had a bunch of those rock 'n' roll wizard and fantasy-inspired songs so popular in the '70s, but my favorite was "Stealin'." It was a different kind of song. One guy on his own journey, out running his crimes, literal and metaphoric—"stealin' when [he] should have been buying." But also, he was on a quest.

My counselor in prison, Ms. Smith, had talked about how I needed to search inward, to dig down to my core. She said I needed to recreate the narrative of my life and own it. I understood it this way because in many ways, the guy in the song was me. She said I needed to be a pilgrim of my inner world and the shrine at the end was me. What if you journey to your inner self and find a Minotaur, and to kill it is to kill yourself because you can't live inside the rage anymore, can't bear the sorrow of being trapped between the two worlds of the animal and the man? Like sitting in the front seat of a Monte Carlo with a revolver with one bullet in the cylinder and a dare? Some nights, my tongue remembered the taste of gun oil and the feel of machine-sharpened grooves in the end of the barrel.

The line that always grabbed me was, "I stood on a ridge and shunned religion." Somehow, it seemed all there. Of course he stood on a ridge. How many holy mounts were there like where Satan tempted Christ, where Moses got the law, where Muhammad ascended to heaven, the mountain tops where holy men sought enlightenment and Native Americans went on vision quests? In philosophy, Nietzsche's madman had come down from an alpine peak to reveal we'd killed God and He was dead. This song was the pilgrimage of the unbeliever to some unnamed ridge to reveal his own epiphany to the world.

I'd heard the song on my transistor radio when I was at Boron FPC. I'd looked out the window from my bunk. The darkness filled the valley up to the brim of the jagged horizon and the night sky above some far-off urban aurora after that. I believed it must've been Los Angeles over the limb of the Earth. I'd shunned the desert religion when I lay under night skies like the one arched over this bluff of inmates and guards. The church, like this prison, seemed open, but it was still a confining space and subject to the whim of authority. To question faith brought righteous condemnation from those you thought friends—to question was to be exiled. From junior high on, I struggled with faith and doubt and spiritual meaning.

A meteor had streaked the sky in a brief fast fire. It reminded me of the time I'd first thought of the sky as some other place, the galaxy and the universe beyond it. We were camped out at the homestead. My dad sat on a rock. His dirty and sweat-stained Stetson rested on the back of his head as he worked the coals of the campfire with a stick. He added some more mesquite branches to it. It flared. It cracked and sighed smoke into the night. "What you need to know about is speed, distance, and time."

Coyotes chased after rabbits in their nocturnal rounds. The weather had been clear with warm days and cold nights. We ate pinto beans and jackrabbit meat from tin plates. Our spoons scraped against the metal, sounding like my dad whetting his knife before gutting and skinning game.

As we sat in the dark with our lone fire burning, he talked about the scale of the galaxy and the universe. How our closest celestial neighbor, Alpha Centauri, was over three light years away. A distance so great it had to be measured in terms of years traveling at the speed of light. We looked into the sky, and he said to stare at the space between the stars. In those lightless spaces, our naked eyes glimpsed eternity, but also the future. He pointed out the W-shaped constellation of Cassiopeia and the boxy shape of Pegasus. "See that smudge of light between them? About the size of a full moon?" We squinted into the dark sky. "The light from the Andromeda Galaxy traveled 2.5 million years to us in that moment. This light had been emitted two million years before Homo sapiens ever walked the earth. It could be gone now for all we know. And think about this: the universe is expanding. Everything is becoming farther apart as it expands into space, so there were stars and galaxies that were visible from Earth in the past but have traveled beyond their visible light. The tip of that light beam is out there in the universe traveling toward us, but we are moving away from it."

After dinner, we kids lay out in the open. I stared into the sky, scanning between the stars, searching the void for what might appear out of it. For the first time, I began to feel the immensity of nature and time. I'd watched the moon landings on TV, and the moon was easy to see. It looked within our grasp and was only a couple days away. But after moving into the desert along the Mexican border so far from anyplace, it seemed we were the six sole survivors of a nuclear war on the desert plain. I'd never realized the night sky held so many stars or how much faint light made up the Milky Way. The artificial lights of suburban civilization washed out all but the brightest stars, but here, as I looked up in wonder, a flashlight felt sacrilegious and the airliner, so high I could only see its traveling lights and a thin contrail trailing behind it, seemed a scratch on the face of God.

Later, I'd think about a blackened future sky, empty of stars and constellations and the possibility of anything beyond us here on Earth. But for me, a fifth-grade kid staring up into the dark spaces between the ancient light, the night was no longer a dome or a vault or a ceiling or the home of gods; it was infinite. The stars gave it depth and meaning. Just because you shun religion doesn't mean you still can't look for meaning in the light.

I asked Gina if I could play the song. She said, "Sure. Give it a spin."

For a moment, I closed my eyes and let the song fill my head. I mouthed the line, "I stood on the ridge and shunned religion, thinking the world was mine." From where I stood, I understood that to shun religion didn't mean shunning the idea of a god or the spiritual or the godlike, but to still be in awe and in wonder of what might be possible. I just didn't know what was possible yet without discovering it for myself.

It was like contemplating freedom. What was possible, and what was just blue-sky thinking to fool yourself? I am and am not free. Was it understanding that we all live under some kind of constraints, and its working within them that gives us actual freedom? Like how an artist uses the constraints of any medium to spark creative thought unable to be accessed without any constraints? I am free within the rules of the State. Maybe not even that free. What of the freedom to break free from your biology, your time, your raising, your ancestors, your culture, your unnamed force like gravity that you can't see but keeps you pinned to the planet no matter how hard you try to jump free? Does it matter that freedom and free will are airy nothings we've fooled ourselves into believing to satisfy our egos like a fortunate person who believes it was only hard work that made them successful? If not, then are those who commit crimes freer than those who follow the rules and laws? I was not free. I was free. No, I was semi-free.

We sat and listened to the album side. When it ended, I checked the time. I wanted to go to the library before I had to head back to the halfway house. We said our goodbyes and promised to get together soon. We would never have the time see each other again.

On Monday, after I'd checked in with Penelope, I rode over to an office building where my former lover worked. The steps to the office building started to fill with office people going to lunch. On one of the last times I'd been here, a fat guy in a suit came through with a cougar on a harness and leash. A fucking cougar. The heat already closed in on a hundred degrees. I leaned against a pillar in the shade, waiting. My former lover worked for a corporate attorney, and I expected her to walk out the doors at any moment. I'd been debating about coming here to see her or just letting it go, but in the end, there I was.

Lynne wasn't the only visitor to come see me at the jail. Bonnie had come to see me. When I was shipped to Tucson, she wrote me letters saying she'd wait for me. Then she wrote saying she'd found someone else. I was not to write her anymore. She said her new man had a gun and was not afraid of me. I knew by that sentence he trembled himself to sleep every night. Men who feel the need to mention they have a gun are, in their hearts, timid and fearful sorts. I wrote her back, saying I wanted to see her when I got back just to say goodbye and her boyfriend scared me not at all. She didn't respond.

We'd reconnected as friends the fall before my arrest. In prison, I thought a lot about the intensity and passion that broke over us and the wreckage of our marriages. We believed we could move on from that and be together as a couple, as if an explosion had much of a future.

I'd just finished registering for classes and was hanging out in the common area at the community college. *Scarface* played on the television. The coke-fueled Tony Montana killed an assassin poised to kill kids, revealing the cocaine kingpin had a sense of morals after all. I wore an Army T-shirt and my camouflage pants. Reagan and Mondale posters, and even the odd one for Jessie Jackson, hung on bulletin boards along with other college fliers.

Bonnie walked up to me and asked, "How have you been?"

At first, I didn't recognize her out of her fast-food uniform. We'd worked at the fast-food place together before I'd gone to Fort Knox and a little bit after I'd returned before I quit. One night, the manager was yelling at me, and I snapped and threw the tomato cutter across the kitchen. All the customers parted as I strode through the lobby and out the door.

Bonnie's jeans hugged her thin body opposite the way polyester slacks had hidden the curves of her hips. She wore a fitted, collarless blouse unbuttoned at the throat. Her straight auburn hair, normally pinned up under a hat, brushed her slender shoulders. Gunshots echoed in the common room as Tony Montana gunned it out with other narco-thugs. "FUCK you, you fucking FUCKS!"

"Hey," I said.

"Things ain't been the same since you left."

Blam! Blam! Machine guns ripped up a mansion.

"Well, I had to get on."

"Kelly was pissed for the longest time."

"I bet she was," I said.

Amid the gunfire and profanity blasting out of the television and students hustling to class or hustling politics, we discovered we were taking the same classes, just different times, and planned to study together. Her husband, Doug, worked some desk job for the Air Force. He took classes too to bolster his promotion potential with an eye to a job outside the service. Coincidentally, I'd started taking Spanish that semester to increase my abilities for my unit or if I went active duty and ended up in Central America where the Contras were fighting.

Lynne and I had moved into a one-bedroom apartment a month after getting married. We had a little box television we watched sometimes, or we listened to records. The apartment had the most basic of second-hand furniture: a chair, a couch, a couple of shelves, a dining table, chairs, and a waterbed Lynne's mom bought us. I'd decorated one of the living room walls with training posters from the armory that broke down Warsaw Pact battle order, ranks and uniforms, armored vehicles, and aircraft. I also had a couple of maps up. I'd fallen in love with maps in high school and studied them in libraries, planning expeditions I wanted to take. Lynne put up some Grateful Dead, Led Zeppelin, Who, and Pink Floyd posters and some photos of our wedding reception.

Doug and Bonnie liked to have us over to their apartment for going over the homework. Some nights, we'd meet at our place. By the end of the evening, we'd be playing cards and drinking wine chased with shots of 200 proof Everclear. Doug and I did stupid shit, like light our spit on fire and blow fire out of our mouths, run barefoot in the street yelling military cadences, and flip each other and spar like clumsy kung fu monkeys. Lynne and Bonnie played records and laughed at us.

Lynne, Bonnie, Doug, and I'd wake up on those mornings after study nights, and we'd all stagger off to our jobs, heads throbbing, mouths dried from too much alcohol and fire. He went to his Air Force job and Bonnie to a legal secretary job she'd landed. After getting laid off from a hod carrier job I'd worked through the summer, I'd started working as a porter in a hotel and worked the midday shift. Lynne hunkered down for a couple of extra hours of sweaty sleep. Lynne had become a DJ at a local strip club and picked up some side work in a club that specialized in fleecing money out of visiting businessmen by selling them expensive watered-down drinks for the illusion they were going to get laid.

Finally, we reached the last of the fall semester and Christmas break. Bonnie and I passed. We'd all enrolled in the same classes for the spring and looked forward to when all four of us would be in class together. We were going to be a juggernaut of studying. Maybe I'd finally found the friends I kept losing every time my dad lost a job and sent us out on the open road again.

Christmas Eve, we readied for drinks, dinner, and presents without any pretense that we were studying. Bonnie and Doug and Lynne and I in their apartment. It was a typical one-bedroom with off-white-painted, textured drywall. The living room and dining room were only extensions of the same space, and the kitchen was divided by a counter—all open. At the end of a short hall were a mirror and a vanity with dual sinks, bedroom to the left, bathroom to the right. An arcadia door let out to a small, fenced space, not really a yard as much as a pad of concrete and a strip of grass for a couple of chairs and a hibachi. On the wall hung photos of them and parents and department store prints of flowers. A couch, a love seat, and a chair woven from a cloth the color of cream before it sours were arranged in front of a stereo system. It was one of those bought at base exchanges, all silver and black plastic with a cassette player, turntable, light-up equalizer, and four speakers not for blasting Christmas carols, but Rush's *2112* or REO Speedwagon's *Hi Infidelity* or AC/DC rolling on a *Highway to Hell.* And what Christmas would be complete without Iron Maiden's "Number of the Beast"?

The whole place was filled with decorations: a fake tree sprayed with pine scent, strings of lights blinking in time like a chorus line of showgirls kicking out the finale, fake icicles, fake snow, fake wise men, and a plastic holy family under the tree with molded, mute animals with dazed looks as if they were searching for something to say. Everything was frozen in the Vegas December. I can't remember if there was a star or an angel on top of the tree. Maybe one of those awkward stars so in vogue that it looked less like the star of Bethlehem and more like a red and silver jet cowling mashed into the tailfin of a '50s Chevy. Maybe. But for sure it was Christmas Eve, and as was our habit, we drank before, during, and after dinner. Then we cleared the table, and the cards appeared like a Christmas miracle—a deck from a casino with the hole punched through so it couldn't be used for cheating.

What did we eat? Did Bonnie roast a turkey? Maybe we gorged on sliced ham and mashed potatoes washed down with high proof holiday cheer. We mused about the holidays, and they popped a bottle of sparkling wine that we all called champagne anyway because we were ignorant, working-class kids. We knew how to make comfort food and knew how to drain booze bottles. We knew the ritual of cutting loose and letting it all go for the sake of the holidays. We didn't know "seize the day" meant anything other than full frontal obliteration. Hello, carpet, my old friend. Welcome to Vegas Christmas. We didn't know how to be surprised at the New Year finding us no better off than before and had no clue that things didn't have to get better. The myth of Sisyphus escaped us even though we'd all read it. Worse, Icarus, for trying to reach above our station. We still didn't know geologic time gave a shit less about our problems and didn't know the Doomsday Clock was a gift from our grandparents to make us appreciate living in the moment. Eat, drink, and be merry for in two minutes, we will all be dead. We knew how to overeat in the name of sacred holiday spirit. We knew how to play cards like in western films. We knew how to get drunk and fuck.

We sat at the table. Was that the night I lost my shirt and ran barefoot out the door into the Vegas winter to climb over the fence to their patio hours later, shivering and blue, standing at the arcadia door, staring at Bonnie and Lynne sitting at the dinner table, Doug snoring on the couch, until they noticed me and brought me in? No. That would be later, when Christmas Eve became Christmas past and we didn't know how the past never left us. Was that the night I flicked my Balisong butterfly knife like castanets clicking metallic time so fast and so smooth I reached some Zen trance as the knife laced through my fingers, scattering reflected light on its own wings? Only in jeans and a motorcycle jacket, I stood in front of the mirror at the vanity, Bonnie by my side in only her panties. Yes. Christmas Eve.

Lynne had said, "Let's play strip poker." The drinks flowed and the clothes fell away and drunken time blinked and five minutes conjured two hours from nothing. Who knew, in the blur, why my wife was giving head to another man on the couch and asking for frosting? Who knows why I led Bonnie away to the bedroom to kiss her gently between the legs until I came up because Bonnie asked for me to check on the other two to make sure they were going all in?

"I am a Christian after all," she said.

They were coupled on the couch, and so Bonnie and I did. In the aftermath, we all sat on the couch, the air redolent with fake pine tree and portent. We agreed it would be one of those crazy drunk things, a Christmas morning to remember. The presents we unwrapped were each other's spouse.

With the new semester, we kept our study schedule, meeting a couple of times a week. Bonnie and I met in private to say, "Wow, wild, right?" "Like, who knew that'd happen?" "Let's remain friends like we were before." And maybe our intent in verbalizing it was to banish the urge to devour each other in great sweaty draughts.

Bonnie and I didn't know it, but the more we said no, the stronger our attraction became until we met every day to have sex somewhere: in the park, in the car, in her office bent over the desk with her bucking wild and her hair flinging, and one night, we somehow even snuck out from our study session with our spouses. We walked to a casino close to the apartment and took the elevators high up to look out over the city from the window in the elevator lobby. She lifted her skirt, showing she wasn't wearing underwear. We clasped onto each other as if the tower was swaying and made love against the wall. We finished and had our clothes smoothed out before the bell dinged and an old couple strolled out flush with loss. People who lose have a certain look when they're heading back to the room. It's kind of a stunned shock, as if they've just been in a car accident. We smiled at each other, and they looked away.

We got lost in lust and booze and the feeling we were about to die. After the first time, Bonnie and I became unmoored from any sense of guilt because they'd started it. We started meeting at her apartment in the mornings before she had to go to work. I raced my motorcycle up and down the streets, waiting for her husband to go to the airbase.

Then the night came after we four studied until we were too drunk to read. The night Doug passed out and I took off to run through the city. The night I came back and stood outside barefoot and shirtless, still drunk and shivering blue on a March night. Can sheer lust and confusion stave off hypothermia? How was it no one killed me, barefoot and shirtless, wandering the streets of North Las Vegas? I slinked past the 7-Eleven's No Loitering sign. How was it the clerk at 7-Eleven didn't call the cops? How was it no one called the cops? I don't know, but I found my way back by some animal navigation to the fence and over it and into the sliver of yard. Why not the front? Bonnie saw me with a start. Lynne gasped when Bonnie's hand went to her chest in shock but, realizing it was me, smiled and let me in as Doug snored on the couch. Lynne smiled. Did I try to kiss Bonnie? Did Doug wake up?

I told Bonnie I needed to talk with her. I led her around to the other side of the fence, the same one I had scaled. How could Lynne and Doug not be suspicious we snuck off all the time? This time was not to the upper floors of a hotel elevator lobby or her car, but just on the other side of a flimsy fence. In my wild romantic way, drunken and full of passion, full of seizing days and riding off like the great adulterer, Lancelot, I begged Bonnie to leave with me. We could split out for LA, the beach. We could remake ourselves out there, become something more and transcend this time, this place. Just get a suitcase of stuff, travel light. Words like pollen covering bumble bees—all sweetness and life and holding the life-ending sting. I had begged her in a parking garage before this night. She had said no then too. Afraid of an unstable life. Afraid of cutting it all loose and showing up in a city with little money and no job and a boyfriend with wild eyes. "No," she said again, and on the other side of the fence, Lynne listened. And it all unraveled with a scream from offstage like in a Shakespearean tragedy. We all fell down. Lynne moved in with Darla, who I didn't know was Lynne's sometimes lover, and her timing couldn't have been better. At that moment in time, the forces of the federal government were building a case against me. What felt like years lapsed in those short weeks. So much time, so little, I didn't know what to make of it. So many lines smeared like mascara on a broken-hearted showgirl.

A week after Lynne left, I found the picture. The 8x10 of Lynne and some middle-aged suit with a horseshoe of hair. A portrait. Her and him at a dinner. A place in fucking Kansas. Kansas. When did she go to Kansas? When I was on a field exercise, oblivious that her "companion" job had led to a little more than hanging out in a club sipping drinks? I'd suspected the maintenance guy if anyone. The stoned, racing-on-coke, Mexican apartment handyman who always seemed to be hanging out, smoking weed with my wife, even before Christmas Eve. She had moved out, so why would she leave the picture where I could see it? To stick me in the eyes? Did she want me to find it? Maybe she left it out so she could clean her conscience of it. To come clean without having to sit me down and say, "I've been balling this dude down on business from a state as flat as my granny's ass." Maybe a message that our marriage was beyond reconciliation or any repair. I mustered the socially accepted rage and acted hurt and betrayed. Even as I did, I knew myself to be a false spurned lover.

I saw Bonnie coming through the lobby and push open the doors. Her eyes widened as if she'd seen a bear. She turned and pushed against the flow of people to get back into the building. People gave her strange looks, wondering if they should run too. My thought was to leave. Fuck her. But I waited. It seemed such a lame thing to want after all the months and her breakup letter. I just wanted to say goodbye. We'd shared such a consuming fire that it filled me when I saw her, as if we'd been apart a couple of days. But really, I think I just wanted to be seen by her. To let her know I'd made it out and I'd be fine without her when at one time we believed we'd die without each other.

The doors opened again, and she was accompanied by a pasty office worker. He puffed up his chest and tried to put on a tough guy face that made him look childish. "You need to leave her alone." Behind them, armed security looked out from the lobby.

"I just wanted to say goodbye." I looked at her. "Goodbye, Bonnie."

I turned and started down the steps into the heat. I thought about telling him that his gun didn't frighten me, but that would have been as weak as telling someone you had a gun. Yeah, I was alright. I wasn't even angry.

The first Friday night that I didn't have to go back to the halfway house arrived. Mrs. Gutiérrez had run all checks, sending out private investigators and other flying monkeys to check on Mike and Joan and Binder and Jen to see if they were legit, upstanding people in the community. Just another way the State wanted to grind you down and humiliate your friends was all I saw of it. In the name of security was just some petty tyrant's excuse to fuck with you.

Lynne had invited me over for dinner with other friends of hers. Her new husband wasn't what I expected given all our wild friends from before. He looked respectable with his button-down shirt and clipped hair. He and another guy in pressed jeans and an Izod polo shirt played some blues numbers. They were really good on the fretboard and at fingerpicking, better than Brew and Flat-Five, but something was missing. It was like my first night in that big room with One and Punch in the barracks room at Boron FPC. The something missing wasn't a sound, like keys clattering or the yelling or a smell of death and disinfectant, and after a while, I figured out it was the feeling, the vibe. The quiet settled over us, and a feeling filled me like when I was a child laying out on the desert floor in a sleeping bag. The danger was still out there, but it was with a strange intuition that I was in time with nature and accepted that I'd either wake with the sun rising or wake as I was attacked out of the darkness.

When I told Lynne's new husband and friend I'd been learning to play but wasn't very good, they offered me a guitar. I started blues in E minor.

"You're right. You aren't very good," Lynne's husband said.

"But you play with feeling," his friend said. "And that's harder to do."

I knew then, for all their technical proficiency beyond Brew and Flat-Five, they didn't have what Brew told me was *duende* and Flat-Five called the pain. It was cool. It's not like those two couldn't find it. It'd just take life bitch slapping them a few minutes. Everyone knows a broken heart, but they just needed to make us feel it up inside us through a minor chord with a flat fifth keeping it dampened down so we knew it was going to be around a while. Like what I was dealing with fresh from prison. It was not going away, so the music had to come from that place of permanent pain that others related to even if they didn't end up living in despair.

Brew and Flat-Five sang these songs about people who knew they were fucking up and committing crimes, and the song told the story. I knew of songs like "Hey Joe" by Hendrix, Johnny Cash's "Folsom Prison Blues," and others, but there were all these old country, folk, and blues songs like ballads I'd never heard about.

I'd seen them with their guitars, but the first time I heard them was walking up a one-lane road to the top of the bluff above the dorms of the prison camp. The road split to circle the summit in the shape of a teardrop, encompassing maintenance buildings, a warehouse, and a radar dome run by the Air Force since the days this place was one of their Cold War posts. I continued up the right side. At the top, I stood a moment and looked out over the desert. All the empty space stretching away made me a little dizzy. It was only an illusion that the land sloped down toward the bluff, but even though I'd experienced it hundreds of times since I was a kid hiking, it still gave me the feeling I was being drawn into the belly of the earth.

I looked back and saw the barracks, offices, and staff housing built into the base of the bluff and more miles of desert beyond that. On the yards at all the other prisons, I looked through chain-link and concertina wire or stared into a block wall, but at this camp, there wasn't even a three-strand barbed wire fence. The only wall was around the staff houses, like their own West Berlin. I laughed.

I heard guitar music rising from the valley floor as I walked up the Teardrop. I stared down the bluff thinking I was hearing things on the wind from a distance, like a mirage of voices chattering. I shook my head and squinted as if it'd help my hearing. As a boy, in all the rural areas wherever my dad found work, I'd hike through the desert or forests thinking I might have heard things that weren't there. I continued past the radar dome where a guy called Molly—because his hair looked like Molly Ringwald's—stared up at it. He believed it was an alien communication installation, and every evening, he paced the fence line with his mouth twitching like he was on the verge of speaking out loud. When I rounded the bend, I saw Brew and Flat-Five sitting on the flat-topped rock, playing a guitar.

Out on the playa, dust devils spun high into the sky. They reached hundreds of yards up and scooted across the desert, tearing at bushes and churning up more sand and dust among the heat waves. A couple of birds got caught in one, but then I recognized they were plastic bags being whipped around. The dry wind flowing uphill dried my sweat and reminded me of a hot wind I felt as a kid. A wind I'd once felt when I'd left the Lake Tamarisk library to get home for dinner. The a/c in the library had been so cold I started to shiver when the 110-degree wind hit me. It felt odd to shiver in such heat, but it felt like a breath, a giant hot breath. Like when I'd first made out with a girl and felt her exhale along my neck and realized how hot the furnace burning inside her was for me in that moment. Did she burn so hot for another? No doubt. But to feel her breath on a wind coming up a hill years later as the desert exhaled made me pause and close my eyes. Where had she gone after all the layoffs?

"I didn't notice those."

I looked from the desert to him. "What?"

He nodded toward the dust devils. Brew checked his tuning. He picked each string with his head cocked like that Victrola dog. "This climate is hard on keeping instruments in tune."

"I've always wanted to learn."

"Why haven't you?"

"I can't tell notes by ear."

"Not many can without a lot of practice."

"I thought it was a natural thing."

"People do have a natural talent for it, but to different degrees. You can train yourself to hear. If you're completely tone-deaf, it'd be hard. But riddle me this: when you listen to live music, can you tell if someone plays a wrong note?"

I thought about it.

He played a blues riff. "Now listen again." He played the same riff, but one note sounded off.

"You can definitely hear the off note."

"See, man, you're not tone-deaf. It's a process of learning which sound goes with which note. Like learning color or smells, for instance. If no one told you what a rose smelled like among flowers, you'd still be able to pick it out."

"True."

"I can teach you. We got time."

The guitar shone in the late evening sun. "Maybe. I'm having a hard time concentrating, so I might not be a very good student."

"It might help you."

The guard they called Flier walked up the trail a little winded. He was round, and the belt he wore looked like a ring around Saturn, with his radio and keys like small moons. With him walked a little Vietnamese guy with a potbelly they called VC because he'd been in the Viet Cong and ended up in the United States making counterfeit passports. He and Flier traded stories about the war. They stopped to watch the sunset.

"The sun rising out of the South China Sea was one of the most beautiful sights I ever laid eyes on."

VC stood there staring at the horizon, hands behind his back. He wore OD green dungarees and a white T-shirt. From where I sat, it looked like his hands were bound and Flier was about to push his ass off the bluff if he didn't give him the intel he wanted. The image in my mind of someone else's war created by all the stories I'd heard.

"Never saw it. Always in the Highlands."

"You never seen the South China Sea?"

"I have, just not at sunrise."

"Oh. Well, I figured it was such a narrow country that you must have gone down to the sea to watch the sunrise."

VC shrugs. "There was a war to fight."

A tall, lanky guy with straggly hair and a blonde beard shot with gray was making a lap when he yelled out, "Don't let him bullshit you, VC. He was a pogue in Cam Ranh Bay chasing after nurses and whores. He never even got his boots muddy." He rattled off something in Vietnamese that made VC laugh. He kept walking and, without looking back, said loud enough for everyone to hear, "And he's a pogue now."

Brew and I chuckled. "Riddle brooks no bullshit," Brew said.

I watched Riddle stride away.

The late sun slanted mountain shadows over the playa. The golden air vibrated. My skin tingled at the electricity drawn up by the friction of dried air over the stones of an arid land. Far to the south, wisps of clouds sketched pencil marks of mares' tails over 40,000 feet in the sky. I felt if I reached out, I could run my fingers through them. The sky, so immense and so close all at once, encompassed the sun while holding the stars back. "Thunderstorms are coming," I said.

"Really?" Brew asked.

"Not today. Maybe two days. Three."

Brew looked around at the desert.

"The moisture help with keeping your guitar in tune?"

He nodded. "It will."

"Cool. Maybe I'll take you up on your offer after the monsoons arrive."

I started back down the south leg of the Teardrop. Three days later, rainwater ran hard down the bluff, driving the inmates indoors or under awnings, cupping cigarettes as they smoked. In the phone banks, men who weren't paying attention while calling home flinched at the thunder and crackle of an electric sky filling the phone lines with static. The sudden rain stranded them in the open wooden booths, reminding me of the Old West photographs of coffins filled with dead outlaws and vigilante victims on public display. They stood in disbelief at all the water so suddenly pouring over the earth. They watched kangaroo rats rush the high ground around them and panic as a Mojave green rattlesnake floated the muddy rapids past the barracks. Its rattle angled up, tillering it downstream for the playa where the water fanned out over miles of ancient seafloor with the promise of wildflowers.

Lynne's husband and his buddy started playing Blind Faith's "Can't Find My Way Home." They couldn't match Steve Winwood's high tenor voice that sounded as if he sang in a castrati boys' choir. They did catch the spirit of the song. It made me long to find my way home, a home. While some said it was about getting off drugs—and I felt that too—it could be about being emotionally wasted from wandering as if lost in a wilderness. Ever since we left our homestead, it felt as if we never chose to leave a place. How can one make a home if it was a layoff notice away from being taken? Then we were living on the road again. That displacement wears you down and begins to haunt you, so you never feel secure. Doomed to wander the earth with no way home or a sense of peace that comes from it. Maybe that was why I identified with the Ancient Mariner or Marlow from *Heart of Darkness*—always adrift in the world with a story to tell. Maybe home was wandering and I needed to make peace with that, just as I needed to make peace with the emotional wreck that was my life and the void that filled me with dread as I came to understand nothing existed beyond death—no heaven, no hell, no angels, no demons, no gods, no afterlife, no soul to return to this scene of a crime and mayhem, and no redemption or salvation or damnation or promises or threats dreamed up by people existed.

In the music, I felt connected and felt meaning in my life. An emotional resonance stirred in me. The vibration of the universe perhaps and the sense of belonging as music played and when I played. Even though I sucked at it, something moved in me with the rhythm of the chords and notes. Not unlike how I felt when alone in the desert with a warm breeze cooling me after hiking through the emptiness. Maybe that was finding my way home.

The weekend ended. I rode to see Penelope before heading to the boiler room. There were some others ahead of me and she gave them referrals. I stepped up, thinking this might be my day. She said it wasn't my day and said she was sorry. Those guys had family in the business and were requested. *Of course*, I thought. I bet they had nowhere near the crazy experiences I had at Boron with ancient wiring and electricians who were electricians because they were assigned to be.

When I arrived at Boron, the guard told me I had to report to the electricians' shop at the top of the bluff, so my first morning, I climbed up the hill. A guy named Zee I'd met at dinner the night before walked along and showed me where to go. He picked at his hair with his plastic fork. "You be careful in there. Electric chair in the waiting." He laughed and turned to the double Quonset huts that housed the assembly plant.

Inside, I met the shop foreman. He had a five o'clock shadow at 8 in the morning, and his feathered and flaked-out hair looked as if he'd been in a windstorm.

"Hey, man," he said. "Call me Flash. Like Flash Gordon and not flash of electricity. Get it? Always some dumbass has to make the comment about it."

The Allman Brothers' guitar jam, "Jessica," played over box speakers mounted in the corners of the high shop walls. A work bench ran along a wall, and there was a tool board and rack.

"Alright, so, man, here." He handed me a metal shower ring with a dozen red metal tags and the number 5 stamped on it. "You take a tool, you leave a tag so we know who has what. You fuck up and they'll send you back to a place with razor wire. Get it?"

I'd just been transferred from the coast and briefly thought of the women on the decks of motor yachts lifting their tops for the inmates catcalling from the fence. Was it worse to be there or in a place with no fences surrounded by hundreds of square miles of desert? "I got it, Flash."

"You and I will be partners. I'll show you around, and you can get a handle on the electric layout of the camp. I been here about six months and hoping for parole in two, so you got a little time before I leave. Sledge, he got more time, but he's kinda slow. Mumbles a lot and has that Thorazine shuffle, though he ain't on Thorazine. Get it, the shuffle?"

"I get it. I've seen it at county lockup." I'd also seen it in a psych ward, but I didn't know what it was back then.

"Too much crack back in the hood, most likely."

I asked, "Where's the guard?"

"What guard?"

"The one who's supposed to supervise us and make sure we're not porking the pooch?"

"This ain't that kind of prison, New Guy."

Flash took me out to run the power grid. Our feed came off the high-tension wires. He told me the voltage, which I promptly forgot except for the fact it was a terrifyingly large fucking number. The job we needed to do, he explained, was to splice a new main power line into the mega voltage line to run the camp because the old one had been pulling amps since the late '40s. It'd be me and him in the bucket and Sledge down below making sure no one got in the way and did something stupid.

"How many times have you done something like this?" I asked.

"Never. I read up on it when they told me what they wanted done."

"I mean you must've done something similar in your career."

"Career? I was a dope smuggler with a cigarette boat."

"Oh."

"Don't worry. It'll be fun. At least I'm not sending you up with Sledge."

Flash took me around the camp with our tool belts hanging on our hips like building supers on a sitcom. I needed to learn the layout of the camp's power grid. He'd learned it from his predecessor because there were no schematics showing how the buildings were wired, where the breaker boxes were, or how to get power back up in the event it went down. I also learned where inmates snuck to do drugs or drink homemade booze or have sex—the nooks and crannies out of sight, in the shade at high noon and unlit at night. I followed him out a back trail that skirted a rise out of sight of the camp and technically out of the camp, but it was the only way to reach a junction box behind the admin building.

I looked out into the empty desert. I thought about being in AZ and the desert through the double chain-link fence and razor wire. Two bozos thought if they took off their clothes, they could slip through the concertina wire unscathed. They'd gotten the idea from the John Wayne movie where a Vietnamese soldier shows the new soldiers how the Viet Cong can slip into their perimeter without clothes on. If you could slip in, then you could slip out, the dumbasses reasoned. How fucking embarrassing was it to be found entangled and naked in the triple rows and stacks of wire because a razor hook had impaled your ball sack? Sometimes the feds didn't need a snitch to catch the criminal.

"This, New Guy, keeps all this side in power." He pointed toward the admin building. The Air Force blue, knee-high box had a brass lock on it. Flash produced a key and unlocked it. We hinged the awkward lid back. A black widow web was woven between heavy gauge wires and relays. She hovered over a heavy ball of eggs.

I said, "Somewhere down in there is the corpse of her mate."

Flash looked at me. "You don't say?"

"I do."

He stared for a long moment as if looking to catch sight of a ship on the horizon. "Lucky bastard."

After he explained the ways the wires ran, we hinged the lid over and locked the black widow, her brood, and her dead lover in the dark.

Flash said, "We better get back before Sledge thinks we run off."

That afternoon, Flash and I went into the admin building. A fluorescent light was blinking, driving the admin people crazy. I learned we needed to change the ballast. We walked through the desks. Flash said hi to everyone like he was your average maintenance guy. All the office people smiled and asked how his family was doing. He joked, "Living the high life on the money I send home."

The light was by a round woman's desk. She looked up and smiled big. "Hi, boys," she said.

I said, "Hi." Her desk had a photo of her and a girl in a volleyball uniform. I recognized her as the younger sister of a guy in my high school class. She'd been a freshman the year I graduated, so she'd be a senior now. I wondered if she lived in staff housing and took the school bus like we did from the mine our fathers worked at an hour away from the school. I thought of her languishing away her teenage years like cavalry officers guarding a stage route. It was funny to me how the staff housing looked like mining camp housing, just like it was funny we both ended up here and we were both in the National Honor Society. I thought about telling the woman to say hi to her and her brother for me, but I didn't.

I set up the folding ladder. Flash climbed up and removed the cover. He started to unscrew the ballast.

"Do you want me to turn off the lights?" I asked.

"Nah. If you connect the wires in the right order, it's not a problem."

The ballast hung by its wires when he unwound the wire nuts. They sparked a little. Flash reached down, and I handed him the new ballast. He screwed it into place. The first wires he twisted together sparked and smoked a little. He handled them with his fingertips as if they were scorpions. He wound the wire nut onto them. The last wires sparked as he hurriedly twisted the wire nut to connect them. He replaced the cover and climbed down.

Flash smiled. "See, no worries."

About a month later, in one of the dorm's common rooms, Flash and I spread our tools out. We needed to run some new wires and install some new outlets and switches throughout the dorms. The warden was afraid the old wires were a fire hazard and sure as hell didn't want to have the place burn down on his watch. What a sight it would be, though. The top of the bluff blazing like a man with his head on fire with the radar dome in the background, visible for a hundred miles or more. I imagined transformers and whatever was in the dome exploding and all the embers raining downwind like Revelation, patching the desert with fire.

Flash turned on the television as I started measuring from the corner of the room to find the wall studs. Every sixteen inches, I marked with a pencil. Flash said, "I don't know why you want to go over to the fire crew. Just sit around in their little-ass garage just waiting. Here, you'll be in charge in a couple of months, and you get to walk around and not be cooped up."

"I'll get to rotate out to the airbase. That'll be cool." Two muscle heads, Oak and Stacks, asked if I wanted to transfer over because one of their guys was being released. I said sure about a second after they asked. We needed a fire crew because if shit went down, no one would get to us for hours.

Flash nodded and said, "Well, you could get hurt on a fire or an accident. I've seen cars roll and spray gas all over."

"I don't care," I said.

He shrugged and chopped the drywall next to one of my marks with a roofing hammer and exposed one side of the stud. "Sure. I can see that. Maybe you get some Air Force pussy."

I put the inch wood bit on the drill so I could punch a hole through the stud where we were going to run the wires. It was a big drill with a handle off the left side to help control it.

Flash marked an X with his pencil on the 2x4. "Here."

"It's good? Why don't you tear out the drywall on the other side of the stud so I can see where we're drilling?"

"We need to leave the drywall intact so the carpenters don't have as much to replace. They whine if they have to do too much work. They start in on, "Save money on materials," you know. Just punch a hole and we'll feed the wire from the end."

I ran the extension cord across the room and plugged the drill into it.

"Check it out." Flash pointed at the television. The space shuttle sitting on the launch pad filled the screen. "Maybe you'll see it land when you're slumming it at the airbase."

"That'd be cool." I watched the astronauts give thumbs up and Mission Control stare into monitors like crystal balls. I still liked watching the launches, but they also depressed me. You're told your whole life you can be anything you want if you set your mind to it, and if you don't, it was your fault because you're a lazy ass and don't want it bad enough or a moron. I bet if I'd had help with math from someone who really knew what they were doing when I was young, I could have made the grade. But when you come from a sink or swim culture littered with mediocrity, that's what you succeed or fail by.

I gave the drill trigger a couple quick squeezes and the motor whirred, spinning the bit. "I'm going in."

The bit sliced away the wood as I leaned in and held the drill steady. It started smoking from the friction, but it was about to push through. I leaned a little harder into it when blue and yellow sparks flew from the hole and flames leapt out.

I was jolted and fell back on my ass as I heard Flash yell, "Holy fucking shit."

My vision fluttered dark and light as if trapped in a flock of birds lifting off. When I shook my head and my sight cleared, I looked up and saw, on the television, the space shuttle exploding against the blue sky.

Flash beat the flames with his gloves.

"Holy shit," I said.

Flash said, "You hit a live wire. I'm going to chop out the drywall on the other side. The carpenters can deal with it."

I said, "No, man. The shuttle." I pointed to the television screen.

He looked over at the debris falling from the sky and the smoke drifting on the wind. "Fucking hell."

Monday, I transferred over to the fire crew.

I left Penelope and her cheery smile. After checking the job boards at the unemployment office, I rode to the boiler room. I locked my bike to the rack. In the bathroom, I wiped off sweat with paper towels and put on pants and a fresh T-shirt. The day was the same monotonous task and dread of thinking, *What if this is the best I can do for the rest of my life?* The second hand on the wall clock moved backwards for a split moment before moving forward, like a pitcher winding up before the pitch. If the Archaic Greeks were writing myths now, this would be the eternal damnation inflicted by Zeus on some wayward god, titan, or some arrogant mortal out to prove they could outwit the gods. What was eternity but a place without time where if a second hand moved, it moved forward, then back, and then forward again? You lose awareness of the sun passing, the moonrise, or the tracing of stars across the night sky. It was why casinos don't have clocks, to keep you eternally gaming and losing, so much so that gamblers forgot to take medicine and collapsed on the casino floor. They'd topple over from the stool in front of slot or poker machines as if pulled down by the soldiers of an invading army or the citizens sucking up to the invaders. Amid the bells and whistles, the call of the Keno runner, "keno, keno, keno," or the incantation of a cocktail waitress, "cocktails, cocktails, cocktails," and a clatter of coins from the change cups they all carried and the coins washing out over the carpet, shining disks flashing in the light. Not hell, but purgatory, a place also out of time but infinitely boring and full of desperation until your fall from the stool and release from all earthly worries, from Blake's same dull round.

The afternoon wore on. I was about to hang up after confirming a woman was happy with her service when she said, "You sound cute. Want to go out?" I heard giggling in the background and figured she and a girlfriend were day drinking.

I paused, unsure if I was being played, but said, "You sound cute too."

"You know my name. What's yours?"

I told her my friends called me New Guy.

"Maybe you can be my new guy." More giggling in the background.

I laughed. Anne was her name, and we arranged to meet Friday.

The woman with tight curls next to me gave me the eye with a smile, as in, "I know what you're up to."

I shrugged in reply, as in, "What's a boy to do fresh out of prison and just wanting some company to while away some evenings?"

I grinned like a damned fool the rest of my shift. Even as I sat behind the desk, I focused on calls, trying not to accidentally blurt out how horny I was. Good thing I had a script to use as I kept losing track of what I said to customers. Before I knew it, my shift ended, and I was out on the street.

Anne said she had straight brown hair, brown eyes, and was physically fit. What guy ever had a woman ask him out over the phone when the phone call is one pathetic step away from telemarketing? My mother warned me to steer clear of women who moved fast, or I risked disease, blindness, or being drugged and robbed of watch, wallet, and a kidney. Sexual freedom didn't mean a person had freedom from common sense.

I didn't care. It was a risk I'd run to be with someone who sounded as fun as she did over the phone. And the expectation, the temptation of sex, the ecstasy, and the warmth of intimacy filled me. I hoped she didn't have hepatitis.

After work Friday, I rode my bike back to the halfway house and got my things to spend the weekend at Mike and Joan's house. I rode there and showered. I had wanted to go to Jen and Binder's place, but it was a longer ride to get there and then back to the address Anne had given me. I didn't want to lag and be late to meet her. Mike and Joan had given me a key to a camper they kept in their driveway. I didn't think the staff from the halfway house would ever follow up on where I was even though Mrs. Gutiérrez said she'd send Mr. Lopez out to spot check. I figured Mr. Lopez would head for a sportsbook to watch a game. Hell, I hadn't even met my parole officer as he was too busy with his caseload of Vegas mobsters and gangster drug dealers, so we talked on the phone.

At Mike and Joan's, I told them I had a date but would be quiet when I returned.

"A date, uh?" Joan raised an eyebrow. "I guess you won't be needing dinner."

I blushed. "I'm not meeting her until later, but I'm going to grab a bite on the way there."

"Hu-huh." Joan had a way of making you feel like she knew all your intentions, bad or good, with a single look and the tone of her "hu-huh."

I had looked up how to get to Anne's place and figured I was a fifteen-minute ride away. Our date was for 8:00 so she could get her kids—both in single digits—dinner and hang out with them before sending them to bed. I'd never dated a woman with kids before and wasn't sure what to do if she introduced them to me.

In the camper, I looked in the mirror and combed my hair. In the low light, I looked shadowed. I thought of the campers we'd lived in as I grew up. To make room in the single-wide we lived in at Mountain Pass, my parents let me live in the travel trailer they'd parked behind it. It was cool of them as it gave me space to hang out by myself, and I made sure I had condoms just in case. When I finally found a girlfriend with whom to make out and then make love without the threat of anyone busting in on us, it was good. Here, I kind of felt like that teenaged kid looking in the mirror, illuminated with low wattage lights and the hope for something bigger and success when I got out of high school. But now, I just hoped for something a little better, nothing grand. There were a lot of miles between the kid I was and the guy standing in the camper.

I locked the camper door and climbed on my bike. The sun still blazed down on the streets. I rode to a fast-food joint about five minutes from Anne's place. In the bathroom, I swapped out my sweaty T-shirt and shorts for jeans and a fresh shirt. At the counter, I ordered a burger and fries combo and ate while I cooled off in the a/c. I was a little apprehensive, but more excited. For a moment, I felt like a normal guy, although I wasn't sure if I'd ever felt like a normal guy. The outsider even among outsiders.

Anne was eleven or twelve years older than me. She answered the door and smiled, glad to see me if I was any judge. Her tank top hugged her body. She was fit and sexy with big, braless boobs that hung to her belt line. With her straight brown hair and bell bottoms, she reminded me of the stoner chicks from high school and the ones I'd gone out with before basic training who loved to get high or have a few drinks and fuck while listening to Led Zeppelin or David Bowie.

She didn't invite me in. Over her shoulder, another woman looked at me. Anne said to her that we'd be back in a couple of hours and stepped out onto the step. "Hey," she said. "You're as cute as you sounded on the phone."

I grinned like a dumbass. "You're as pretty as you sounded."

Her turn to grin, but hers was tinged with that 'yeah, right, asshole' look. We got into her Reliant and drove out to Glitter Gulch for .75-cent import night, where that big-ass forty-foot electric cowboy, Vegas Vic, hollered out, "Howdy Podner!" as he thumbed the way for all of us suckers, and across the street, Vegas Vicky kicked up her giantess gams. People milled up and down the sidewalks, wondering where they should lose their money. The casinos were open to the streets, so all the noise of change falling from slot machines and the cheers of craps tables spilled into the street and echoed off the buildings. It was like daylight. You could look up and see a black slate beyond the tops of the buildings. U2 had filmed their music video, "I Still Haven't Found What I'm Looking For," there a few months before while I was still in prison out in the Mojave Desert. Litter to glitter and I hadn't found what I was looking for either. *Funny*, I thought. A bunch of sullen Irishmen came into the desert I grew up in, had trained for war in and been imprisoned in, and, in short order, created music that touched all of that in me. Bullet the blue sky and streets with no names, red hill mining town and with or without you, running to stand still and not finding what you're looking for all echoed my life. Maybe I should have gone to Ireland and skulked around and lost myself in their landscape. Make the Irish go, Oh, man, he gets it.

We walked by the barkers at the entrances who held out fliers with drink specials, coupons for free slot pulls, and buffets as they called out to the tourists, trying to lure gamblers into their place. "Loosest slots in Vegas!" "Cheapest buffet with prime rib and fifteen different desserts you can eat!" "Free booze if you're playing!" "Step right in and be a winner!" "Single Deck Blackjack!" "Best lounge acts in Vegas!" "See the best Elvis in town!" Smoke from thousands of cigarettes and cigars twisted in the flashing lights.

I stood in front of the casinos under the bright and flashing lights of a carnival on steroids. The last time I'd been in Glitter Gulch was the New Year's Eve before my arrest. Lynne and I had braved the shoulder-to-shoulder crowd on Fremont Street, drunk from our pre-flight ritual of getting liquored up before heading out. We knew the casinos would card us and send security to escort us to the street without so much as a have a good evening or a kiss our ass. We watched as an uncommon hush fell over the people as the first fireworks went up at midnight above the Union Plaza Hotel. Then a cheer went up and thousands yelled, "Happy New Year!" Whistles and horns followed the yells, and the booms of explosions in the sky echoed down Glitter Gulch. Lynne and I hugged and kissed as if things were okay and the new year was going to make a difference in our lives. It did, but not all change is good, just like some dreams are nightmares waiting to unfold.

Anne and I gambled a little, drank screwdrivers, and watched different lounge acts. We wandered about, taking in the vibe of the surreal wonderland. The land of the eternal bachelorette party, of people who thought they were poker players like Doc Holliday or riverboat gamblers, those who high-rolled in suits looking as suave as 007, the endless tourists who could have been in Disneyland or the Great Mall of America blowing through souvenir money at the same rate. Anne and I wove our way through the crowds. I'd never been on a date in a casino before, but it seemed a completely Vegas thing to do, as normal as going to the movies anyplace else. She made me laugh out loud and made me remember all the small, fun things a couple could do just hanging out.

We drove back to her place. The curtains opened and I saw her friend's face checking on us. I'm sure there was an agreed upon time limit where her pal would call the cops if we weren't home—an APB on a strange, yet attractive loser. Anne turned off the ignition. She smiled and leaned in. We kissed, and she said thanks for the fun. "Let's do it again," she said.

I asked, "How about tomorrow?" I didn't have anything going on, and her kiss made me want to see her soon.

She laughed. "Sure, same time."

I got on my bike. As I started to pedal off, I felt wobbly. I'd drank too much. Released from the pressure of going back to the halfway house, I didn't feel the need to stop drinking. The only thing I needed to do was get to Mike and Joan's. It was just after 11:00. It felt so early in the evening. No one telling me it was time for lockdown or curfew or forcing me to sit in an empty apartment as if it were a bomb shelter and to leave was to risk dying of radiation exposure. It was an odd feeling, to be this free, pedaling through the still hot night. I used to love to ride Bad Bob on summer nights like this one. The heat off the engine and pipes, the heat off the street, the heat of the air as it flowed around me as I raced someplace and sometimes no place at all. I had trouble sleeping and at times felt so restless I'd just get up, dress, get on Bad Bob, and ride. Lynne used to worry it was something bad or about her, but I assured her it was some restlessness in me I didn't understand.

The old feeling came back. But I had far enough to pedal to the camper that I was sure the urge to wander aimlessly in the night would be sated.

Back at the camper, I lay in the bunk and couldn't sleep.

I went to visit with Lynne. She asked if I wanted to join her and her new husband on an encounter. Her mom would be there. "The last time did you good."

I was not so sure. Of all the months Lynne and I lived together, we were sober very little. One of those weekends, her mom had paid for us to go to an encounter group, and no booze or drugs were allowed. No sex either. *Some encounter*, I thought. I didn't want to go. What a lame way to spend the weekend. All I knew about encounter groups could be summed up as people who sat around and cried about their loser lives. Boo-fucking-hoo. But because I loved my wife, I went.

I remember the hippie playing the acoustic guitar as the encounter weekend wrapped up—"Almost heaven," he sang, "West Virginia." Neither place I'd been. Most everyone else is a blank except my mother-in-law, the guy I think she was balling, and the reason I went, my wife. Well, also the monk who also looked like a hippie and arrived late Sunday afternoon. What sticks out is him giving the Eucharist and blessing my wife with the sign of the cross on her forehead, as does my refusal to be blessed, even for free wine. This happened a couple of months before my arrest and right before our marriage blew apart.

The encounter group felt like the irrigation canals crisscrossing the desert our parents warned us kids to stay out of no matter how hot the day and inviting the cool water. Below the smooth surface, powerful currents threatened to sweep us away and wash our drowned bodies into another county where farmers walked rows of alfalfa or jojoba beans. They cautioned us not to try and save those being swept along for fear we'd be dragged in. It felt as if a demonic creature lived in the canal, waiting for unsuspecting children. Imagine my surprise to see a bunch of holy rollers one Sunday baptizing kids at the canal's edge. At least the white robes would make their bodies easier to spot as they bobbed in the stream. Unlike the monk in his Franciscan robe, where only the glint of a crucifix would shine from dark water.

In the mashup of tent revival meets psychotherapy, strangers urged me to remove the mask I showed society and get in touch with my true self. It reminded me of POW training in the Army. What I really wanted was a drink, but that wasn't forthcoming. My parents warned us of people who insist you adopt their paths to spiritual or psychological salvation, as if what keeps them from killing themselves will give your life meaning. My parents also warned me about drinking booze, but there I was hankering for a beer and a shot.

Like I said, this was right before my arrest, where I'd be isolated with a different group of strangers. The prisoners were mostly alright guys. They knew everyone wore many masks and didn't care. Jailhouse preachers and religious fanatics, though, had no room for multiplicity and saw people as saved or damned. I discovered too that I could go a long time without booze.

I refuse to believe heaven is almost like West Virginia. True believers are horrified by a person's lack of faith. It's as if the existence of skeptics disproves their dogmas. Without any evidence, a surprising number of them will murder you to save your soul—a human sacrifice for their god. Your death a validation of their faith's truth. They've discarded whatever masks they'd worn and revealed themselves as killers as remorseless as a canal's current sweeping gasping children toward blue water.

Within the bubble of the community center, they set up groups to get us to shed our social masks. "My mask has a mask," I quipped, and no one laughed. What if I shed one social mask and all I did was put on a new social mask for this group so they'd quit pestering me and let me take a nap? Funny how the system wanted me to put on a mask for the parole board which they all knew was a false front. I took part in talking circles and trust exercises, and on the last afternoon, we opened letters of support and small tokens sent by loved ones.

Lynne and her mother had asked my parents to write. They sent letters of support, alright. Keywords: losers, jellybeans, hippies, man up, psycho-bullshit, cult. Dad had quoted Louis L'Amour's words about ancient gods still walking the earth in lonely places where worshippers no longer came. He said to take three rocks (enclosed in the letter) and make a pile out of them. A god might wander by, looking for a little of the old sacredness and worship, looking for an offering, to be needed again. He wrote, "I'm not saying they're not out there, but in the end, it's only you and a pile of rocks."

I sat there in the plastic chair with the group staring at me. I'd read Antoine de Saint-Exupéry: "A rock pile ceases to be a rock pile the moment a single man contemplates it, bearing within him the image of a cathedral." Not so much the rocks themselves are sacred, but only our belief they are. How else to imbue meaning in life? I think about all those days in my childhood I wandered the desert in search of something mystic. Some sign of this spirit world, this other thing living among the bones of the earth. Why would it not reveal itself to me? What did it mean to go out on spirit quests and always return having sighted nothing? Had the land been emptied of spirits, and I only chased after the memory of a long-gone race, all the sacred rock piles vacant?

My dad's letter ended with something to the effect of: "Get the hell out of there and stay as far away from those emotionally stunted pussies as you can." Tears streamed down my face because my mom and dad responded in a way they saw fit and not what was expected of them. The group leader singled me out, the tough guy soldier, to show how my letters had uncovered something in me I didn't know. How my loved ones had finally honestly opened up to me. He was wrong. My folks didn't know how not to be honest with their feelings, even if it made someone cry from either pain or joy.

After reading letters and hugging, we had a big lunch, the monk came and blessed some people, and the hippie played his acoustic guitar, starting off with "Country Roads." A feel-good time, but not quite heaven. We left, and aside from Lynne and her mom, I'd never see any of those people again. I hope they got what they paid for. Can you buy your way into a new self? Maybe in America.

A week after my first date with Anne, I scored tickets to see AC/DC. I hadn't been to a concert since Lynne had sweet-talked a security guard to let us through to see Yes without tickets—a tame, progressive rock band with a cool laser show. The hard rockers from Australia would be the opposite, with songs of hard drinking and drugs, rocking, and casual sex while riding on the "Highway to Hell." Listening to them was a full-body experience because you felt the music in the basement of your nervous system, and it stirred up all the primal urges. It made you feel like going out and enjoying all the sins you could rack up because it was better to die young and leave a pretty corpse, as Lynne was fond of saying, than to stay home and mold like forgotten food. No wonder religious zealots hated it. It made them feel human.

The concert was going to be on a Monday, but I was allowed to stay out on more nights after having gotten a job and not fucking up. Anne was excited when I told her. We'd been going out to wander Glitter Gulch. We'd gone and had our photo taken with $1 million at Binion's Horseshoe. The display was 100 $10,000 bills sandwiched in Plexiglas in a horseshoe-shaped frame all lit up. It was odd that a million bucks could look so cheap and fake, but that's Vegas. We got the photo back. Anne held it out at arm's length and then pulled it back in. "Hell," she said. "I thought I was getting fat, but it turns out my tits are drooping."

The day of the concert, I rode my bike over to her house. Clouds covered the sky, and it sweltered. Thunderstorms passed over, and a light rain fell. Most of the rain evaporated before reaching the streets. The sharp crack of thunder after the flashes of lightning made my heart jump. I felt exposed on a bike along the street. I kept waiting for the hair on my body to stand up or for the smell of ozone to fill my sinuses. What would I do if it did? Close my eyes and keep riding? Maybe jump out of the way, find shelter in the gutter split seconds before the bolts came down? It all felt so silly. Die on the way to see a woman to go to a rock concert. I pedaled to a store and locked my bike quickly to a rack and hurried inside.

Other shoppers were doing their business, but a cashier stood and stared out the big plate windows that made up the store front as if having never seen a thunderstorm before. I understood and felt it too, reacquainting myself with the power of nature. When we lived down on the homestead, I'd experienced my first thunderstorm outside in the elements. We huddled in a tent with the wind collapsing the walls and water rising to flood the tent floor, soaking everything not above high water. The seams began weeping, and my brothers and I sat as the flashes of lightning chased away the dimness of the tents for a fraction of a moment. We looked as if caught in grandma's Polaroid flash with our shadows washed away. The aftermath of the flashes left us temporarily blinded until our eyes readjusted until the next flash. We lay in our sleeping bags as the rolling thunder carried in the wind against the sound of running water which we hadn't heard in months since the last monsoon season. We kids had often played at being pirates or sailors bracing to round the Horn. Out on that desert plain filling with water rushing all around us, we lived like shipwrecked sailors on a small raft under a tarpaulin hoping for the storm to pass without striking them dead or dragging them under the waves with water coming over the sides.

The cashier and I stood watching as the rain hurled against the earth. Vegas was on a flood plain, and the urban planners, in their rush to pave the desert, didn't build storm drains, so the streets became canals. Then water breeched the curbs to flood the parking lot. Trucks and cars threw rooster tails like speedboats. The rain started to let up, but we still looked out on a shallow sea and slipstreams where fast water flowed.

A shopper interrupted. "Excuse me, miss."

The cashier sighed, maybe wishing to be on a ship's deck during a storm instead of here in this air-conditioned retail shop. She smiled at me as she turned to help the old man. With her black hair and brown skin like those who'd sailed open boats across the Pacific, she must have felt something. The storm must have stirred some feeling of the old explorers in her like it did in me. I wanted out of this place and time so bad and still didn't understand how to get out, to get away, and be someone else out on the sea.

I worried about being late to meet Anne, so left the store, chancing the lightning and the receding floodwaters. All those light poles and tall buildings, I hoped, would attract the lightning instead of me.

Her older sister answered the door. She introduced herself, Candace, as she gave me the once over, as if I might be a match for someone other than her sister. She was there to watch the kids, who were still up. I still hadn't seen them. They were eating ice cream at the dining table, sizing me up like suspicious cops. I waved, and they grinned and giggled as if they'd been caught stealing candy or cookies.

Anne came out from the back of the house. She wore her standard tank top and bell bottoms. She went over and hugged and kissed her squirming kids, who kept casting curious looks at me. I smiled at them, and they giggled more.

"Alright, kids, you behave for your aunt. Understand?" They nodded, spooning ice cream into their mouths.

I waved bye to everyone, not saying anything but smiling as if it was great to meet them all. I didn't feel awkward so much as not knowing what to say except bye or have a good evening. Everything sounded fake in my head. When I thought about saying something, I was afraid it sounded sinister or like a pervert—"Have a good evening. I know I am. Hahaha." Subtext and the art of not sounding creepy.

At the show, we started drinking and missed the opening act—some band from Seattle. We made it to our seats and, like everyone else, stood on them and yelled as we rocked out. After the show ended, we started making out in her car. She asked if I had somewhere private we could go. We hadn't made love yet, so I figured this meant we were close. We were so wasted we decided to walk over to the stadium entrance and get a cab.

We staggered to the door of the camper, and I fumbled with the key. The door hinges squeaked. She giggled. I shut the door behind us and turned the lock. We tried to be quiet, but I felt we sounded like a truck loaded with monkeys rolling over on the highway.

We got on the bed. Our hands ran over each other. We kissed more and started taking each other's clothes off.

She whispered, "Be easy. I ain't been with a man in a couple of years."

"Okay."

"And don't look at my stretch marks. Oh, man."

I didn't notice stretch marks in the dim streetlight filtered by thin curtains. I noticed the heat. I noticed the dust swirling out of shadows. I noticed the way she suppressed her moans as her body trembled and her skin quaked. I felt some magic of my past life, but the past disappeared as present absorbed me. The moment melted away and resolved itself into the black.

No sooner did I enter her than she grabbed my hips and whispered in cadenced breaths, "Fuck me hard. Like it's the last time you'll ever fuck."

Afterward, we lay in each other's arms to catch our breath and let our skin tingle together before we dressed and slinked out. A dog barked at a neighbor's house, and a motion light came on. We paused like escaping cons at the verge of the fence and freedom as the guards' searchlight beams scanned past us. Still giddy from sex and booze, ears ringing from rock 'n' roll, we laughed, and she snorted. I was sure we'd wake Mike and Joan and all their neighbors. We slipped away with the scuff of boot heels and giggles and wandered into the Vegas night. We found her car and drove to a casino for breakfast and coffee and made talk of jobs. She worked as a receptionist in a doctor's office. In high school, she'd been in a rock band and had dreams of making it big like Grace Slick or Stevie Nicks. "But, you know, I got knocked up, and living in a van traveling to gigs with a bunch of guys became too hard." She sighed. "Then I had to be a mom. Got a job doing what I could, which was answering phones and setting appointments. Kind of like what I did with the band too."

I said, "You know, my skills are in jobs I can't have. My college career was cut short by an arrest, so I answered an ad in the newspaper because I'm qualified to dial a phone, and they don't care about my recent past."

"You do have a smooth phone voice," she added with a grin.

"At least I have that."

Over the next couple of weeks, we wandered a lot of casinos, saw movies, lounge acts, or just sat in cafes and chatted about the day and ended up drunk in her bed before midnight with her kids asleep in the other room.

We never talked about a future. She never asked me about my plans or what I saw my future like, and it was a good thing as I had no vision. Having been arrested during the semester, my GPA was wrecked. Not that it was great before as I'd started going off the rails. I wanted to go back to school. But study what, I wondered. Not that I could afford it. What good was it to get a degree when no one would hire me except telemarketers because I was an ex-convict? I couldn't even get a job as an electrician's helper. I wanted to strike out and get experience that I could eventually write about. But for now, here I was, in the dark and feeling okay. With Anne, I didn't feel the emptiness of all I'd lost or the dread of a future I couldn't fathom, only her warmth and the way she made me smile. We lay together, her head on my chest, as music drifted out of her radio on the nightstand. We just breathed. We wasted the night deep under the light of stars already long dead, and it was nice.

I'd begun shaving when a knock on the halfway house apartment door nearly made me cut my neck. I had a headache, and it made me blink it was so loud. The blows to the door made me wonder for a split second if cops were about to stream in and knock me to the floor. For what, I didn't know, but since my release, my first reaction seeing cops or hearing a chopper or a loud knock at the door made me think I was about to be arrested. Here in this apartment, it might be a random sweep by Mrs. Gutiérrez with the aid of some marshals, and not necessarily to haul me off right away. I'd slinked in the night before a little tipsy, but Ms. Randall didn't notice, or she did notice and was now informing on me after some second thoughts about letting me slip through. I'd acted as straight as possible, which, thinking back on it, probably made me look drunker, like the way a kid tries not to look guilty with a snake in his hand behind his back.

I wiped off my face and went to the curtains to look out. It was Captain and his Great Dane. I opened the door and looked at my reflection in his Aviators. There was still some shaving cream by my ear.

"Good God, man. Did I catch you shaving? Go and finish while I go see if old Lopez has the spread for tonight's game." He turned around and made his way over to the office. His dog loped by his side and then lay down in the shade of the building.

In the bathroom, I reapplied some shaving cream in the spots that needed it and finished in a few swipes. After rinsing my face and toweling off, I put on a clean shirt. I had to be at the newspaper boiler room in a couple of hours, and the day was already heating up.

In the office, Captain and Lopez were griping about the shit season the Dodgers were having when I walked in.

"I tell you, Lopez, it'll be a hand of God, freakish occurrence if they cover that spread against the Astros."

Lopez reluctantly nodded. "I had such high hopes after last season."

"Hope is the handmaid of disappointment, my friend. Just take it game to game like a good old-fashioned aerial dogfight. We can only play the numbers, not bet on hope. The bookies—I mean sportsbooks…" He gave a 'you know what I mean' look over the top of his Aviators. "…make money off all those home team fans and their hopes this'll be their glory days. I tell you, no amount of hope can get a pitcher throwing strikes when he's slumping. Even God Himself can't interfere on the mound then."

From the back, Mrs. Gutiérrez came out with a folder in her hand. "I know we are not loitering in this office and talking about gambling."

"You are correct, good ma'am. Might I say you're looking lovely today."

She blushed as she eyed him.

He continued. "No, not gambling per se. We were talking about hope and divine interference in baseball in relation to how certain fans might bet on a game. Purely philosophical or theological in the case of the Dodgers this season. Surely, a priest will be needed for last rites."

Mrs. Gutiérrez smiled at him. "At least Fernando is pitching as if

God is with him."

"That is a fact and evidence the whole team is not without some divine guidance."

Captain looked me up and down. "Well, you are a sight better, my flown felon friend."

We left the office and went out under the trees in the courtyard. The shade and breeze felt nice, but I could feel the heat building. The grass was already taking on that smell of water and dirt being pulled out through its roots, smothering our senses like heat waves.

"Now listen up," Captain said. "I have it on good authority that you are in a boiler room. Phone work is no work for a respectable man such as yourself. Now as it turns out, I need a trusty assistant to help me do some jobs. Now I know what you're thinking. We are not talking anything that might involve jail or prison time. I am a craftsman, son. A bona fide craftsman in the fine woodworking trade. I spent many hours in the base woodshop turning out many a finely wrought cabinet while waiting to fly off in the name of freedom. Now I know you know your way around the good side of a pair of dykes and have a history of hod carrying—although that ain't fit work for a man of your education and skills—and can be handy in general, so you can fly with me. Now I know you're thinking, "What if the law calls to check up?" Don't you worry about the PO. My friend, who supervises over at a certain warehouse, has a friend who will say you work for him if anyone calls and if anyone shows up." He laughed as no one ever showed up. "Well, you are out on an errand getting widgets or entertaining customers."

I rolled my shoulders when he said hod, thinking of the miserable summer I carried one.

His dog got up from the shade and wandered in a circle before taking a crap.

Still looking at me, he asked, "What do you say?"

"I say you're going to need a shovel and a bucket." I nodded toward his dog.

He looked toward her. "Or a flag to stick in the summit."

I agreed to go with him. I'd be learning some construction skills, earn a bit more money. He gave me a name, an address, and a phone number to give to Mrs. Gutiérrez as my new place of employment. She asked me about the boiler room and giving two weeks' notice. My plan was to work there for the evening shift so I could make more money to help get an apartment when I got out. She nodded with what seemed like approval, but it was hard to tell.

That morning, I didn't go by the union hall. Tomorrow, I'd be out with Captain and wouldn't have time to go by the hall anymore, so today didn't make much sense. I thought about going by just to tell Penelope I'd gotten a freelance construction gig and would be back when it ran its course but didn't.

I made it to the boiler room earlier than normal to talk with the supervisor. When I told him I'd gotten a day job that paid more but wanted to keep working evenings, he fired me. He said I needed to be available to take any shift and if I couldn't, then I was gone. I needed to be dedicated to them. I'd heard my whole life that the company wanted your undying loyalty but would dump you on a whim. Fuck him. I left, passing under the mortal eye of the clock and out the door into the inferno of a Vegas summer day.

The next morning at 7:00, I signed out, and Ms. Randall smiled at me. She wished me a good day and to not get into any trouble. I nodded and tried to look as if it were general advice she gave out all the time the way sidewalk preachers hand out copies of the *Book of Psalms*. In the back of my mind, I wondered if she was alluding to my brushing up against curfew, or maybe she didn't believe I hadn't been drinking when I was feigning fatigue. I put it out of my mind, not wanting to believe she knew about my bad behavior. Afraid, maybe, that thinking about it would somehow reveal the truth the way bad poker players reveal they have a good or bad hand.

I stood out front when Captain pulled up in his Maverick. It had some dings and rattled and smoked as he braked. I climbed in. He pulled away as if leaving the scene of the crime or on the way to commit one.

"Where're we headed first?" I asked.

"Breakfast," he said. "Now reach in the back and grab a couple of cans out of that cooler. We need to get the day started." He looked in the rearview mirror as if someone might be tailing us, which wasn't as paranoid as it sounded.

I reached into a cooler in the backseat and found it full of ice and beer. I didn't hesitate to pop two open and set his in the cupholder between the bucket seats. I grinned as I did it. I'd been swooped up in the magnetism of skating against the law and being bad, and the risk felt like a kiss from a woman who wanted you bad. It felt like the vacuum inside me was being filled with something. We were two freelancers out in the city. It beat the dread I normally felt. Here in the Maverick, we were two men poking at the great bear of society. We each knew the consequences but swept aside the concerns for feeling in the moment of freedom, the glow of doing what we wanted and dodging the warders who found purpose in breaking the spirit of those who didn't fit into the mold anymore.

He pulled into the parking lot of a casino restaurant between Henderson and Vegas. He downed his beer, then stuck a pouch of chewing tobacco into his cheek. He offered me one, but I declined and downed my beer.

In the casino, he slipped some quarters into a poker machine and hit a straight after drawing one card. He hit the payout button and sang, "Know when to walk away," as the coins clattered into the metal tray.

The cafe in the casino had booths around the perimeter, a counter with stools, and tables through the center. Captain sat at a table right in the middle of the place. I sat across from him. The waitress came up with menus and glasses of water and set them down. Her name tag read Marlene.

"You can keep the menus, Marlene. We'll have steak and eggs, hashbrowns, two Bloody Marys, two cups of coffee, and if you'd send the keno gal this way, we'd appreciate it. I have recently come into some money and want to see if the numbers are lining up for me today."

"How would you like the steak?" she asked with a slight smile.

"Why, rare, of course," he smiled back at her. "How's Hal been doing?"

She said, "He gets out next month."

"Why, that is good news. Tell him I'll be looking for him and not in the bad way that ex-cons sometimes look each other up."

When she left to place our order, Captain snapped a keno card out of the rack on the table. Every table had one, like salt and pepper. He marked some numbers, and when the keno runner came around with her tray, he gave her the ticket and a twenty-dollar bill.

As she took the card from him, he said, "Now I know the odds of this paying out are as good as a chihuahua in a dogfight ring, but if it hits, there will be a little something for you too, miss."

"Always appreciated, Captain."

"Oh, hell." Captain fished out a fiver from his wallet and put it on her tray. "We should never make tipping contingent on our bad fortune in gambling matters, especially when the odds of winning are as bad as keno's. That's just bad manners and shows poor raising."

The keno runner thanked him and went off toward other tables, calling out, "Keno."

The food came, and by the time I finished, we'd had two more Bloody Marys and I felt like one of those fat lizards flopped on a rock waiting for the sun to warm their cold-blooded bodies to action.

Captain had played four keno cards and hit one for $275. He bought breakfast, and when I offered to chip in, he flagged me away. "Nope, my flown felon friend, this is a bona fide business expense." He looked at his watch. "Lunch will be coming soon. We'd better get our engines turning and burning and get some work done."

He drove us into an old neighborhood where we had to pass through a gate. The house was set in some willow trees next to a pond with cattails and other brush around the shore. Some mallards paddled around on it, and other birds darted through the branches of the trees. It looked like a wetland. The adobe house had big windows that reflected the sky and the surroundings. It looked ancient, blended into the land. I couldn't be sure it hadn't always been there, formed in some volcanic press and left behind, a geologic oddity that'd become a home.

A woman opened the door, sleek blonde hair pulled back, diamond earrings, black long-sleeved pullover, capris, and ballet flats. She waved as Captain parked in the driveway.

We got out of the Maverick. I stood for a second and steadied myself against the car to keep from staggering. From the back of the car, we took our tool belts and put them on. As we walked toward her, a breeze stirred the willows, and their branches swayed like bead curtains.

A smell came up off the pond of water and decay. My mom had planted a willow in the backyard of the house in the suburbs where I thought I was going to grow up. We kids watched it grow, and when it grew tall enough and leafed out, we'd hide in it, pretending to be in *The Lord of the Rings*, waiting on trolls or goblins to pass by us on their way to the mountains. It was from that house we moved to the southern desert to homestead. Living in the wild, we lost the notion of trees planted in yards. Scraggy desert trees, little more than bushes, dotted our plains, and the big cottonwoods and white oaks along creeks and in the foothills before the big pine forests of the mountains all grew wild. The two were the difference between a dog and a coyote.

The woman, introduced as Diedre, held her arms out to Captain. He gave her a big kiss on the cheek at the door before we entered. In contrast to the outside, the interior had a modern design of glass, stainless steel, marble tile, black leather furniture, and, between some neon light installations that looked like hieroglyphics, abstract paintings hung on the walls lit by track lights. Floor to ceiling windows looked out across the pond like a diorama. Low bookshelves flanked a fireplace, and photography books sat on the coffee table. Classical music played low, and the sound came from all around as if out of the air around me.

"Son," Captain said. "I need to go into the back and put the finishing touches on a cabinet project I started yesterday. As of yet, I need no assistance, so hang around out here until I'm finished. Feel free to look at the books. I know you are a man of exceptional reading, so you know the value of time spent with books." And with that, Diedre led him into a hallway and out of sight.

I'd never been in a room like this. It was like being in a movie set in the New York loft of a famous playwright or novelist, and then I recalled the movie, *All That Jazz*, and the director/choreographer Joe Gideon's apartment. I wondered at the order and sleekness, the precision, that still had a lived-in vibe. The couch and chairs looked comfortable—worn in and not worn out—and one chair had a book face down in it—*Bright Lights, Big City*—and although I wanted to, I was afraid to sit down. I was afraid to take off my tool belt and set it somewhere. It might break up the flow, mess up the order, or scratch something.

I wandered over to the windows. On the patio, a pair of Morris chairs looked out toward the pond. Between them was a round side table on which lay *The New Yorker* magazine and a coffee cup. I wondered where the door was to get out there. Maybe through the kitchen. My alcoholic haze made the air flow around me as if I stood inside of a mirage looking out. The sun made the pond a bright mirror. The sky looked blue-green, clouds scudded over the water, and the grasses and brush branches along the edge created a frame of mirrored images. The ducks on the pond were upside down and wavered as they swam. One flapped its wings without taking off and rested again. I marveled at them inverted among the clouds and the water when I realized it was their reflections in the rippled water and I was having trouble seeing what was real from the reflections around them.

I shifted my gaze to the distance. Over the trees, Sunrise Mountain stood above the horizon. as if molded then fired in the kiln of the sun, and then the sky was so bright I blinked and looked away. I turned back to the room and noticed the music again. I didn't know what was playing, but it was familiar to me. I'd listened to classical music on a transistor radio in prison over my headphones long into the night as the others slept. Some days, to piss off some asshole cons I worked with on the rescue squad, I'd play it on the engine bay radio. Classical music became my form of rebellion and breaking down what people expected of me and who they thought I was.

My dad mocked opera as high-class screaming, but I heard something else. Even without understanding the words, I felt something move inside me, exhilaration, joy, and was even brought to tears, just as any non-vocal music can do. Even before prison, I listened to some classical music and wanted to learn more but didn't know how to start, and Las Vegas wasn't exactly a conducive place for a poor kid from the desert to educate himself. There wasn't even an art museum or any galleries, all of which I wanted to visit.

But in me too was the feeling of embarrassment. To ask questions or to go to a symphony was to invite ridicule. I didn't own a suit, and as far as I knew, you needed a tuxedo to go. I didn't have any friends who knew. I didn't have money to buy cassettes to experiment with as I was afraid I'd spend money and not like what I'd bought. Fear, though, of looking like an ignorant bumpkin and feeling inferior to those who'd been educated and had sophistication and taste kept me back. I'd just listen to the radio and read on my own. Maybe someday when I could afford it, I'd go to a symphony. But, like standing in this house that I so badly wanted to live in, it seemed as good as wanting to be an astronaut and fly to the moon. I gazed around at this bubble of another world that was about good books, music, film, and conversations about art and history and science where people who said things like, "What most people don't understand," actually knew something most people didn't understand.

"Can I get you something to drink?"

She startled me out of my daydream. *What would it be like to be with a woman so sophisticated?* I thought as I turned. "Some water would be nice."

"Sparkling or still?"

I had no idea what she meant, and the puzzlement must have been obvious.

She smiled. "Sparkling is mineral water with carbonation."

I felt like the stupid peasant. "Sure, sounds good," I said, trying to sound hip.

She went to the refrigerator and came back with a bottle of Perrier and handed it to me.

I cracked the cap. The pressure releasing felt good on my palms. I couldn't help but think this was what greedy, shallow yuppies and stupid preppy kids with money drank and not necessarily the sophisticated intellectuals I'd imagined.

That night, in the halfway house apartment, I took out my transistor radio and tuned into KCNV. I sat on the not so modern and sleek couch, leaned back, and closed my eyes. The ringing of tinnitus was smoothed away, blended into the sounds of the orchestra. Through the cheap headphones that I'd carted from prison to prison to here, the music sounded far away and thin the way my mom's voice carried over the desert when she called for us to return to camp. But still, the authority and emotional power of the sound came through. I wondered what it'd be like to see a symphony live, to feel all those instruments playing in an enclosed space. I knew the difference between listening to a record or a song on the radio and being at a concert. The magnification the difference between lighting a match and fireball and detonating a 55-gallon fuel drum. I loved the way the music came in my ears but seemed to drift throughout my body, traveling the web of my nervous system and charging something in my spirit, and joined the deep current of my unconscious mind. It made me escape me. It created a place I existed but didn't, a dark forest of sound where nothing mattered but the vibrations of this created universe, a place as important as breath and my heartbeat.

It took me back to Boron when I would tune into the classical station out of Los Angeles. Around that time, Halley's Comet was in the sky, and after seeing it one night, I listened as the station played a series of astronomy-inspired pieces. The DJ said, in her BBC voice, the next piece technically wasn't inspired by astronomy, but because Stanley Kubrick used it in *2001: A Space Odyssey*, we now connect it with space travel. She said, "Kubrick uses the introduction, 'Sunrise,' from Richard Strauss's tone poem, *Also sprach Zarathustra*, inspired by Friedrich Nietzsche's philosophical novel of the same name. Nietzsche asserts, again, God is dead and talks about his concept of the Übermensch, the overman, who must transcend society's conventions and values to improve humanity for everyone."

I'd owned the *2001* soundtrack and noticed how she said Rikard instead of Richard. I'd never heard it pronounced like that before. "The overman is like Joseph Campbell's hero who ventures out and struggles and, in overcoming obstacles, brings back a boon for his community. It's not about dominance of people through violence or manipulation, like some will have you believe, but an improvement of society and shaking people free of old superstitions and power structures that hinder the intellectual and spiritual growth of society."

I wondered about those who lifted society up, transformed it for the better against my earlier belief that the will to power was acting to dominate society by force of will for one's own purpose. My philosophy teacher said Nietzsche was the most misunderstood philosopher and explained how his sister, a Nazi, helped pervert his philosophy for Hitler.

The DJ went on. "It is this transcendence of humanity Strauss captures, and his music reflects Kubrick's theme of evolution from ape to man and then man to Star Child when he uses the opening bars."

She went on about the majestic opening of Strauss's piece "in perfect intervals in the universal key of C major that resonates in all humans and elevates us."

After listening, I did feel invigorated, as if the trumpets and timpani backed by the orchestra created a current over the airwaves and electrified me. I felt I could overcome all of this and step outside my existence. I wasn't unlike the ape men in the beginning of *2001* where one breaks free of scrambling around and grabs a bone to use as a tool. Here, though, what can I do? How must I search? I do know none of these sons of bitches could be counted on to give you a break, so then, as Nietzsche knew, you had to go it alone. What I would eventually need to do.

The DJ said, "We mustn't forget that Nietzsche also said, 'Life without music would be a mistake.'"

Even in prison, I felt the meaning of her words, of life with meaning in transience. I nodded off during Gustav Holst's *Jupiter* and woke with a start at my alarm clock's ring. Sun filled my room. I sat up and looked at the mountains illuminated in the early morning pastels of filtered light. I thought of all the stars and planets and Halley's Comet beyond the blue of the sky and how it's only in the dark we can see the immensity of the universe.

In the halfway house, a car horn and gunshots woke me. I sat up on the couch. A string concerto I couldn't identify played. After a few minutes, I turned off the radio and went into the kitchen to make dinner. When the water in the old pot started to boil, I broke some spaghetti noodles in half and dropped them in. I stirred them to keep them from sticking together. Leaning against the counter, I looked around at this dive of an apartment and thought about the house on the pond. It wasn't only money holding me back or prison or not having the drive to learn.

In my mind, I heard the voices of family and almost everyone around me in the mining towns. "Getting above your raising." "Hoity-toity fancy music." "Artsy-fartsy." "A bunch of jellybeans talking about writing." "Think you're better than us?" Sometimes it was made to sound like a joke, but it was often enough said with contempt to wash away any pretense at the excuse of, "Just kidding you." Why was I being judged as a sellout? I loved rock 'n' roll and heavy metal and blues and bluegrass and Texas swing and outlaw country too. I resented having people try to fence me in.

I became wary of trying to learn more from others without sounding like an idiot. When I talked about things I'd read, I feared mispronouncing words or getting some bit of knowledge wrong that would unmask me as a poseur. I mispronounced epitome as epitōm and winced at the condescending grin as a more sophisticated friend corrected me. You're trash, boy, and we can hear it in your speech. Which was true, but I could still strive for the house on the pond.

Keeping the headphones on, I heated some red sauce from a can, and after draining the noodles, I mixed them together. Earlier, after we left the house by the pond, Captain and I made a couple of stops at other of his friends' places. I didn't do anything but stand around with my tool belt on like an extra on a movie set.

Every morning, off we went in his Maverick with belts full of tools, a cooler full of beer, sometimes his Great Dane, and all the intentions to do some honest work. We spent a lot of time driving around, drinking beers, and doing odds and ends at his friends' houses, most of whom were beautiful women. We ate at the casino restaurant between Henderson and Vegas and had cocktails. I started chewing tobacco when he offered it. In short, easy money, and I never had to buy the beer even when I offered. Captain said drinking was like flying a fighter jet. "You push it right out to the edge where everything feels great and you feel the warmth of the afterburners pushing you on like you are being embraced by the almighty God, but one more push and things start shaking and begin to come apart." You are always one drink away from too many, and that's the sweet spot. I knew what I needed to eat to mask any residual fumes, and even though I'd relied on peanut butter, I liked the spicy stuff. Like the horseradish served with the prime rib where we had lunch. I'd also learned to check to see who was on duty before slinking back to the halfway house.

Lopez was always listening to a ballgame or sports radio as he pretended to do filing. Ms. Randall was somehow always just far enough back from the desk so she couldn't smell me when I signed in. I knew the peanut butter and horseradish were magical thinking, but such was the power of superstition and risk.

On Friday, Captain paid me out in cash. It was three times more than I made in the boiler room. That put a grin on my face. He dropped me off at the halfway house. I signed in with Mr. Lopez, who was listening to a ballgame on the radio.

Mrs. Gutiérrez emerged from the back office with a clipboard. She gave me the once over and said, "I didn't know you chewed tobacco."

"Once in a while," I said. "Not all the time."

She turned away without another word and pulled Mr. Lopez away from his game to look over some documents. She told him, "You need to go follow up."

He looked resigned as the ballgame entered the seventh inning.

I left them. From the payphone, I called Anne.

"Hey, let's go to a movie tonight," I said. "Just got paid."

"I can't tonight. Got kid things to do. Tomorrow?"

"Sure." I still wasn't used to hearing about someone needing kid time instead of going out, but she was worth it. With Anne, I felt I was realigning myself with the free world.

"I tell you what, though." Her voice lowered, became conspiratorial. "If you're out roaming about after ten and got nothing better to do, why don't you slip by?"

"I will."

"Let yourself in the side gate and tap on my window."

"It's a deal."

Hanging up, I started to head to the apartment for a shower when I thought to call Binder. He might be off and up for doing something. As it happened, he and Jen planned to go to the drag races, and if I got over to his place in an hour, I could ride along. If I got there in thirty, I could have a cheeseburger he'd grilled up and a High Life to wash it down.

That sounded like a plan. The track was out in the desert, northeast of town and north of Nellis Air Force Base. I'd have to hurry. They'd leave without me, and I did want a burger and a beer.

My dad had been a drag racer. I have faint memories of him and my mother at the track with a fast-looking car. He held a trophy, one of many I'd seen around the house. He'd also tell stories about racing cars in Kentucky as a teenager before dropping out of high school to join the Air Force. It wasn't on tracks, though. It was against other guys on public streets, and there were stories about trying to outrun the police over backcountry roads that cut through the woods. He'd also tell stories about his father and his brothers outrunning revenuers and other moonshiners during Prohibition in their juiced-up cars like Robert Mitchum in *Thunder Road.* As a boy, it felt that ever since the automobile had been around, my family had been souping them up to elude the police and other shifty folks and go faster than other people on general principle.

At the races, Binder's brother-in-law, Ronnie, had a car in the heavy class. A 1969 'Cuda with a 426 Hemi sporting dual Holly carburetors, Hooker headers, fat racing slicks, and a 13.4-second quarter mile. He raced the brackets and just had to dial in his time and try not to race over the time he thought he'd run the race in. He had a wicked reaction time. We all cheered him on and drank beer in the revved uproar and smoked rubber lingering in the desert air. I walked around the waiting area and the pits, marveling at the cars. The amount of money spent blew me away. One guy's paint job cost more than any three cars I'd ever owned, and that wasn't even getting to what he spent on the engine and drivetrain.

After the races, I pedaled across town to Anne's. It was close to midnight when I got there. A dog barked a couple of houses down, and a hound further off howled in response. Moths flew around porch lights, and nothing moved along the streets. I locked my bike to the fence and went through the side gate.

Her bedroom light was on. I rapped lightly on the window. In a few moments, I saw her face and smile as she parted the curtains and opened the window.

"I about gave up on you."

"My uncle took me to the races, and they went late."

I climbed in and tried not to fall in a heap like a sandbag tossed to stop rising floodwaters. Even as I was crossing over the sill, she pulled off my T-shirt. I stood and swayed a moment, still feeling the beer I'd drank earlier. Anne grinned at me as she pulled off her tank top and slipped off her panties. As I unbuckled my pants, she unsnapped them and shuffled them down. I pulled her close to me as they fell to the floor. I stepped out of them as I guided her to the bed.

"You smell like burnt rubber," she whispered.

"The drag races will do that."

I kissed her neck as she held on to me. She put her hands on my shoulders and slowly pushed me down the length of her body. "Let's see how good a kisser you really are."

At four in the morning, she woke me. "You got to go."

"Crap, I sure do." I dressed quickly and climbed out of the window. I leaned in and we kissed hard and fast as if, at any moment, somebody would come busting through the door. Once I had my bike on the street, I began to pedal for Mike and Joan's. The smell of exhaust and burnt rubber still clung to my clothes, but I also smelled Anne's hair and her body. It was like I could reach out and hold her as we stood in the middle of a fire.

It was over 90 degrees out. Even though I wasn't baking under the sun, I started to sweat as I pedaled. A car crept up the street behind me. I looked over my shoulder. It wasn't a cop. Just some old hatchback. Why would he be creeping on me? An old enemy? A new enemy? I slowed down to let him pass, and he didn't. As I started to speed up, I thought about turning back to Anne's. I coasted up into a driveway and stopped, ready to fight whoever came out of the car or take a bullet. Fucking nerve-wracking, the verge before chaos. The car slowed. A newspaper at my feet, the *Las Vegas Review Journal.* The driver shook his head at me and continued down the street.

Rolling again, the breeze felt good over my body. At this time of morning, few other vehicles rolled up and down the streets. It was between casino shift changes and too early for the normal day workers. The city still hummed, though, from the all the electricity running through it to power the lights along the Strip and downtown. The glow a dome of light miles wide like an umbrella to keep night from falling on the gamblers still hustling for a win.

I slept until the heat became unbearable in the camper. That evening, Anne and I went to the movies. We watched *Howard the Duck* and then went out to eat afterward at a small casino. I liked these smaller places that felt a little more run-down and local like the people who mostly came in there. Not many tourists doing this beaten path with all the glitz and shows of the big-name places. A different attitude, and it showed. Still, with the noise and lights, it felt like, with a little luck and the right bet, you could walk out a winner with a pocket full of hundred-dollar bills.

Anne talked about her week and how her ex-husband was being a dick again and not paying child support. The bills piled up, and the kids needed clothes and food. Her job didn't pay enough. "Watch the doctors with their Porsches and Beamers, Rolex watches, and country clubs, while I struggle to feed my kids if my ex decides he don't want to pay. I should be able to support my family on just my salary."

It was the first time she'd talked about her kids, ex, or the struggle of living. She looked exasperated like I remembered my mom looking as she sat at a table not unlike this one with a stack of bills and a checkbook. Anne sighed and looked at me. In her eyes was a weariness I hadn't seen before.

"Can't make more money, can't stop the bills, can't make the ex pay up." She reached out and squeezed my hand. Her hand felt warm.

I wasn't oblivious. I grew up with my parents always repeating the Merle Haggard line, "If we make it through December," and witnessed the death of dreams we'd hoped to accomplish. The first time I realized the struggle could end not the way we plan was at our homestead.

"Know what I mean?"

"I do, yeah."

We'd been visiting my maternal grandmother. She lived in Glendale a few hours north in the same house where her husband had planted a juniper tree when my mother was born. I was only thirteen, so not privy to what the adults were up to or even the state of our lives. I didn't know we were on the cusp of abandoning the desert to move back with grandma until dad could get a job and save enough money to start over. We survived on pinto beans from a hundred-pound bag, Spam, canned goods, and jackrabbits. We kids thought it was all part of making a life in the desert and not dwindling money. I didn't know about not being able to find work or not being able to just live off the land because it was owned by a bank who would foreclose on you like they'd foreclosed on millions of farmers since the American Revolution and cast you onto the road and not lose sleep or miss a meal in doing it. I couldn't know about cars and repossession and stranding families thirty miles from overpriced groceries. So many things a boy didn't know, like the hardness of a banker's heart or the promises of work that never materialized or wage theft.

As far as I knew, it was just a visit and we'd return to our frontier home and continue building the adobe house and start raising chickens, a cow, grow a garden, and we kids hoped we'd get horses. We drove into a low front. Rain had been falling, and the gray clouds muffled the sky and hid the sun. I knew more rain might come. If we were lucky, we'd get home in time to catch the dry washes full of rushing water and race our small wooden boats we'd built from scrap wood.

We turned up the dirt road. The new Ford Torino we'd moved here in was gone. We now rode in an old, dingy white Dodge Dart that had a red hood from a different car and was tied down with a hank of rope. From the paved road, Turkey Creek was a couple of miles away, which we'd have to ford if the water wasn't too high, and then the homestead was another mile and a half or so beyond that. In the rain, the desert caliche gets slick, but luckily, the road had been graded and graveled, so we didn't slide much. Once we crossed the creek, there was only one other home on our way. They'd had a double-wide trailer hauled out and set up instead of building a house and had corrals with horses. They had invited us over a couple of times in the past, and we got to ride a little, just in circles no better than a pony ride at a carnival.

I sat behind my dad, who drove and kept looking out the side window to see if the washes were still running and scanning the clouds to try and determine if more rain was headed for us. Sometimes you could watch a storm front with a gray curtain of rain between the clouds and the ground move and see the bushes buffeted by the wind and rain before being swallowed into the gray. Once, I'd stood and watched as one came toward me, wondering what it'd feel like when the gray front crossed over me. The wind gusted hard, and I leaned my skinny body into it. On my skin, I felt droplets of mist and rain the wind had carried, but when the misty front reached me, the rain fell hard in big, fat drops that stung and, in the wind, felt like I was being hit by crystal shards. The mist rolled around me, blotting out the horizon. The fog drifted through the mesquite and yucca plants, leaving me in a land transformed into terrifying ghosts in spiked helmets with long horns and scaled armor. I'd read that the Norse believed the underworld a cold and misty place ruled by the goddess, Hel. This storm front was that mythic place as I stood and squinted against the pummeling rain.

But I saw no rain coming. Just the clouds and the wet desert saturated with gray light.

I can only imagine my dad said, "Fuck" or "Shit," when we got to within sight of our camp. I can only imagine my mom's steely-eyed stare and her stoic's face set as if in an FSA photograph from the Depression. I looked out the window. My brothers tried to look over me. Our place had been ransacked. The tents trampled. The small camp trailer's door open and flapping on its hinges. Our possessions strewn through the mud and papers caught in the mesquite branches like giant moths impaled on sticks by children. Deep ruts cut by truck tires crisscrossed where we used to sit and eat by the fire and the spot where we'd toss our sleeping bags on the ground and fall asleep staring into the darkness of space and all around the place we'd lived and worked to build something for months. One rut had carpet cut out of the camper stuffed into it. I didn't know why, but later, when I was learning to off-road in the desert, I discovered that whoever had done this had become stuck. Truck tire treads filled with clay spun and dug them into the earth. The carpet had been wedged in front of the tire and forced to slide under as the driver gave the engine gas. The carpet created a surface so the tire could grab traction and move the truck forward. Their footprints pocked the ground all around, and knee and hand impressions dotted the mud where someone had knelt to work the truck free of the mud. They had to do it several times to get back out to the gravel road and speed away, leaving their destruction and disaster behind them.

We left our homestead. We moved to grandma's. I still wore my belt knife I'd worn in the desert until one day, walking back from a market where I'd bought an ice cream with money grandma had given me, a cop pulled his prowl car over and asked me why I carried a knife. I didn't know what to say. Just that I had lived in the desert and most kids had knives because they came in handy. He told me I wasn't in the country anymore and needed to leave it at home now. It looked like I was up to no good and looking for trouble. I told him, "Yes, sir," as I had been taught to do with cops and went back to grandma's. I took off the knife and put it in a box with my pack, survival kit, canteen, and canteen belt.

Anne and I ate and had a few drinks while we listened to a one-man band lounge act before heading back to her place. Her sister was asleep on the couch with the television on to an informercial selling real estate dreams of making money. It was the first time I noticed how disheveled her place was. A stack of papers and mail on the counter, dishes in the sink, toys and clothes on the floor, and a general untidiness that the low light made seem grimmer than it was. But after our evening talking about finances, hardships, and the struggle of finding decent-paying work, I felt I'd stepped back into the places I'd lived as our family was lost between jobs or working overtime so hard we lost any energy for anything else at home.

Anne went to the fridge and got a couple of beers. We slipped into her room, leaving her sister snoring to the false promises of the infomercial. We stripped off our clothes and climbed into bed and drank while the radio played soft rock. *This could be the end of the line*, I thought. What if I woke up bald with a potbelly and thirty years had gone by, and this is as far as I'd gotten working to make others rich?

We fell asleep in each other's arms until she woke me at 4:00 am to go. I dressed and started for the window, but she stopped me. We went out through the living room. She opened the door for me to slip out onto the front porch. She kissed me and said to come by later. Maybe, she said, I'd like to join her and the kids for a drive out to Lake Mead and swim away the heat. "Sure," I said. "That'd be nice." Even though I thought being around her kids like that might be awkward. She kissed me again and said to come back around 1:00 pm. I didn't need to bring anything except trunks and a smile.

I didn't have swimming trunks. After a side trip to Kmart, I made it to Anne's place just after 1:00. Candace, dressed in shorts and a T-shirt, stood at the trunk of the car loading in some beach chairs next to a cooler. She smiled when she noticed me, still with a guarded look.

"She said she'd invited you, but I bet her even money you wouldn't show. Now looks like I got to pay up."

"Hard to turn down a trip to the lake in this weather."

"Right." With a smart-ass grin, she said, "You'd better lock up that beauty of a bike before someone runs off with it."

The kids had on shorts and T-shirts with their swimsuits underneath. Anne had on a one-piece swimsuit and cutoff Levi shorts. We rolled the windows down and headed out. Candace sat between the kids in the back as they giggled and held their arms outside the car to surf their hands in the wind.

At the lake, I helped set up a shade canopy and carried the cooler from the car to it. I'd learned to scuba dive in this lake and had taken more than a few trips just to drink beer and swim.

The cool water embraced me as I waded into the lake. I dove in. The deeper I went, the colder the water until it felt like I was passing through sedimentary layers of geology. My lungs ached. I started for the surface. I rose from the water some distance out. The sun reflected off the water, causing me to squint against the pain of it. On the beach, it looked as if Anne and the others were the survivors of a shipwreck and I still out on the sea yet to make it to the shore.

I swam back in. The kids ran through the water laughing. Anne and Candace kept eyes on them as they drank beer.

Anne went to check on her littlest. I sat next to Candace on a towel. She drank and then said, without looking at me, just straight ahead, "You hurt her or those kids, I will have you killed."

The way she said it reminded me of a mob boss. "I won't."

"As long as you understand that."

I just nodded and drank my beer.

We made it back after dark with the sunburned kids and Candace asleep in the backseat.

Lynne invited me back over for lunch, so I went the day after going to the lake. I felt like a hunk of glowing beef jerky from too much beer and sun. After our sandwiches, we went to the living room. The guitars sat in their stands, and I asked if she minded if I gave one a strum.

She smiled. "Go ahead. I know those two gave you a little grief last time."

"The curse of not being very good but still wanting to play." I played through twelve bars and smiled, then played the intro to "Stairway to Heaven."

"Ooooo, Zeppelin!"

"I thought you might like that."

She asked about how I started to learn, and I sat back a moment thinking about it before telling her. It seemed years ago, before we'd ever met, much less met, married, and divorced.

On the bluff the first day I sat in with Brew and Flat-Five, they'd started playing and explained what they were doing.

Flat-Five started strumming some chords with little changes in them. "Listen for the one, New Guy. Count out, and if you can always make it back to one, you'll be learning to keep time."

"I'm that guy who gets lost clapping along with the band. I look around and realize everyone else is clapping at a different beat."

Flat-Five laughed. "Shit, New Guy. You can mark time. You was in the Army. Marching is keeping time."

I thought not just about marching cadences, but songs we sang as kids. Christmas songs, folk songs, and all the patriotic songs to indoctrinate us to blindly love our country. I remembered singing with my family in the car on Sunday mornings on the way to gather with aunts, uncles, and cousins at grandma's after church for lunch. "Over the river and through the woods to grandma's house we'll go." Our high voices buoyed no doubt by the expectation of root beer floats and pie in the afternoon.

Flat-Five pointed out the frets on the neck. "You want you pointer finger to be right up on the third wire with you fingertip and you ring finger on the fifth fret."

Brew strummed. "Alright, now. Follow along with me."

He tapped his foot in an exaggerated way that sounded like Frankenstein's creature limping down the street. Just down at first until I kept time with him, and then he started using his pinky to press down on the seventh fret of the A string and let off. I heard the blues rhythm playing and tried to match him. I faltered but kept at it. My fingers started to hurt, so I let go of the neck and shook out my hand.

"Keep at it, New Guy. You fingers will come around," Flat-Five said.

I smiled at the two guys.

They started playing, and I followed along as best I could. When they stopped, I shook out my hand.

Brew explained the first chord was G. "That's our root." The second chord was C the fourth. "If you count G, A, B, C is the fourth and D, the next chord, is the fifth. What you need to know to start is the blues progression begins like this. Root, fourth, and fifth. In the 12-bar blues we play, four measures of the root, two of the fourth, two of the root, then one of the fifth, one of the fourth, back to the root, and then finish the twelfth bar with the fifth."

Flat-Five said, "You can do a turnaround for the 11th and 12th bars so you can either bring back to one to keep on playing or finish the song."

"Cool."

I handed the guitar back to Flat-Five. He took it with a grin. "Look, man, we get you some rhythm going and then get you riffing." He played the first few bars of "Mannish Boy." He patted his guitar. "Just stick with us, New Guy."

"I don't know if I got what it takes."

"Man," Flat-Five said. "Don't let thinking get in the way of the groove."

"Yeah," Brew said. "It's a visceral thing. I saw you were feeling it. Just you keep at it."

"Maybe you could sing some white boy blues about how you momma didn't make you biscuits and gravy enough," Flat-Five said.

"Or how you were late returning a library book," Brew added as they laughed.

Flat-Five said, "We just fucking with you, New Guy. Everybody gets the blues, especially here. I mean, you ass is in prison. Now tell me that ain't blues. You just need to tap it and not be so uptight about it."

"You got to pay your dues if you want to sing the blues…and you are paying some dues," Brew said. "But blues is more than having hard times. It's about feeling those hard times so much you can make other people feel them because they hear theirs in you. See, it's not about you. It's about all the others."

"You singing for them," Flat-Five said.

Brew said, "A self-centered prick like Chicklet had hard times by having the feds break up his banking scam fucking investors out of their nest eggs, but he couldn't sing the blues because he thinks only of himself, and everyone knows it. People don't relate to that."

"Except other douche bankers," I said.

"You find it in youself honestly, and others feel it in their guts too."

"That's the art, man," Brew said.

"Plus, New Guy," Flat-Five said, "singing about hard times and playing music make life a bit easier. You know what I'm saying?"

"Especially way the fuck out here," Brew said. "I have to fill all this space with music."

I stared out across to the far mountains. As a boy, I'd never thought about having the blues. It was a southern thing that used the Mississippi

River to travel north to Chicago from the Delta and points in between. My parents' music had the laments of coal miners crushed in dark shafts, of truck drivers on the road their whole lives, and of cheating lovers and drinking booze to forget. And having some pride in poverty and a nostalgia for some golden country life, which I couldn't understand. My family had lost everything from cars to houses to land to idealism. Dad had lost jobs from mine layoffs caused by corporate incompetence or crooked employers who shafted him and, by virtue, his family. We'd picked up and moved in an old truck with a camper and parked along desert roads on the way to another mine or a promise in a sawmill that was so much dust. We wanted to believe any guy who worked hard enough deserved a shot at a home and a steady check so his kids could grow up in the same house and go on to do better, but even as my parents held on to the belief and the hope, I saw the breaking of the promise over and over again with each time I left friends behind and in each new school where I was cornered by the local boys who saw in me the threat that their good life could be swept away in a flurry of pink slips. They weren't wrong. My blues flowed down dried rivers, rose on heat-shimmered playas, and lay exposed like the guts of mountains dug up as raw, unsmelted ore. Depression, melancholy, feeling down and out, and the sense that everywhere I went, disaster followed like so many buzzards over a dead range cow. I imagined music vibrating with the rattlesnake's hiss and rattle, sounds a person can confuse with harmless dried gourds or seed pods on a hot west wind as harsh as the August sun on a fieldworker's neck. But for all the heat that makes snakes race and mirages shimmer, the desert is a cold and lonely place. The music needs to capture the isolation of a boy wandering lost in the moonless desert night where the stones sucked the heat from him while coyotes howled, drunk on the hunt.

Lynne and I lazed about the house for the rest of the afternoon, listening to Led Zeppelin records, lost in our own thoughts. Maybe hers were of the past, maybe her future. Or more likely, she was just lost in each measure as it washed over her. No past, no future, just the present in time with the music in a state of wonder.

Captain had a friend who had a friend. A friend who owned a tire store. "New Guy, I have found you a bona fide job. One where you can make some dollars and be a proud and productive member of society, and it will pay you a damn sight more than the pittance I am forced by circumstances to pay you—and you know I'd pay you a lot more if I could, but I have large expenses. You know I told the judge that if he sent me up to the pen, a wife, an ex-wife, a girlfriend, and two hookers were going to become destitute. Well, as you know, the judge didn't listen, and now I'm making up that lost ground. Don't get me wrong. I have greatly appreciated your help and valued it very much, but now is the time for you, son. This job is going to help you to freedom. And as you know, my boy, freedom is all we really have. Even if the bastards throw you in the can."

While I loved being around Captain, I didn't really work for him except to keep him company, get him a beer, and occasionally grab a tool from the car. We visited a lot of places with beautiful women. As I waited around looking useful, he disappeared to finish some job he'd already started. Only years later did I think he might've been a gigolo. Of course, maybe he did just want some company and to get me out of the boiler room.

I thought about stopping by the union hall but wanted to be at the tire store when they opened. I rode my bike up to the tire place and applied. Ron, the manager, asked me about my automotive experience. I gave him the spiel like I did for the mechanic at the garage that told me to get a certificate or get fucked. Ron didn't ask about my felony or quiz me about my plans or even act like he gave a damn about my past. He nodded as I finished telling him about the tires we mounted on our muscle cars up in the mountains. He laughed at the thought of all-terrains on a hot rod so you can tear ass up dirt roads. He went into his office and brought out a couple of button-up mechanic shirts. "Extra-large should work," he said as he handed me the shirts. "Just wear jeans and boots. We open at seven. Sound good?"

I said yes, elated.

My parents were happy to hear I had a steady job that paid reasonably well when I called them that evening. It felt nice to share good news with them. A small win is still a win.

The next morning, I was out in front of the tire shop waiting on Ron when he arrived at 6:45.

Anne shook me awake. I opened my eyes, groggy, not coherent, and out of breath.

"You sounded like you were having a nightmare."

I didn't know where I was, lost. My senses lingered in the dream world, and I thought I was in prison and Anne the face of a guard we called Stasi rousing me from my bunk for the count.

The last time I was shaken awake by someone like that was in prison. My cellmate, Punch, woke me, and it brought back an odd sensation from when I was a kid. My brothers and I swam in a concrete irrigation tank under palm trees at the grapefruit orchard before moving to Lake Tamarisk. It must've been thirty feet deep. The water had been piped in from the Colorado River to irrigate groves of grapefruit trees. Even in summer, the water made us shiver. The gray concrete sides had algae growing on them, giving the water a greenish tint. We dove down to touch the bottom that felt impossibly far as I kicked and kicked, thinking I had somehow become lost in a bottomless tunnel of water. It became colder and started darkening as I, however slight and skinny, kicked against my buoyancy. My lungs began to burn. I kept going. I felt my younger brothers turn back toward the surface with the swish of bodies and of arms clawing for the light. In my moment of doubt, the air in my body depleting, I thought to turn back. But I touched the slimy carpet of algae growing on the bottom of the tank. I flipped around and pushed against the weight of the water, gravity, and my own breathlessness and, in that moment, dreaded something would grab my ankle and anchor me to the bottom. But I kicked. Above me, the silvered light of the surface seemed so far away like a smudge of stars through cirrus clouds. I could see the silhouettes of my brothers' legs and arms treading water. As I swam, the slow blacking out began even as the water started to fill with greenish and golden sunlight. Waking up from a nightmare was like breaking the water's surface and sucking in that first breath of desert air against the burning of the lungs after resisting the impulse to breathe while struggling for the surface. What else could I say? "Sorry."

My cellmates went back to bed. I lay and looked out the window. Moonlight on the desert floor shimmered like water. The light and shadows twisted mesquite bushes into sailing ships adrift, praying for wind while the Joshua trees dotted the sea with arms raised up as men overboard do when waving to attract rescuers' attention. How was I on this island? How was I to un-shipwreck myself?

Anne looked at me. I finally shook off the haze and confusion. I began to recognize my surroundings and sat up. "Sorry," I said.

"It's okay. It happens to all of us."

I couldn't sleep because of the strange electricity that ran through my body at times, especially like that. I lay next to Anne, and my brain spun with no place to go. It wasn't like I was even thinking about anything in particular. My thoughts skipped around from what was I going to do tomorrow to what was I going to do with my life. Again and again, I worried. What was I going to say to the court-martial when I had to go? Where was I going to stay? Binder said I could stay with him and Jen. But for how long? Ron had said if I worked hard, I could eventually manage my own shop and maybe move up to corporate. To me, that sounded like taking a little poison every fucking day that burned away a part of your soul until you finally died an excruciating death from it, empty and with nothing to show but plaques and a house in the suburbs your kids will fight over if the property values haven't gone to shit. What was even my future with Anne now that I was getting closer to release? I liked being with her. Her kids were okay, but in general, I hated kids, didn't like being around them very long and didn't want to have any of my own. Joan mocked me once when I expressed this sentiment to her. But it was how I felt then. I liked Anne a lot, Candace's threats notwithstanding. I knew she liked me a lot, so I'd try to make it work with her. The kids weren't too bad.

The digital clock numbers glowed red. When they lit 3:30, I got up and dressed. I woke Anne gently by caressing her check. The light from the street, through the curtains, created a half-light, like a charcoal drawing. She shifted and opened her eyes. I told her I had to go. She nodded and puckered her lips for a kiss. I bent down and, after kissing her, said I'd call her tomorrow.

I let myself out and made my way back to Mike and Joan's camper.

Then one night, after riding the bike from my Uncle Binder's place in North Vegas, I rapped on Anne's window. She let me in as she always did, and we made love. I was a little tipsy, so when she said I must leave and not come back, I laughed.

She said, "It's not a joke."

I asked why.

But she just said, as she pointed between us, "We, this, can't work out."

Part of me wanted to refuse to leave, make her realize this was a mistake, but the side that remembered the despair and chaos of a marriage falling apart knew better. I saw and heard how resolute she was. I thought of her kids in the other room. I thought maybe tomorrow she'd call me back.

"Okay," I said. After dressing, I climbed out, and she closed the window and drew the curtains. I stood there a moment, confused. Then I felt like a weirdo for being there in the shadows, thinking the distant siren breaking the night was for me.

I made my way to the street. Nothing moved in the neighborhood except bugs throwing themselves at streetlights.

I wandered the streets at a loss. I decided to go—felt compelled, really—out toward the edge of town where I knew the darkness was to clear my head and think. Going out into the desert at night brought me a strange serenity.

Before prison, I went on an insomniac motorcycle ride out here when I felt things were collapsing around me. Tonight, I thought about another restless night when I left Lynne sleeping and rode. I'd been preparing to go to Officer Candidate School. In my working-class mind, the officers did all the boring paperwork unless they were generals, and according to the stories my dad told me, all new officers got good men killed because most "couldn't pound sand down a snake hole." My class of boy needed to be the one who got shit done. The backbone of the Army was all the sergeants, the noncommissioned officers (NCOs). Like the struggles between labor and management, the glory belonged to those in the field, those who worked and stuck with it and got the job done. Seemed a betrayal to go off and be an officer. Was it maybe a fear of responsibility? The fear of fucking it up in a high-stakes game and being held accountable to the dead and their families and friends? Maybe. But I was going anyway.

The first weekend of OCS, I met the other happy few from the battalion and a couple from the Military Police unit. The Guard flew us up to Reno and drove us in an Army van to the training facility up in the mountains above Carson City. The other new cadets were so cool, focused, and squared away. We tankers acted driven to be great commanders like Patton and Rommel. But in my heart, I wondered how driven to be officers we really were if we had been plucked from the enlisted ranks by a test given one weekend at the Guard armory. None of us had tried for West Point or even the ROTC at any college. We seemed tentative combat leaders of chance. Those citizen soldier leaders who wanted to help their community but were not necessarily so gung-ho as to have a tank or a barracks named after them.

We rode in the van and talked of qualifications and badges, getting to know each other—college students, waiters, construction workers, casino porters. All of us were young, wanting to learn and experience as much as possible. We wanted to go to Airborne School. Ranger School. We wanted to go to Dive School. Jungle Warfare School. Mountain Warfare School. We wanted all the training and all the shiny badges to pin to our uniforms. Be leaders in the Lean Green Fighting Machine and defenders of freedom and the American way. We were heirs to armored divisions that rolled down the throat of Nazism and Fascism and choked it to death. We stood the great armored line between democracy and communism, a legacy left over from the last great armored war.

The van pulled through the trees to the training camp. We shared rooms in the cabins and made beds and organized our gear for our weekend stays as if we were back at Fort Knox. We wore helmet liners painted black with the insignia of the State of Nevada National Guard with its motto, "Battle Born," painted on the side.

Every month, I'd pack my gear and fly to Reno on Friday evening and take the gutless Army van into the mountains and then back down on Sunday. The only remarkable thing that happened was that, one Sunday, a woman in a Porsche 911 convertible pulled alongside the van and flashed her tits at us and then sped off, leaving the van struggling to do the speed limit no matter how hard our driver mashed the pedal.

The one weekend a month up in the Sierras didn't feel quite real. One weekend of training a month. To switch gears from being a casino worker for four weeks to being a STRAC cadet trying to find the groove of saluting and learning about all the admin jobs officers did. I thought it'd be all battle planning and strategy and tactics and how to make war. Most of what we learned was how to order supplies, how to discipline troops, how to spot and discipline non-hackers, how military law at the junior level worked, and how many forms the Army had and how to fill them out. The joke went: Always use the last form to order forms to order more forms to order more forms or the Army would come to a standstill because you couldn't order any more forms. Our training officers stressed the importance of attention to all the minor details that, if overlooked, brought an advancing army to a stop. Oh, fuck! No fucking fuel, you idiot officer! Hey, stupid, where's the food! The fucking bullets! Fuck the food, where's the bullets!

For our summer drill, we were flown to San Luis Obispo and then bussed to the Guard's military camp outside the city to train under the auspice of the California Cadet Corps and be yelled at and trained with cadets from all over Nevada and California. Before we left, our cadet commander told us to wear nice clothes so we'd look respectable when we showed up. Not a seasoned air traveler, I showed up at the airport wearing a Black Sabbath concert T-shirt with "War Pigs" on it and jeans. The plan included a night in a hotel before being picked up in a van and driven to the training barracks. I figured I'd change into my uniform and away we'd go. Something happened and our flight got canceled, but the airline bumped us into first class on the next flight. We flew in fine fashion, but our luggage languished someplace between Vegas and the Pacific Ocean. Our ride arrived. The other cadets, even in rumpled clothes, looked respectable. I became self-conscious. It struck home when a training officer yelled at me, "Well, what do we have here? Move it, Cadet Black Sabbath! Get in line!"

I finally got my uniforms the following day. We learned to land navigate, including a night course where one cadet got lost and chased up a tree by a free-range Brahma bull. We learned about plastic explosives when the instructor demonstrated the Big Bang by molding a vagina and penis out of C-4 and then detonating it. We fired all sorts of American and Russian weapons. And we even started to learn the basics of leadership. I began to learn all the things I had dreamed of learning as a kid sitting in my room with a makeshift survival kit, Army surplus canteens and belts, four merit badges, and the aching desire to be tested.

This was less about the pushing of requisitions and signing papers and more about the physical struggle. I fell in love with it again, and even with my Black Sabbath snafu, the officers praised me for my *esprit de corps* and ability to learn and act quickly in tactical situations.

If I could've stayed at the training academy and not gone back to the world, I would have. Reveille and the loudspeakers blaring a selection of rousing martial recordings, like George C. Scott's Patton speech from the movie, *Patton*, marching songs, the Scottish skirl of bagpipes with the beat of their drums, or "The Star-Spangled Banner," as we hustled to get dressed and into formation.

When I returned, though, to home and civilian life, I mind-fucked myself into believing flying away to training one weekend a month to Carson City was the difference between making things work out for my marriage and not. I quit OCS and went back to being a Specialist Four.

In the dark, I thought of all the justifications I'd used. What seemed so important at the time I couldn't go on? That I didn't want to be there in the first place? I ran into a guy who had already dropped out of OCS in a gun shop who offhandedly said word for word what my dad had said: "Fucking NCOs is the backbone anyways." Was it the fear I'd be trapped into doing menial admin work and never go regular Army, never see Airborne School, and be forced to leave the field? Lynne? The love of a hippie stoner chick who dropped acid and said, "The inside of the stars is the birthplace of the soul," "The desert loves the sun more than rain," "This is why they call it tripping," or "Whatever, I must be high"? All these things got shaken together in the cocktail shaker of my rattled mind.

Out there in the dark on that Vegas night, I felt the drifting. I chose nothing so much as it chose me, and I rode it out or changed my mind in confusion as to what to do. And if I did one thing, like go regular Army, I'd miss out on getting my education. I was taking Army correspondence courses while still going to college. Better to stay then, but what the hell was I educating myself to do by taking random classes with no major in mind? I was headed for a major in Trivial Pursuit.

In the desert, on a rise far enough away, it looked as if I stood on the rim of a bowl. In the bowl flickered the lights of stars and the long smears of neon nebulae as cars traced the streets like meteorites through the blackness. Above, worlds spun away through space, so cold in their distance, but felt closer to me than the city lights. I imagined sailing between the stars and strained my mind as if concentrating hard enough would transport me out there. Soon enough, a noise in the city drew my attention back to the earthly lights. What was I doing here, and what was the point of it? Some sad collection of bones and flesh with no more sense than a coyote pulled by forces of nature, history, and family even as I misbelieved I controlled how I lived my life. We country kids believed we roamed an open range through life, but really, we found ourselves stuck following a fence line strung out by someone else. If you did cut the wire and go your own way, you might find yourself exiled from your family and friends and have to start over, find a new community. It's a good feeling to realize you broke away. But maybe becoming the outlier, the black sheep crossing the fence, was also ingrained by those same forces that give the illusion of freedom to those marching down the fence. I thought of Thoreau and most men leading lives of quiet desperation but realized most don't even know that desperation was their lot.

I thought I had discipline, but discipline to carry out orders and perform tasks quickly, efficiently, and perfectly was not all the discipline that existed in the world. I didn't lack self-discipline when driven toward goals like being a good soldier, like when I worked out every day before basic training. I worked hard at being a martial artist. I studied and memorized military things as I had memorized the constellations, planets, and all the space missions when I wanted to be an astronaut when I was a kid. I wrote a report for high school history about Viet Cong booby traps with hand drawn diagrams and was the only kid in my high school to read Che Guevara and General Erwin Rommel's books. But for all of that self-discipline, I lacked it in controlling my darker urges to drink, race cars and motorcycles, sleep around, and act like a fool.

At the dark edge of a town built and sustained on bad impulses, I didn't realize I was struggling with competing desires that would never mesh. The insomnia, the drinking, doing poorly in college after having been an A student in high school, and being a disciplined soldier at the top of his specialty.

With a battalion out in the field, I felt good and focused, at home in a strange way. I didn't have to consider anything outside the bubble of my platoon and my tank's steel womb. I had tasks needing done, a crew needing support, and that was all I needed to worry about. No bills, no timecard, no other people but those I shared the common goal with. Guns cleaned and operational; gas mask strapped on along with my M191A1 pistol and M3 grease gun; ammo secure; radios on the right freqs; passwords and authentication codes known; light and noise discipline; gear secured and tank squared away for operations; briefed on the day's mission; what's my job; and no matter what, watch the land for lines, glints of glass and metal, movement, and the distant dust and smoke of an armored column beyond a ridge; scan for distant birds that might be ground attack aircraft, like the Cobra attack helicopter or an A-10 Warthog; keep focused and sleep only when told to. No Guts, No Glory. Who Dares Wins. Always Faithful. Make the other poor son of a bitch die for his country. Drive on, drive on, drill sergeant, drive on! Steel on Steel. Shoot to Kill. Kill for Thrill. Shoot, Move, Communicate. Lead by example. Kill Russians. Kill communists. Kill, Kill, Kill. Swift, Silent, and Deadly. Battle Born. She wore a yellow ribbon for her tanker far, far away…

When I went out on training exercises, Lynne mailed letters pretty much every day. Thick, handwritten love packets of looping teenaged letters in purple ink, sprayed with perfume and containing clippings from the newspaper comics. And somehow, I felt so close to her when I opened those fragrant letters, closer than being within arm's reach of her. Some of the guys said, "You volunteer to go out too much. She's going to get sick of it, and the letters will stop."

"Jody's got your girl and gone," as the cadence call went.

The breeze on the outskirts of the city drew toward the heat in the heart of downtown. The cooler air cannot help but be drawn in. That night I'd left Lynne asleep and rode out here, I finally felt exhaustion fill me. I rode on back home to my hippie wife. I undressed, smelling of exhaust and leather, and slipped into bed next to Lynne. The waterbed sloshed a little, and Lynne shifted in her sleep. I pressed my body against hers, feeling her heart's warmth on her smooth skin. She'd showered away the smell of fast food and cigarettes, and her blonde hair felt wonderfully soft. The smallest of intimacies, something I needed but was still too ignorant to know it. She asked if everything was fine.

I kissed the back of her neck and said, "Yes." I loved being with her as much as I loved being in the field. In the end, I'd lose both.

But now I had no one to go home to. Not home so much as a camper in a driveway to sleep in. All those things that happened had happened in the confusion of trying to live a life with conflicting desires and no way to select all. Here I was, sleepless in the desert on a bicycle looking out over Las Vegas, haunted by the knowledge that if I'd remained in OCS, I wouldn't be here now. But as my dad always said, "Coulda, woulda, shoulda. Get on with it."

I rode the borrowed bike out of the darkness and into town to a camper I didn't own and couldn't strike out across the country in even if the law allowed me. It didn't matter how hard or how far into the desert I rode, I was still there.

I'd often thought about my last day as a cadet in every prison bunk I'd lay in, all of which were not so different from the camper bunk. One of the officer trainers called me to attention as I packed my gear in the barracks on my last Sunday. She came up to about the center of my chest. Her black hair was pinned back under her cap, and not one strand escaped. She was starched. Her uniforms remained immaculate even after running us up and down the mountains of the Sierra Front or if she stood in front of a class instructing us on some basics of being junior officers. Crisp, clean lines, military bearing. The crossed pistols of the Military Police on her collar caught the light. "Jesus, Mathes. You have the mind of a steel trap. I can't believe you've given up on yourself."

I stood there, mind fatigued from competing stresses and no sleep. I felt like the ancient Sibyl of Cumae who said to the children asking her what she wanted most of all: "I want to die."

At the tire store, I began to learn all about tires, rims, and how much men didn't know about tires by when they opened their mouths. A guy came in and wanted a "high-speed" balance on his tires. Ron laughed and told him it was included for all cars and nothing special. The guy insisted he wanted the ultra-high-speed balance in excess of 100 mph. Ron explained we didn't have a machine that was capable of balancing for such speeds. Pissed, the guy said his tire guy in Texas did it for him on the same machines we had in the bays. Ron shook his head. "How much he charge you for that?"

That first week, I learned Ron liked to host crew parties. He invited me to play a game called wallyball on Friday with our guys and some guys from another tire store. Wallyball was volleyball with the net strung between the walls, and the walls were in bounds. Only the floor was out of bounds. The day of the game, I made sure to have a change of clothes with me and tennis shoes because boots were forbidden on the court.

Ron gave me a ride with him in his sweet Mustang—a '68 fastback. We went by a 7-Eleven, picking up snacks and a case of beer on the way to his house. At his house, before he put the beer in the cooler, he put Pink Floyd's *The Dark Side of the Moon* on the turntable and let it spin. He popped two beers and handed one to me as he went into his room to change out of his work clothes.

I loved Pink Floyd. My friend, Blaine, from Mountain Pass and I used to listen to them and think about madness and music. Lynne had a friend everyone called Roach (He told his mother it was because he told everyone they'd lived in a roach-infested apartment in NYC as kids. She was scandalized even after he told her it was just a joke). He had all their albums, rare collectors' items, concert posters, and the like all over his room. They got high and rapped about the deep mysteries of Syd Barrett's disappearance, reappearance, and madness and how it shaped everything after like he'd been some kind of holy man. The summer after I graduated high school, their movie, *The Wall*, came out, and I went a few times to see it. I'd been listening to the album since 1980 when an English teacher played it during our classes as we wrote about the different apocalyptic scenarios. It weighted my high school years with an emotional and psychological resonance. But at that moment at Ron's, their music came back to me. "Comfortably Numb," "Young Lust," "Wish You Were Here," "Shine on You Crazy Diamond," "Time," "Brain Damage," and the other songs filled me now with a different set of emotions and thoughts to consider. Is it nostalgia if music from the past makes you understand something about your present? The music stirred me and tapped into something elemental in me about prison and keeping time while searching for meaning in it.

The first time I heard "Several Species of Small Furry Animals Gathered Together in a Cave and Grooving with a Pict," I did wonder at what they were trying to tap into with their music. In prison, I began to think about the origins of music and time as I learned to play guitar. I discovered it did come back to a cave, not so much a Pict, but I felt there had been some grooving going on.

We believe the earliest art was sacred and not just Paleolithic graffiti or early landscape and animal painters of a pre-pre-pre-Romantic bent or cave-dwelling abstract expressionists. We must believe their art wasn't only decorative or something they did as a diversion in the fire-lit caves to pass the time like so many hobbyists. They were using art to create meaning in their lives and to join with the divine. It follows, in these caves turned first chapels, that the artifacts on the floor were also part of a religious ritual, and those artifacts included drums and flutes. These instruments are a technological wonder.

It boggles the mind to think about someone who saw the wing bones from vultures and swans and imagined a flute or saw mammoth ivory and thought, if I carved that into a rod, that'd be a start. I think of all the hits and misses, especially with ivory, until they landed on a design that worked. With a knapped stone, a craftsperson delicately cut the rod lengthwise with serrated edges to make the two halves that can lock together again after each side has been scraped to create an air passage. The craftsperson then drilled finger holes so they could play music on the flute. Any kid who learned to play the recorder can play a recognizable tune like "The Star-Spangled Banner" on these 45,000-year-old instruments. I think of all the trial and error to discover the placement of the holes that would create a perfect pentatonic scale. They did this while also trying to survive in a hostile environment. Even so, I like to imagine being there when they created sounds in patterns that had never existed before. The awe of discovery of beauty. I wonder if it moved them spiritually.

I wonder if spiritual awareness arose in tandem with our ability to keep time internally and with others to make music. It makes me think if their music had a sacred aspect, then their paintings are an illuminated manuscript on a rock face. While Paleolithic researcher and filmmaker Marc Azéma makes a case for the Chauvet cave paintings to be like a cinema in the flickering firelight, I see it more as a theater backdrop where the performance takes place in front of it, and as the performers enact the hunt or the journey to some far place, the landscape and animals behind them shift and waver, adding depth and mystery, but also a spiritual/metaphysical enactment of survival.

They marked time in their minds, felt it in their bodies the way I did, or as Nietzsche wrote, "We listen to music with our muscles." Time became more the day to night, moon phases, and the seasonal shifts tied to edible plants and the migrations of herds and flocks and schools of fish. These people discovered time inside them, and it led to finding a new meaning in the world around them and unlocked the spiritual world. I want to think music and art gave them solace in a dark and unforgiving world. It gave them a way to pass to the next generation what they felt important for physical survival and salvation from dread, from the void. It gave them a way to appreciate life and feel they could manipulate the future with the help of planning and a dash of providence. Time pulsed through them and around them, and they were conscious of it like a fire wavering in the cold. They marked their mortality as they conceived of an eternity and discovered their soul.

At night in the half-lit barracks of the prison, amid the snores, farts, jumble of words of men talking in their sleep, and the regulated footfalls of guards making rounds, I thought about the Paleolithic people. We shared the same darkness and the same way to wait for day.

In prison, I thought about my grandmother dying while I served my time. I imagined getting the news of her on her deathbed. I fretted about her asking for me in her last moments.

Brew had skipped out when he heard his father was dying and the warden denied his request to go to his father's deathbed. No Moses coming to set him free. No King Cyrus to send him back to the Promised Land. No. The pull of filial obligation tugged harder than the fear of two more years. What's two years if your dad's slipped into eternity and you never sought forgiveness from him? Why? I can hear him say to me, "Because you must atone, friend, atone."

He needed to go say the Kaddish with his people, to help make meaning of a life he messed up. He skipped out over the desert to a car idling a liturgy on the side of the dark road.

I bet he didn't see his father. The marshals knew he'd arrive at the hospital, so they would be posted at all the entrances and his father's door for good measure. The cops had time on their side. They worked in shifts, had nothing better to do while drinking coffee and collecting a paycheck, while Brew was but one man, with one destination, from a long history of running out of time.

I wondered if I'd skip out like Brew. Or would I reason we wrapped ourselves too tightly in the notion of seeing someone before they die? Maybe it eases the passing of the dying to see a descendent one last time. To see proof that something of them will go on in the world when they're dead. I didn't know.

In the caves where the first humans brought their fire, art supplies, and musical instruments, they left handprints. To be exact, they left the negative space where their hands had been. Paint marked the outline of the hand, one after another. It is conjectured that they believed the cave was the entrance to the underworld, as is the tradition from other mythologies. Not a representative of or a symbol of, but the actual entrance. In the case of the hands, it's believed the spirit world was behind the rock walls of the caves. So to place your hand there and leave a negative image of it was to touch hands with the spirits of your ancestors, to exist in *nunc stans*. Is it making peace with mortality or a sign of reverence? Maybe both? Maybe it was like the way we show an open hand when we greet to show we are unarmed and have no ill will. All those hands waving to eternity, waving goodbye to the dead and hello when they cross over. Maybe it was like when visiting time ended in the county jail, and I put my hand on the safety glass when my wife put hers against it, our hands separated by half an inch, she in the living world and me in the house of the dead.

But the dying. What did I think I'd find standing beside a woman's deathbed—redemption? Or a way to regain some measure of grace? To witness the end of a dream?

I think about it now all these years later. I might've followed the Jewish blues man's suit. Absence in an imprisoned state messes with the mind differently than when you walk among free people. Sure, there is the clock time physicists calculate and recalibrate because of gravitational time dilation and relative velocity, but there is also the mortal time we live in, measured in breaths and heartbeats, filtered through a mind that doesn't measure but feels time. Because so much is outside an inmate's control, the importance of moment, of gesture, gets magnified with the gravity of a holy mission. We make a pilgrimage to touch the dying, the holy relic which made us manifest in this world. A living, breathing connection to the past about to vanish to dust, gone. We confront the reality that in time, we might become the oldest connection between the dead and everyone still breathing.

We know Paleolithic mourners created funerals. They discovered the transitional moment where mortal time ends and eternal time takes over. Standing at graves with funerary objects and a body prepared for traveling into the afterlife, they acknowledged the importance of ritual for both the living and the dead. They realized the sacred nature of time. I wonder if they sang and played music on their instruments made from once living things.

It's not hard to imagine escaping into the desert I knew like an old lover. Brew and I, we felons flying, strike out across the wilderness, dash across the desert under the impossibly bright night skies where stars hang like twinkle lights in the trees over a child's garden party, across the vast open spaces where coyotes lope and yelp, over the mountains, and across the river to the far side, to death's other kingdom—the past. The kingdom we live in, the kingdom of time. To grandma's house I'd go.

At the wallyball game, I got trashed. When Ron got me back to my bike at the tire store, he asked if I was okay to ride. "I don't want you swerving into traffic and getting plowed over."

I told him I was fine. Nothing to it. I slung my pack on and waved at him. He looked as if he was in a fish tank where the water wasn't being filtered well. He waited while I unlocked my bike. It felt like a monumental effort.

"Seriously, man. Lock it back up. You can crash at my house."

"No, no, I'm good. I have to get to a place I'm allowed to stay at."

He shook his head and got out of his car. As he led me back into the passenger seat, he said, "You can tell me where you need to be." He locked the bike on the rack and got in.

By some magic born from patience and having listened to a lot of drunks talk, he got me to Binder and Jen's. It was just after 9:00 in the evening. Binder was at work, but Jen brought me in and fed me—which I later threw up—and put me to bed. I lay there, not sure where I was or even who I was. So drunk I was nothing but an incongruous bunch of sensory information that didn't make sense. My teeth tingled. There was no I, just the body floating in space, the organism and its suffering. The I had gone missing.

A few nights later, I saw Bridgette walking along the street as I coasted my bike up to the halfway house. She looked me up and down. "Hey, why you been a stranger?"

I shrugged. Her glazed eyes and crooked grin caught the streetlight. I smiled back.

"Come party with me."

I felt almost like the time she'd crawled through my window when Captain had sent her. I wanted her again. Alluring in the half-light, I wanted to follow her into the shadows. "Sure, where?"

"Couple a places down. Follow me."

I followed her to some apartments not unlike the halfway house and locked my bike to a fence. We went in. Through a haze that smelled like nail polish and paint thinner, I saw, around a dining room table, a Black guy, a white guy, a Black woman, and two Hispanic women passing a crack pipe. I knew about crack but hadn't seen people smoking it. Everyone sat slack and smiling except the Black guy, who looked around as if the cops might bust in behind me. They all looked like students, well-washed, wearing polo shirts and nice blouses, and not like anything a person would consider a crackhead.

My first thought was to leave. I abhorred hard drugs and wanted nothing to do with them. But my desire for Bridgette put a hatchet in any good sense. The craving for her touch and sex filled me. I missed Lynne. I missed Anne, and when she dumped me, I was filled with a dread that I'd never find another woman. After having been isolated for so long, I felt like a person who nearly dies of thirst and, when rescued, drinks too much water, not out of need but from sheer craving. Bridgette took the pipe and lighter and took a hit. She offered it to me. I shook my head and declined.

"Why not?" the Black guy asked.

"I don't want to," I said. "Not my thing."

The white guy eyed me. "You a cop? You have to say if you're a cop."

What a joke, I thought. "Undercover cops don't have to say they're a cop if asked."

They looked more suspicious.

I offered, "I'm at the halfway house. They piss test me."

They didn't look convinced.

"Ask her."

Bridgette smiled. "Yeah. That's where he stays."

The Black guy got up. I readied myself for a throw down, but he just said, "I got to go." The white guy and the two Hispanic women followed him out.

"Guys," Bridgette pleaded with them. "Come on."

They just said they'd see her later.

Bridgette sat on the couch. She took another hit and set the pipe on the coffee table with an overfilled ashtray. She patted the couch next to her. When I sat down, she guided my arm around her shoulders and cozied up next to me. "Do you want me?" she whispered.

"Yeah." I kissed the top of her head.

"I want a boyfriend."

Before I could say anything about rushing along, she said, "But I can't have one. Not like this." She sank a little in the couch and into my side. "Not like this."

I kissed the top of her head. She pushed me back from her side.

"Not like this." Her grin from earlier turned to a frown as if she were contemplating a mystery. She looked at me, eyes flattened. "I need to stop."

"Okay," I said.

"If you want to be with me, you need to wait."

Not sure what she meant, I said, "Let me hold you again. Like we did last time."

She shook her head. "No. Not like this."

"No problem," I said.

"You need to leave. I will find you when I'm better. I need to stop. This needs to end."

I nodded. "I get that."

"Then you can be my boyfriend."

I got up to leave like she asked. At the door, I looked at her lost in thought. She looked like a guy I'd seen in county the day I'd been arrested. Some dude in so much trouble, surrounded by so much chaos and despair, that he turned inward, and on the wooden bench under the fluorescent lights, in the clammer of a drunk tank, the smell of unwashed men, secondhand smoke, and booze, he looked like a monk gone into deep prayer. I left, shutting the door behind me, and went into the night.

Back in the halfway house, I sat on the couch in the half-light staring at the crack in the wall. It pulsed like a blood vein. My eyes twitched as I shifted my vision. I thought about how Lynne and I came to the end. It was only a few days from my arrest, as the feds finished building their case against me. Lynne and I broke our life between what we could still recover from and what would forever separate us as lovers.

Suicide is painless, or so the song goes from *M*A*S*H*, but not if your wife storms out the door after a fight. Over what? Maybe me, maybe her, maybe some nothing new. Me and her and Bonnie and Doug and not putting love affairs behind us even after the promises of a bright Christmas morning. No, it was April when everything came crashing down around me and all the others close to me. April, the cruelest month. The month of battles. Of Passover. Of crucifixion. Of resurrection and the promise of rebirth and revelation. The month of my arrest and of a suicide attempt clean and clear as the white paint on a front door. The door slammed behind her, and she kicked it or hit it hard with her purse. She yelled something. My bad ears only heard muted shouting until she broke down in tears, huddled against the step. The door creaked as if it breathed against her slumped weight. Did she have the razor with her when she came over, or did she take it out of the bathroom before leaving after one of our epic fights? Had she carried it with her the way a spy carried a cyanide tablet, just in case? When I was an angst-ridden teen, I took comfort in the small caliber revolver in the glove box of the family car. Knowing an exit was possible somehow made life less of a trap. I knew she didn't take one the night she came over and pointed the revolver at me. Cocked the hammer back with glassy eyes, strung out on weed, speed, and bad love. The night I took the revolver away from her and unloaded it. No, a night closer to the day I'd walk into the armory and be whisked away for 18 months without a break.

At our apartment, Lynne slumped against the door. She slit her wrists and smeared blood from the Judas hole down to the threshold. Holy fucking Christ. I had heard her bang against the door, and I ignored her. I ignored her because we yelled and kicked at things. We both had missed the memo that yelling and screaming solved less than shooting someone or running away to LA. Nothing but raw ape passion. She pounded again on the door. I imagine her now. Imagine the blood running down her arms from her upraised fists banging on the door. I imagine the slow panic stirring in her guts that I was not going to open the door. The banging stopped, and I imagine I thought, *About fucking time*, before I heard a loud and clear wail. A wail I knew I will never forget. A wail more desperate than I have ever heard even in the depths of prison or when a fishing ship I crewed on threatened to buckle in a gale or as fire roared up a canyon years later when I was on a wildfire crew and we were not sure to live. The wail came up and out and wrenched the night as if torn from the soul of the earth. A visitation from the Holy Spirit. It cut so deep that when it stopped, it left a vacuum, and all the traffic's rumble and all the roar of electricity surging in the city stopped. The quiet enveloped everything, and I became frightened like when I was a kid and thought I saw the devil's reflection in the night window of my bedroom. I forgot the anger, swept away into the vacuum. I opened the door. The blood streaming down the door glistening in congealed streaks. Graffiti of the dying.

I stepped out of the apartment. Lynne staggered for an apartment where a friend lived. The gay couple looked out the window from their apartment and let the drapes drop and came out. Not terrified, not mad, not smug, nothing but the fear of concern. Someone called an ambulance. I applied pressure to her wrists. I held her wrists as if we were arguing and I was trying to keep her from scratching my eyes out. I held them harder than that. I did not want her to die. I loved her still in that way one must. I could not stand the thought of her gone from the earth. Could not stand the thought she'd be gone from the earth, into the void, over me. I was not worth it. The paramedics came. They whisked her away, leaving me swathed in receding blue lights under the blue-black night, smudged in red-black blood like the rouge, hair dye, and glitter of our first wild night dancing the "Time Warp." I shook from the want of a fiery drink.

The day after, and just days before federal agents intercepted me, I visited Lynne in the psych ward at the hospital where they had taken her from our apartment. She had a dazed look of broken wonder as if she were having ecstatic visions of angels, a blue gown that made her eyes pop, and white bandages incandescent on her tanned wrists. She showed me her stitches, those little black tick marks on an unnumbered clock. In the moment, I was numb. I didn't know how to react or what to say. "Glad you're alive." "What the fuck were you thinking?" I had not been taught how to sit with a woman in a room like this, in this space between life and the loss of all her tomorrows.

We sat at a table as other patients looked around in a state of amazement, like they'd been able to pass by a riddle-talking, winged cat out of Ethiopia or were simply amazed at the magic of breathing air. Maybe those awestruck faces were why people used to believe God touched the mad. Others shuffled in broken-down slippers, mumbling and drooling as they doddered along. I did not know it then, but I'd soon learn in the county lockup that inmates called it the Thorazine Shuffle, the name of the worst dance ever invented.

Part of me wanted to believe it was dramatics, a selfish act to get back at me, and her wounds superficial, tempered with the wrongheaded notion it was a choice. I'd learn people were compelled by forces out of their control toward suicide and how madness escaped the quaint ideologies of freewill and self-reliance. Then, I was the boy in heavy boots stomping through spider webs, ignorant of the damage I left behind. The longer I sat with her in the ward, I felt the cracking in my numbness but was still too much of a dumbass to let that crack open wide. It'd work on me over the years until I learned to see compassion doesn't cost anything.

When I was a Sunday school boy, I'd heard the story of Jacob wrestling with an angel. The teacher showed us pictures of this ancient main event. I thought, *How could a man wrestle with an angel, this great force from Heaven who helped cast Satan and his band of bench-angels into Hell?* The wings alone seemed indomitable—a hurricane of flapping to hoist Jacob high and drop him on his head. Take that, human. Jacob had lied to his father on his deathbed and stole his brother's blessing and later deceived his uncle. But after the struggle, the angel dislocated his hip. He was blessed and seemed to have changed his ways. With the sunrise, he was renamed "He who wrestles with God"—Israel. What was it about the struggle? As a kid, I took the story literally and wondered if change and redemption only came through an actual struggle with a celestial being and suffering a wound. Surely, I was not so strong.

But as I grew, I shed the myths of my youth. I realized no angel had descended from Heaven. Jacob had dreamed alone in fearful sleep in his camp. Who among us has not had lucid dreams shaking us awake with a gasp and a muscle cramp, not sure of where sleep and waking ended? An undigested bit of beef? Not likely. Perhaps Jacob was troubled by doubt and the guilt of his betrayals. He had to strive against his own worst enemy, not some outside force, but his own flaws and weaknesses. I was in pain at Lynne's despair, but not in that real way where the meaning really lived. I had yet to wrestle with the angel of my blame, my own selfishness. One night, though, I would and would for many nights after because I wasn't strong enough to do it in a single night. Some nights, I'd wake in disarray and discover the phantom of her love, like a lost limb, absent but pregnant with a lost lover's touch. A person might find grace there, under the story, if he was lucky. But in that April, in the season of death and rebirth, I was not. I was just a boy.

Ron took me to lunch, and we split two pitchers of beer. When we got back to the tire store, a blonde woman wearing a plunging V-neck and a high miniskirt asked me if I'd do her a favor and put on a more expensive set of rims. In my drunkenness, I thought, *Sure, why not?* I fixed her up, and she handed me her phone number with a wink. I smiled as I went back to working on another car. About forty minutes later, she called the store. One of the front tires fell off the car. Ron was pissed. He sent a tow truck for her and brought the car to the shop and made me do the work of fixing it with he and her standing over me. I never called her.

I had this little voice saying, what the fuck? You do not have one good prospect, and just going along with everyone is like being trapped in the belly of a ship as it hits the rocks. I needed to figure out what to work toward before I really fucked something up. I vowed to curb pushing the rules and stop drinking. Like Bridgette had said, this needs to end.

I figured, after the night of the company party, I'd stay sober for the last couple of weeks in the halfway house.

On a weeknight, we'd all met up at a Mexican restaurant. Because there was an open tab and the company rep said to order whatever we wanted, it became a margarita and tequila shot drinking contest. None of us had any self-restraint, and I couldn't help but keep drinking. There was in me a hunger to appear as a normal guy. A working-class guy who could drink with his friends and co-workers, and at the same time, a guy who held his own while drinking.

Rows of empty pitchers stood on all the tables. I'd consumed so much margarita salt my lips began to crack. Instead of ordering water, I ordered a pitcher of beer. We left and went out for more drinks. I nearly got into a fight with a bouncer at a bar who I thought was being rude to a stripper. "Fuck you, asshole," I yelled as the others dragged me out the door and into the parking lot. The guys from work stuffed me into a car and started for another bar. I wanted to go over to Anne's. She'd never called like I'd hoped. I wondered how she was doing, still perplexed at the sudden end of our relationship. We seemed to be doing so well. We didn't fight or argue about anything. I put her out of my mind, knowing the pointlessness of it.

Someone dropped me off in front of the halfway house. I expected Ms. Randall, who looked the other way when I had been tipsy, but not blind drunk. But no, curses no. Mrs. Gutiérrez had come in to straighten up a paperwork snafu and was still there. They always had snafus, but she usually only dealt with them during business hours and not this late. I saw her in the back. She looked out of the back doorway as if she'd seen the creature from the Black Lagoon. Ms. Randall smiled apologetically up at me, knowing she couldn't let me go. I knew even as I scribbled my name on the sign-in sheet and slurred a, "HOqwei uhajhsfi doadaduh o?" to her. I'd burned my luck like a scorched grilled cheese after midnight.

Mrs. Gutiérrez hustled into the office as fast as she dared and told me to hold on. She opened the cabinet and produced the breathalyzer. I didn't think she was smiling as if to say, "Ha! Got you!" but rather, "Ha! I am fulfilling my purpose and justifying my job!"

She put a little filter-looking thing into the device and handed it to me. "Here. You got to blow into this." She held up the plastic box with its tube pointed at my face. I turned that breathalyzer green as a leprechaun's blazer.

"You are drunk, sir," she said.

At first, I wanted to say, "Some detective you are," but only nodded as I swayed like a palm tree in an August wind and said, "Yadl fjadh."

Mrs. Gutiérrez's looked utterly disgusted and shocked. I wondered if I'd been the only guy in the history of her career to speak the glossolalia of the drunk. She put her hands on her hips and told me to report back to her tomorrow afternoon as my pass was revoked and I would only be permitted to go to work and back. "You will come right here after work and make not one, and I mean not one, side trip."

I shrugged. I'd done so well too, drinking in moderation, planning, and covering myself. I supposed it was like the kid in high school who liked to capture rattlesnakes and had never been bitten until the day he was rushed 70 miles to the closest hospital. He lived but lost his hand.

In my blurry vision, she wavered in and out of existence as if slowly passing from this world. Standing there, I felt the Earth moving, and it made me woozy. Vomit rose to the base of my throat, but I held it down. She said something like, "Let me help you to help you."

I said, "Majd fad," and staggered off to my apartment past a giant pile of dog poop. In the apartment, I threw up so hard I was afraid my eyeballs were going to pop out into the toilet. After I recovered and cleaned up, I made a grilled cheese sandwich and then passed out until the alarm buzzed at 0600 when, with a headache and wicked cotton mouth, I put on dirty clothes and hitchhiked to work where my bicycle was still chained to the fence. The smell of vulcanized rubber gagged me all day long. Why would anyone ball it up so close to freedom?

Hell if I knew.

PART III

THE THERAPIST IS IN

"Doctor, my eyes have seen the years
And the slow parade of fears without crying
Now I want to understand"

Jackson Browne, "Doctor My Eyes"

When I walk in, the frigid air feels fake the way grape soda tastes fake. A dream of cold I can't wake from. The heat of the desert feels more intense than the coast. I've only been at Boron a day and have been told I need to visit with the prison therapist. Ms. Smith sits behind her desk. She wears a pale white blouse with grid paper blue lines like I'd used in math to plot x- and y-axis problems and to create worlds for playing Dungeons and Dragons. I swear I can see the lace of her bra, a slightly off-white contour map, through her gridded blouse. She asks how I got here.

I don't want to give her a wiseass inmate response like, "Judge sent me" or "The marshal van brought me." So lame, but what does she want? So I ask, "Do you mean from the beginning?"

"Sure." She straightens her legal pad on her desk that doesn't need straightening. "Just go ahead and tell me what you want to get the dialogue started."

"Okay, doc."

"Oh, I'm not a doctor. I'm a certified therapist, but not an actual doctor." She indicates a bachelor's degree in psychology on the wall: UCLA 1985. If she went to college right after high school and took four years, she's a year older than me. I think about this and feel like a child in the chair. I close my eyes a moment. That amplifies the ringing in my ears, so I open them again.

I look at the nameplate on her desk. "Alright, Ms. Smith." I think about mistakes in judgement and fooling myself into believing I'd gotten away clean from the whole fiasco only to be arrested right out of the armory and paraded in front of television cameras and reporters and their stupid questions as I tried to maintain my military bearing. As I think about what I don't want to talk about, I must look doubtful of Ms. Smith's qualifications.

"I know the judge said you needed to be at an institution with psychiatric support and you were expecting a doctor, but I'm what you've got. Don't worry. I've been highly successful."

"I'm sure you are." In truth, I'm not expecting anything. I haven't talked to a regular doctor, much less a shrink, since my sentencing. I'd been transferred between different prisons without talking to anyone. This recycled Air Force outpost, miles from any town, certainly wasn't a thriving center of psychological therapy. I wonder how she knows she's highly successful just as much as I still wonder why the judge and prosecutor thought I needed a psychiatric evaluation anyway. "I'm just trying to figure out what to say. I haven't really talked to anyone about it."

"No problem. Take a moment."

I don't want to talk to Ms. Smith. People where I come from don't talk to psychiatrists or therapists. That's for rich people from the city. We poor people suck it up and keep going. Your feelings got hurt? Too bad. That's life, and "No one promised you a goddamned thing," as my old man said. He'd rub his forefinger across his thumb and tell us kids, "This is the world's smallest fiddle playing 'My Heart Bleeds for You.'" I wonder what she's required to report to the warden or the parole board.

She wants to know about my life from the beginning? Before this shitshow? Some people say they wouldn't change anything about their past, bad or good, because all those events made them who they are. To hell with that. I want to be the person I could've been and not who I became.

I've been forgetting. The trial of forgetting what an awful fuckup I've been.

She says, as if trying to move things along, "Tell me about your wife."

Memory and desire… Desire. I'm not seeing the ghosts of people. It's like having lucid dreams so vivid I can see them. I see Lynne standing behind Ms. Smith. My wife with her top pulled down, the straps of her blouse loose around her elbows as her hands are held in front of her like a surgeon who's just finished scrubbing up. The cold air puckers her nipples, and goosebumps rise over the curve of her breasts. Blood streams from her slit wrists, dripping to the floor from her forearms with a metronome's tick, tick, tick.

"She's basically a good person," I say.

"That's good," Ms. Smith says. "Does your wife still keep in touch with you?"

I close my eyes a moment, listening for the goon squad on the other side of the paneling. A sound of heavy men in armor whose breath raises the room temperature and sweat mixes into the ventilation system like so many masturbating fools at the adult video store. They have to be there. You can sense it down the block, on the street, on the other side of a plywood wall. Is that the tick, tick, tick of a Super 8 movie being spun like a wheel of fortune at a carnival or the rapid jacking of rounds into the chambers of guns ready to blow holes in me? I know they have to be there, waiting in the crepuscular light.

"Yes," I say to her.

The a/c whirs in Ms. Smith's office. I sit and shiver a minute. Her white blouse has small roses on it like she's been splattered with birdshot. "What was your favorite class in college?" Ms. Smith asks.

"Philosophy."

"A philosopher warrior."

I sit for a moment, trying to think of something to say. I've been coming in for several weeks. She was guiding me through the parole process, but she also had me journaling and thinking about identity and self. "To help you, we need to dig in and discover who you are at your core."

I say, "I read this book by Walker Percy about a guy searching outside himself for some kind of meaning, but he only becomes distracted by trying to sleep with his secretaries until he screws up and has a come-to-Jesus moment with his aunt. I can't remember the name of the book, though."

"Interesting. I'll see if I can find it."

"My philosophy teacher says a pilgrim searches outside himself for meaning, but a guru searches inside."

"We will do both. You need to search within yourself first, though."

Ms. Smith acts like she has it all figured out, but I'm not so sure. What is it she hopes I find?

"Okay," I say. "I guess if you search on the outside, you should at least be able to go and search and not be stuck in a prison."

"Well, yes, but also, pilgrims know where they are going. They have a sacred or holy destination, and sometimes they have a traditional route, like a path or a road."

"Not much use to me. I don't believe in that sort of thing."

"Then it's a good thing we're starting with looking inward."

"*The Moviegoer.*"

"Excuse me?"

"That's the name of the book. He also goes to a lot of movies, and even though he puts a lot of meaning into the lives of movie stars, it's still an empty diversion."

She writes the name down on her legal pad.

I'd seen the pictures in *National Geographic* or *Life* or some magazine of pilgrims at Lourdes, the Indians going to a Monkey Temple, and the Hajj in Mecca with throngs of people circling and throwing rocks at the black block shrine.

I ask, "So if the pilgrim's journey is about a trip to a sacred place, what is the journey to the inner self?"

"It's a sacred journey too and as arduous as any pilgrim's."

I thought of the encounter weekend Lynne's mom had paid for us to go to. That was arduous, but not in the sense Ms. Smith was talking about.

Ms. Smith says, "Over the last few sessions, it sounds like you were being pulled in different directions, between the worlds of training to be a top soldier, a serious college student, and a party guy."

I think for a second. "No one ever said I couldn't be all three."

"From here, it looks like you couldn't."

"Ouch."

"Did you start getting into any mischief or breaking the law? Maybe risky, dangerous behavior outside of the ordinary."

"Breaking the law? Besides underage drinking?"

"Yes."

"We didn't get into any more mischief than the average kids. Matt and I'd do some light shoplifting for kicks or race our motorcycles around the city. We'd have a blast taking the curves on Joe W. Brown by the country club after midnight as fast as we could, leaning so far over our bikes that our bodies made acute angles with the asphalt. Every time I did it, part of me wondered if I'd lean too far and catch my foot peg and send myself skittering like a pinwheel down the street."

"What else?"

"I mean, there were some times that were wilder than others." I think about it.

Brenda worked with me on the closing shift. This was when I had been working at the fast-food place a few months before I'd moved out of Blaine's. She'd been giving me rides to and from work after I wrecked the Green Rocket—a 1976 Plymouth station wagon. She wore these big round glasses in purple frames like butterfly wings which magnified her eyes. Her teeth needed braces, but she had a cute grin. She drove a sweet white Monte Carlo with a blue landau roof. A 350cc engine rumbled under the long hood. She started hanging out and getting buzzed with us. One night, Brenda was complaining about her boyfriend she'd moved with from Chicago.

"I just want to go home."

Wendy said, "Just load your shit and go."

Brenda said, "It's not that easy. He has relatives living in the back. They'd call and rat me out before I could get my stuff loaded."

"I'll help," I offered. My childhood notions of knights-errant helping damsels in distress and my old man's southern/chivalric code kicked in. How could I not offer to get her out of the glittery Sin City tower?

"I want to sell the Monte Carlo and catch a Greyhound home."

To minimize the confrontation she wanted to avoid, we'd roll up in the afternoon when the boyfriend was at work. She'd pack as soon as he left, then tell the relatives she needed to go into work so they couldn't argue with her leaving without good reason. Then she'd pick me up and go back. We'd keep it quiet so as not to disturb the back part of the house, load her stuff into the car, and off we'd go.

Brenda lived on the outskirts of town in an older house surrounded by bushes and withering trees. I backed the car into the gravel driveway and popped the trunk but kept the car idling. She kept hauling boxes and suitcases out. I started getting nervous. The trunk filled. I folded the driver's seat forward. She handed me a thick stack of clothes on hangers. I wondered how she planned to ride the bus across country with all these things. Trying to stuff the clothes in the back, I leaned against the folded seat. The horn BLARED. I hit my head against the doorjamb. The seat corner contacted the steering wheel again. HONK! Shit. I figured some old-timer with a shotgun would be out on the porch any second.

Brenda rushed out, not even bothering to shut the house door, and jumped in with a philodendron, its long trailing vines like a wig from a swamp creature costume. I'd already gotten behind the wheel and shifted into drive. In the rearview mirror, I saw a guy with a wild beard step into the driveway. I stomped it. The tires rooster-tailed gravel and dust as good as any James Bond smokescreen. The man ducked back behind the house, and we were gone.

Giddy with escape, we stopped off at a liquor store I frequented and bought a bottle of Jack. We found Wendy and Matt and ran loose over the city stealing street signs after dark. Matt or I rode shotgun with a wrench, a ratchet with a socket, dykes, and a screwdriver while Brenda stayed behind the wheel. Wendy and one of us guys hunkered in the back looking behind for cops or concerned citizens, which happened that night. Some dude in an old Bronco pulled up behind us as I jumped in with a High Voltage sign. He honked his horn and flashed his lights, then got out. Brenda floored it. The dude got back into the Bronco and started chasing us. He followed us through subdivisions and out into the city. Brenda and I traded out positions on the fly when we hit a straightaway. Matt was saying we couldn't outrun that Bronco unless we made the highway. Man, my heart ripped, and I felt like I had the power of the sun pumping through my body. I was on electric fire.

As we flew past a park, I slammed on the brakes and spun the wheel hard over into the parking lot. The tires shrieked. We whooped as the car fishtailed. It was Vegas. A city of risk big or go the fuck back home. We were running hard, wrapped in the beautiful moment, seeing no further than the headlights. What was the dawn to us? Nothing but an uncashed check.

I jammed on the gas, and the big block 350 roared. We jumped the rounded curb. The suspension compressed and flexed, whump-whump. We sparked concrete against metal and caught flight for the briefest of seconds as if we were Steve McQueen in *Bullitt* or any number of movie car chases tattooed into our psyche. Everybody screamed in the light and the flight. Part of the park had been manicured with soccer fields and playgrounds and the other part left semi-wild with cottonwoods and sprawling patches of brush. I aimed to cut out on the far side to a long, dark stretch of two-lane highway with nothing but desert between Vegas and Laughlin. Just kept it floored as if barreling to break through some border town roadblock.

The citizen stopped in the parking lot. We laughed and laughed in the howl of wind through open windows and the sound of the deep-throated engine. That night, Brenda and I made crazylouddrunkenlove, nearly knocking the coffin down when we rolled into the sawhorses. I thought for sure we'd wake Blaine's batshit crazy relatives.

In the morning, we got off the floor and got dressed. We drove down to the bus station with the front end wobbling a little. I helped her check all her boxes and bags and gave her cash for the Monte Carlo. She'd given her plant to Wendy. I waited with her until departure time. The loudspeakers called out destinations and arrivals in a scratchy emphysema voice. We stood amid the swirl of people. A blonde teenager with trembling lips and feathered earrings asked anybody walking by if they wanted to get fried. She was frying, and it was a glorious trip. "Man, better than fresh powder."

When Brenda's bus came, she kissed me on the cheek, pushed her glasses up her nose when they slid down, and said, "Thanks for the swell going-away party." The doors hissed closed behind her, and she was gone back to the Midwest. For a moment, I felt as if there should've been something more. But what? There in the buzzing crowd of travelers, I puzzled about what that more might have been but only had a vague emptiness. I drove on back home with a few browning philodendron leaves and the High Voltage sign lying on the floorboard. Sunlight through the mostly empty Jack Daniel's bottle speckled the sign with amber and diamond light. The brain-searing sun made such beautiful patterns through the liquor and glass.

What do you want to know, Ms. Smith? That I see the shadows of guards as they cross by windows during the night count the way a rabbit sees the shadow of the hawk in the day? The quick flash of a flashlight searching for bodies. A quick rippling and gone. That I wonder if they're ghosts of convicts wandering the dark corridors of the past? That sometimes I hear the shadows rippling the way water ripples against a boat's hull? That I can't sleep? That I lie in my bunk and face the wall with my hands clamped over my ears and my mouth wide open in a silent scream like a horror show mime so I won't wake anybody up?

Sometimes the waking nightmares are things that were almost tragic. It reminds me of when I waited in the car when Lynne and Darla went into a house to get Darla's stuff out. Darla had been Lynne's friend since junior high, so Lynne didn't hesitate to volunteer our help. "We just need to get her stuff away from the scumbag. He's holding it hostage."

I watched the shadows cast on the living room window in case a Punch and Judy show started. If it did, I was going to roll in and stop it. I had my .44, and I just waited. My guts were seized with horror at the thought, but I needed to keep my fucking mouth shut so that Lynne and Darla would have the confidence to get what they needed done. They needed to know I was dependable and not some pussy. Lucky for me, and everyone involved, the guy just wanted to be rid of her. But in the middle of the night, so many things can go wrong. Darkness confuses everything. In the artificial gloaming of streetlights, shadows waver with the current, seem to breathe, and you couldn't recognize the dog from the wolf, as the French would say. In the electric twilight, an open hand can appear as a gun, and who shoots first lives. I thought of men gathered in a graveyard offering condolences to my grieving widow.

I don't say that to Ms. Smith, but I wonder how much she really wants to dig in. I have a hard time believing she really cares. She must listen to so many whining convicts. It feels like that much compassion and empathy doesn't exist in one body, in one heart. My old man mocked the whiners from the war, saying they just needed to get over themselves. The war was over, and what they needed was a solid kick in the ass or a slap like Patton gave a soldier who couldn't hack combat and not to be babied. When the judge ordered me to be sent to an institution with psychological counseling, it puzzled me. I'm not crazy or insane, just a normal guy. But here I am, and what I've seen and felt since then might have made me crazy, but those stories can't be told on a counselor's time frame. It's just how it works. I open my mouth, and nothing comes out because all I can hear are the stories my old man told of lost friends in firefights for this higher good and not the prison stories of revenge tragedies that go down between gangs or wronged prisoners settling scores where the dead are shipped off without fanfare. My old man's stories were a survival manual—a how-to guide for his kids to gather the lessons of a survivor and not the rantings of some loser who couldn't cope. So I tell some stories to not look like a fool and waste Ms. Smith's time, but it's important the stories don't reveal the complaints of a non-hacker.

She writes on her legal pad.

"Ms. Smith," I say. "How am I supposed to find the sacred on this inner journey when it's all like an unholy chaos?"

She smiles. "Like an accident investigation, you need to sort through the wreckage to get at why it happened. Then with that understanding, you can come to terms with it so you can live a life free from it and make sure it doesn't happen again."

I shiver for a moment as if I've just felt the cold blowing from the a/c. I wonder about accidents and answers. One night, Lynne was driving us and some friends on the highway when a coyote bolted in front of us. She swerved, and we started skidding. The car fishtailed and started to spin. She rotated the steering wheel, hoping to straighten the car out and not slide off the highway. Someone from the back yelled, "Jesus take the wheel!" In that moment as the car left the road and we soared into the dark, all I thought was, "Jesus doesn't know how to drive. He walked everywhere."

Ms. Smith leans back in her chair. Her lemon-colored blouse has daisies on it and seems like a mirage. "I want you to think and journal about pivotal moments that redefined your life. Those moments where you felt you had some control, but you actually had very little due to outside influences. Think about how you did something out of an urge you can't really name. It wasn't rational, but you tried to rationalize it anyway. And think about how reflecting on it now may help you uncover who you are and allow you to break out of negative structures inhibiting your growth."

"I'm not sure, you know?" I say. The a/c whirs.

"That's not important. What's important is the process. You just start. Write anything from your life in the last year before your arrest. Write and keep at it. Don't overthink it. Just let your mind wander through associations and back and forth through time. Let it go. Get lost in thoughts. Don't worry about editing or how it sounds. Just get it out on the paper. Eventually, it'll open up your unconscious, and it will lead you to it. Trust the process."

The noise from the fan is enough to muffle the sounds outside or in a room next door. I think about the goon squad—those cyborgs in government service, the faceless, blunt-force end of the judicial system. Even at night, I sometimes think I hear them, ready to jerk me up and drag me back to the prison on the coast, but not before beating me into a different man.

"I'll do that, Ms. Smith," I say.

I leave her office and take my notebook to the Education Center to work at a table where no one will bother me. Some guys are reading or watching videos with headphones on for college credit. Mr. Zachary talks on the phone in a whisper and gives me the head nod when I sign in. I sit at a place in the corner and open to the next blank page. I stare at the page and click the black government pen and write the date and stare at the pale blue lines like mortar holding the bricks of words.

My memory at times becomes vivid. Like the night gunnery exercise where I didn't miss one target and hit three targets in six seconds in one engagement. I was lucky to have a fast loader and a commander quick at the control to put me on target. I loved watching the tracers fly from the main gun muzzle. The glowing tails sailing downrange through the dark. Sometimes they skipped after impact and streaked into the night sky like fiery rocks breaking free of the earth. After that drill, I became the battalion's top gunner.

On my first morning of a field exercise with my unit, I awoke in the dark in the large tent we'd set up the evening before when we arrived. I'd grown up mostly outside and had lived in tents and campers for months on end, but there was something about waking up before dawn in that oily-smelling canvas tent with a dozen other guys. I'd slept in my clothes with my boots next to the cot. My dad had told us kids about guys who had to scramble around in their underwear during an attack. When I saw it was about thirty minutes to reveille, I thought to get up and be ready before anyone else. But I wasn't first up. Outside the tent was Sergeant Clayton, smoking and watching the horizon as it paled. He'd been in Vietnam, and his head was funny shaped from a crushed cheekbone. His head had been trapped between the hull of a tank and the turret in an accident during a firefight. He'd been driving, popped up above the hull, and fumbled lowering the seat when the commander ordered it as he swung the turret around. He let the smoke trail from his lips. He looked at me and nodded. "It's always coldest before the dawn," he said. Our breaths swirled like a new weather front of cirrus breaking an immaculate sky. We huddled in our field jackets, shivering. "Soon, though, we'll be wishing for it." He dropped his smoke, crushed it, and walked off toward the chow tent.

It made me remember winter on the homestead when the temperature seemed to rise before sunrise. We huddled in our sleeping bags, condensation gathering on the tent ceiling and freezing. The wind picked up and then stilled. A light ticking sound made me sit up and unzip the tent door. In the moonlight, snow fell over the desert. Light flakes, the first I'd ever seen in the desert. When the sun rose, filtered by stratus clouds, all the yucca plants and cacti held snow as if they were frosted Christmas treats. But the snow wasn't that deep. Our snowmen only stood about a foot high and had a thin layer of dirt covering them.

On that first field exercise, I learned any gear designated as expendable and unused at the end of the weekend went home with someone. Batteries, rations, and ammunition were all to find their way into duffel bags and backpacks heading home. As an armored unit, some guys brought a lot of stuff with them. One guy had a portable television, and many others brought coolers, cases of soda, and snacks. All that shit I saw as inessential and a sign of weakness. I only brought my issued backpack that had everything I needed to survive and fight.

But Ms. Smith wants this defining moment to explore or to find clues that lead her to the answer of why I'm a fuckup. Most nights, I relive the moments as I struggle to sleep in a prison bunk. I wonder if there is no moment. The wind that knocks the barn down blows against it for decades. Something should have been done long before the last gust came. I wonder at the same feelings I have no name for that have visited me for years—the sweeping blackness where all the work feels pointless, wasted time, and not feeling important enough for anyone to care. At OCS, I wondered, who would follow my orders? Who would follow my command? At the time, I felt these things in my guts but didn't have the courage to name it. Was it fear of having a breakdown because I was weak and couldn't handle the pressure under fire? If I'd stuck it out a little longer and found that confidence, I wouldn't be here. Maybe.

I set my pen down and leaf back through the pages filled with scrawled words. I think about moments that stood out in basic training, so many. But one comes to mind, and it's because I ended up thinking about stories that my dad told us about Vietnam. His defining stories were always ones I'd never be able to measure up to unless I too went to war.

I'd grown up only worried about if I finished or not, but in boot camp, I figured out how pushing yourself wasn't the point. We pushed each other. That first week, the drill sergeants ran us hard, and anyone falling out with a pulled muscle or twisted ankle was left for the jeeps following us. "Leave them in the ditch!" Drill Sergeant Goforth yelled. "They haven't earned the right for you to stop." We still ran like a ragged, losing football team taking the homecoming field knowing we were going to suffer an ass kicking. Not yet a team, a squad, a platoon, just a gaggle of individuals.

We formed up on the parade deck. The Disney Barracks—named after Major General Paul Disney, a World War II veteran and first commander of the Armor Training Center at Fort Knox, and not Walt of Mickey Mouse fame—were a set of rectangular red-brick two-story buildings. Double doors faced the parade deck and passed through a breezeway to the front and the street. Drill Sergeant Goforth stood before us. "You worthless dicks are going to run around the barracks and beat me to the front door. Understood?"

"Yes, drill sergeant!" we yelled in unison.

"Platoon! Dismissed!"

We all took off running as he turned and walked through the double doors and through the breezeway to the front door before we could even break around the last turn for the homestretch. He stood on the steps as we herded together like a bunch of cattle reaching the pen at the end of the chute.

"Back around and form up, you pukes! Go!"

We milled around puzzled.

"Now! Move! Move! Move!"

We scrambled back around the building. Private Hunter, a pale white guy from some rust belt town with all the opportunities of a ghost town, had a pulled hamstring. He limped and had not made it to the front before we stampeded past him. He limped back to the formation as Drill Sergeant Goforth stood with his arms on his hips. We stood at attention. "Again! Platoon! Dismissed!"

Drill Sergeant Goforth stood inside the door as the first privates made the steps, triumphant. He stepped out on the stoop. "We made it, drill sergeant!" one guy shouted.

The drill sergeant stood, arms akimbo, flawless pressed uniform, high-gloss boots, campaign hat squeezed down on his head like a bottle cap. The rest of the platoon finished running up behind the recruits who'd made it first. "No, *we* didn't! Again!" Once more, we held at attention on the parade deck, breathing hard. "All together now.

Platoon!" Drill Sergeant Goforth paused. He grinned. We trembled in anticipation of the command but didn't move because they'd trained anticipation out of us in the first weeks through push-ups and squat thrusts for moving before the command. His eyes squinted as if sizing up cuts of meat to buy.

In that moment, I knew we were trapped. Private Hunter would never make it, and he wasn't quitting. His face measured in equal parts pain and determination. A story my dad told me as a kid struck. He told of a time when his Huey, hit with heavy machine-gun fire, piled into the jungle a long way from any firebase. The crew chief, blown against the bulkhead, was alive but unconscious. Everyone else had been hacked apart by shrapnel and rotor blades. My wounded dad extracted himself from the wreckage and carried the first-aid kit, an M16, and the crew chief to safety, evading the enemy for days. He told the story in an offhanded way, and in it was the code: you do these things for your crew. You do these things as naturally as never leaving your rifle behind. You, son, carry your fellow soldiers. I did. You cannot do any less.

Drill Sergeant Goforth's command caused another mad scramble. I paused and called for Private Lee to help me carry Hunter. Lee, a Black man from a small Southeast Texas town, grabbed one of Hunter's arms. We slung Hunter between us and ran like he was the hungover groom for the wedding. We made the steps in time for the drill sergeant to tell us to turn around. Sweat ran down our bodies. The humidity swirled around us like a riptide sucking us out to sea. One more time, Lee and I carried Hunter before the drill sergeant released the platoon and ordered us to have our nasty asses back on the parade deck in thirty minutes. Hunter thanked Lee and me. We said, "No problem."

In the education center, I close the notebook. *I haven't let everyone in my life down*, I think. I get up to leave.

Mr. Zachary asks, "What are you working on?"

"A personal project," I say. "Military history and blunders."

I walk up the gravel path to Ms. Smith's office. A guy they called Pigtail had been busted drunk on homemade booze, so they shipped him off to the coast. He was one of those never-miss-mass-and-communion convicts, and I'm thinking about how fucked up it is that they couldn't have just helped him out here. A little blood of Christ and some forgiveness for our sins with a Hail Mary. Repent by having to be in a desert prison hours from anywhere. He's headed to an island with a high fence, a guard tower, and razor wire, but it has a sea breeze and women who flash their tits from motor yachts at the inmates crowding the wire. Oh, damn.

I knock on Ms. Smith's door, and she calls me in. Her blouse is white and printed with sprigs of lavender. They have a soft blur to them. I take the seat in front of her desk.

"I've been thinking," she says, "about the dichotomy between your discipline and being a wild child. Did you create boundaries between the military and your private life?"

"You see, Ms. Smith, I didn't ever drink on duty, even when it was permitted. I was even a little self-righteous about it. Once, at Camp Roberts, I sold my beer ration. We'd finished up our summer deployment and were having a little party before lining out the tanks and trucks to move to the staging area. Wetz got so wasted he couldn't drive the tank, so I volunteered to do it. I was supposed to ride up in the loader position and watch the central California hills scattered with oaks go by, but I loved driving too. Besides, Top and the platoon leader knew I was the kind of guy to step up and help, so that's what I did. Wetz and I had become friends, and he was fucked up, but that's okay. I had him covered. It wasn't like anyone was shooting at me. He'd left us in jams before. One time, he invited me and another guy from the platoon out to breakfast and dashed on the check. We didn't have any money, so I asked to use the phone and called Lynne to bring some cash."

I sit a second. "He always did stupid shit like that. I'm just glad I didn't go with him after his girlfriend kicked him out. His girlfriend moved in some other dude while Wetz was at work, so you know she'd had it lined up for a few weeks. Wetz was pissed because he still had his things there, so not only was this douche bag fucking his girlfriend in his bed, but he was also playing his records and going through his shit. Besides, Wetz needed to get his clothes, uniforms, military records, and his other things, like paraphernalia. A real shouting match with broken windows and a police visit."

I feel old, like I'm recounting some tragedy from my long-gone youth when it had only been less than two years ago. I look at my hands with scarred knuckles and burns in the palms from a cigarette lighter where I burned myself to freak out some loudmouth. I rub them together, feel the pulse in them like two birds' hearts in my palms.

"You were saying?"

Ms. Smith breaks my thoughts. "Right. Wetz had a nosebleed. I knew it was from cocaine. The first time we went to work out at the gym together, he offered me a line of coke to get the blood pumping. I'd said no thanks. That shit wasn't for me.

"I saw him with a guy from second platoon who was a cokehead, and they'd disappeared into a hull of a tank and came out sniffing and wiping their runny noses. I think everyone knew, but no one wanted to make a big deal about it unless something bad happened. But even then, we'd try to stretch the rules around them enough to protect them. We had a code. My old man told stories about hillbilly blood feuds. In one, a relative shot and killed a moonshiner from another family out of revenge. Neither side would talk to the revenuers or cops. We took care of our own business.

"With Wetz, we all knew he'd been going through a rough patch after his breakup with his girl. He needed to be carried a moment, and we were his platoon.

"Wetz went from talking too fast to a drunk, incoherent mess before we finished squaring away for the column to move out. Riding in the hull was out of the question, so Corporal Kincaid and Sergeant Fromm loaded him into the back of a deuce-and-a-half truck with a new private to make sure he didn't die a rock star's death among a bunch of duffel bags bouncing along a dusty country road."

Ms. Smith writes on her legal pad.

"Don't get me wrong. I can party with the best of them."

"So I gather from some of your stories."

"What good is sitting alone in your room?"

Ms. Smith smiles. "I love *Cabaret*, but it's not really a good template for living your life."

I shrug. "Sitting alone in your room isn't much of a template either."

She smiles again. "Maybe someplace in the middle then." She writes something. "How's the journal writing going?"

"Fine, I suppose."

"Can I read it?"

I sit up straighter, caught between saying no and looking like I'm hiding something and saying yes, which I'd rather not.

She must read my discomfort. "No judgement. I just want insight into how to best help you. Part of the healing process."

There's the word again. Healing. I don't need healing. There isn't anything to be healed or cured. I just need out of here and a chance to prove myself honorable again. She looks at me, and her gaze is like a missionary who comes to the door to save your soul from yourself.

"Sure," I say. "I have nothing to hide."

"We all have something to hide," she says.

October is ending. Ms. Smith has a jack-o'-lantern on her desk. She has painted her eyelids and her fingernails black and has on deep blue lipstick. Her blouse is black with red poppies like bullet wounds blooming. She smiles when I sit down, and one of her teeth is missing—covered with black wax. I smile back.

"I love Halloween," she says.

"It doesn't show," I say.

She laughs.

"It's Lynne's birthday too," I say.

"I'd love a Halloween birthday. What did you do to celebrate?"

Two Halloweens ago, I'd dressed as a soldier. Clever for a kid in the Guard. What did Lynne go as? A hippie possessed by the spirit of the dead? We went to our favorite bar where our favorite bartender wore a tux and told everyone he had an offer they couldn't refuse. Lynne dressed as a flapper. That was it. She called everyone darling, said "Jeepers Creepers," sang "Life is a cabaret," and did some vaguely 1920s dance moves. She smoked her cigarettes through one of those long cigarette holders and drank gin and tonics. She told everyone to call her Zelda, "Mad Zelda, darling."

Why did I wear my uniform? Did I put it on because I felt like an imposter, or was I just lazy? Do you dress like a normal nine-to-fiver if your everyday getup is punk? Is it really a costume if you dress like a regular job? Maybe if you painted your face white with some blood trickling down the corner of your mouth or put on some fake fangs. Zombie Hippie. Ghost Biker. Vampire Hooker with Angel Wings. Ambulance-Chasing Lawyer Run Over by Next of Kin. Dismembered Construction Worker. Franken-Cop with an Attitude. Poltergeist Soldier coming to the end of his own days because the house would soon be empty, with no one to hear the crashing of pictures and glass against the floor. Do angry ghosts still rage with no one home?

In ancient times, we dressed in costumes to trick the spirits into believing we were one of them. We shifted our identity and camouflaged ourselves out of terror. In our modern times, we dress up as an excuse to act like someone we aren't—to escape everyday life. For one night, we walk among the spirits who wander the earth in search of the living to kidnap.

At the party, I started feeling down with all the drinks flowing and Lynne's laughter like music. It crept over me like how the darkness comes in the open desert—the long twilight and then the black. It wasn't like I was upset or angry or anything had happened out of the ordinary. In fact, it was a ripping good time with dancing and drinking games and everyone masked or painted and loose in the joy of life disguised from death.

As a boy, I'd wear parts of my father's Vietnam War uniforms and later, in high school, bought surplus battle blouses and pants to wear. After I came back from basic training for the National Guard, I'd wear my camo pants off duty as part of my "image." Here, I'd found an old flight suit and paratrooper boots in the supply cache and wear them all the time now. I laugh. I'll end up, two years later, dressed like a poorly outfitted soldier on the edge of the frontier where the supply caravans only make it once a year if they didn't get ambushed and looted. What does this cycle of cast-off uniforms mean?

Ms. Smith writes in her notebook. "It's part of manifesting what you want to be. In a way, you are living proleptically. You feel, unconsciously, if you masquerade long enough, you will become the thing you desire."

I wonder.

"You have to find a new way to dress to break free of the cycle."

As we end the session, she tells me I must try harder with the parole board next time. No amount of desire will overcome the will of the State without the penance of paperwork.

I leave and walk back up the bluff to watch the sunset. The radar dome blushes with the last light, and Molly stands under it, staring at it like a pilgrim who has arrived at a holy site. He mumbles, and his mouth twitches as he rocks back and forth before walking around it, always ending up at the same point he started from. Other inmates jog or walk past, and some pause to watch the sunset. I can hear Flat-Five and Brew playing just around the bend. I figure I'll turn around and not talk with them. I don't much feel like singing any blues. The desert cools as I stand there. A guy they call Frog sprints by several times as the night spreads over the sky like blood on a gauze pad.

On this Halloween, I think of Lynne as I watch the stars materialize as if out of nothing. Her birthday. Twenty-one. Beautiful. Blonde. Stoned. I haunt this bluff, this falling darkness, living but not living. Pallid skin of the undead. Not dead. Not living either. No chains to clink in the night. But a ghost for sure.

I sit and stare past Ms. Smith in a wisteria printed blouse to the wall behind her like I'm looking through the telescopic sight in the gunner's seat. I can see the distant desert, the soft, sand-colored shapes of tanks and armored personnel carriers in the reticle. It's as if I'm sealed in the hull and living in the smell of gun oil and cordite from thousands of depleted uranium rounds fired downrange.

"How it happened," I say. "Hell." I've never actually told anyone.

We'd had gunnery practice over the weekend, and when Top asked for volunteers to come in and clean the weapons, I said I'd be there. Four of us rolled in, set up folding tables in a room next to the armorer's shop, and laid out the bore brushes, rods, solvent, gun oil, and rags. I stripped down an M240. It was the weapon mounted left of the main gun in the hull that the gunner and commander controlled and fired. It was a Belgian weapon, and just for that reason alone, I felt it superior to anything else we had. After laying each part out, I threaded some solvent-soaked patches onto an eyelet at the end of a rod and pushed it through the barrel. I swapped out the eyelet for a bore brush and scrubbed it up and down. When I ran down clean dry patches, I looked for any residue and didn't stop until a patch came out as white as it went in. I had a little angle flashlight I could shine up from the breach to look down the barrel for a visual inspection. I wiped down the breech and used what looked like an OD green toothbrush to knock away dirt, grime, and powder residue before wiping it down again. I moved on to the bolt, recoil springs, and trigger assembly, making sure the only thing on the metal was a thin coat of oil like my old man had taught me to do.

I reassembled the weapon, worked the action, and felt the comforting slam of the bolt going into the breech. It felt solid and life-giving like the way an axe sinks into a round of wood. I ran a cloth over it to wipe off any fingerprints and set it aside to be counted.

Wetz arrived late to the armory. He tossed his motorcycle helmet into a chair as he scanned the table. "I thought we needed to be here at nine."

Sergeant Gonzales, a Black Cuban who had a profile for a beard, said to him, "And you're still an hour late if it was. You got here in time to sweep."

We counted the weapons, and we had one extra M60. I read the serial numbers from each weapon as Sergeant Gonzales checked the inventory sheet to confirm we had an odd child out.

"You wait here." Sergeant Gonzales disappeared into Top's office. About a minute went by when I heard Wetz in another office. I looked in to see if he was okay and saw him stuffing the disassembled extra machine gun into a duffel bag.

"What the fuck?"

"It ain't got no home. I'm giving it one."

I looked at Top's office. "You're going to get busted."

"No, I won't. Just run interference for me."

I shook my head. Fuck. I walked next to him, covering him as he left the armory with the duffel bag over his shoulder as casually as going home. Outside, he said, "Let me put this in your car. I only have my motorbike."

"Shit."

"I'll come get it. Don't stress."

It was too far, but I couldn't go back now. I fumbled with the keys and opened the trunk. He dropped it in, and it clunked like a body. We went back inside, and nothing was said. A week later, each of us from that morning were called in and interviewed about the missing weapon that had belonged to Bravo company. I lied. The weapon was behind my couch. Lynne and I were headed to divorce, and she was moving out in a few days to live with her girlfriend, but I couldn't hide this from her. "Fuck the pigs," was all she said.

Wetz hadn't shown up to get it. He wasn't returning calls, and when I went to his house, he wasn't fucking home. When Top asked me if I knew anything and I said no, my stomach burned with shame. What the fuck was I supposed to do? They said anyone with information could turn it in with no questions asked. To me, that was code for no questions will be needed because we got you, and I couldn't tell them the real story without it sounding like I was a ratfuck covering myself by throwing Wetz to the cops.

I got terrified the cops were going to execute warrants to search our places, so I took the weapon to Arizona. I had an uncle who worked for the railroad in Kingman. I told him I needed to stash some possessions because of my pending divorce.

That afternoon, I made the trip there and back to Vegas, and not an hour later, a snot-nosed guy with red-rimmed eyes who sounded like he was doing a Tony Montana impersonation showed up, telling me he was Wetz's friend and that I needed to take the weapon to a place close to the Utah state line in two days. I called Lynne to ask if I could use the car to go back to Arizona tomorrow, but she needed it. She told me I could use the car any time after. That was good for me to get to Wetz's guy, but I still needed to get it back from my uncle's place. My motorcycle wasn't in shape to ride to Arizona, so I called Matt.

We had been best pals for a long time. I knew he'd help me and be cool.

It was a quick trip in his Ford pickup. I didn't want to sound like a punk, but I told him the story of what went down and how I'd been stuck with it.

"To who?" he asked.

"Some guy. He's going to send it to the Contras."

"Fucking-A righteous, man."

During the trip back from Kingman, I kept glancing at the speedometer because it felt like Matt was driving 30 in a 70. When Matt finally dropped me off, I hurried into my apartment. I put the weapon behind the couch as if it'd somehow be magically hidden. I sat a nervous wreck overnight. I stayed awake and looked out the window every time I heard someone walk by or the neighbor's television switched on too loud or car lights swept across the curtains. A few times, I went for walks around the block, looking for anything out of place and white vans like you see in the movies where cops are on stakeout. I tried to walk casually and not too fast and definitely not run.

I was relieved to see Lynne through sleep-deprived eyes. One more trip and this nightmare would be over. I loaded the duffel bag into the back of the car. I looked around to see if there were any vans parked along the street and listened for helicopters over the neighborhood. Was anyone just loitering around on the sidewalk who didn't belong? I got in the car. I looked around again. As I turned the ignition, I had the vision of a bomb exploding like in dozens of mob movies. The car started.

I pulled out onto the street and headed out of town. Every mile, I kept expecting the highway patrol to pull me over. Any second, I worried, I'd see a black helicopter swoop low over the road with armed guys standing on the skids with the speaker squawking for me to pull the fuck over or die. Mile after miserable mile. Until I went down a gravel road and drove up to a single-wide trailer. I scanned the area and got out. A Jeep CJ-7 was parked among the mesquite bushes. Up a rickety set of wooden steps, I went to the door. The metal door felt cold and sounded tinny when I knocked. A big dog barked, and someone yelled to shut the fuck up.

A fit white guy with a buzz cut wearing cuffed jeans showing off his Doc Martens opened the door. "You here for what?"

"For I was told to bring you something." I kept my voice even and focused on anything out of the ordinary, as if anything about this was ordinary.

"Alright. Let's see it."

"It's in the car."

"I'll wait."

I walked down to the car and, for a second, thought how it might feel to be shot in the back. I looked for helicopters and dust clouds of vehicles crossing the desert. I listened for the shuffling and measured breathing of a SWAT team readying to emerge or the lone crack of a bullet from a distant ridge after it sailed through my heart.

I brought the duffel bag up and went inside. Cigarette smoke hung in the air. The wood paneling with the grain that looked like water stains, the shitty carpeting, and the linoleum were like in any of the trailers I'd lived in as a kid. The dog barked from a back room. I unclipped the top of the bag and took the weapon out and assembled it. I set it on the table and knocked over some empty beer cans that clattered to the floor.

He picked the weapon up and worked the action. "It's fucking clean, bro. Fucking real clean," he said with an all-American grin.

He gave me an envelope full of cash, and I left. Relieved, fucking relieved. I just needed to get back to Vegas before being swarmed by cops.

Ms. Smith regards me for a long moment. I feel like she's waiting for me to say something else.

She flips through the pages of her legal pad. She stops and reads something, then goes back to the page she'd been writing on. "Why did you keep sticking by Wetz when he was clearly trouble? I mean, you can talk about being loyal to family and fellow soldiers and friends in need, but that doesn't mean you have to resort to covering up crimes." She pauses. "You hadn't known him that long and ended up here."

I puzzle over the question. I have been locked up longer than I'd known him back on the block. So strange how time passes here. At some moments, it feels as if everything had happened yesterday. But now, with that question, I feel ancient, like I've been here all my life and I'm trying to remember why. "I'm not sure."

She smiles. "I want you to think and journal about loyalty and betrayal in your life other than Wetz. Just free associate and see where it leads you."

"Sure," I say. I feel a widening gulf between me and every person I've ever known. I can't see their faces in my mind but feel them as faint presences. *It's funny*, I think, *how the past doesn't exist except in the way that dead things fall to earth and dissolve into it as either fertilizer or poison.*

I yawn before I enter Ms. Smith's office. I had lain awake most of the night again. I had this strange energy that filled me. When I was free, I couldn't rest until I'd worn myself down to where I just couldn't stay awake. I'd go walk about the city or ride my motorcycle out into the desert night and get lost in all the darkness and space bounded by the horizon etched in the distance. Here, I'm trapped in my bunk, and my body and brain vibrate like a Jacob's ladder arc snapping and popping. I long to hike out across the desert and just go until I can't see the glow of any electric light or hear the hum of wires or smell the smog exhaled from millions of engines.

Some people are terrified of the dark, but most people are killed in the light. Streetlight, daylight, by the fluorescent light, under sodium lights, in the headlights, "by the bright silvery light of the moon," the bioluminescence of a scorpion sting, or starlight so bright you'd swear the dead were three steps from heaven. My bunk is the top, and below me sleeps a farting old man who'd been convicted many years ago of bank robbery. Across the room from us is a heroin dealer from somewhere north of Cali's Central Valley who snores and stops and breathes again as if being birthed. Perpendicular to us, against the short side of the room, is an old Black Panther whose breath rattles like wind through dried-out mesquite seedpods as he wastes away from some disease no one knows.

From my bunk, I can see out the window and across the dark of the dried lake to the razor-backed ridges and mountains that were islands once upon a time. The odd lights of cars streak like comets along the distant desert highway, and some lights further out might be ranches, pumping stations, or gas stations. But nothing compares to the Milky Way stretched above that makes our dimly lit prison camp glow. What is it about the paint on old barracks? Even at Fort Knox and Fort Irwin, the old barracks radiated the starlight. Maybe it was the lead paint from the old days, or maybe it had absorbed all the isotopes of Cold War nuclear testing and the radiation of depleted uranium cannon rounds streaming from the bones of soldiers. It'll kill us, but maybe we'll go out glowing faintly like the radium watch dials we all wore growing up.

I'd been thinking about what Ms. Smith had asked me during our last meeting. Right after she asked me, my first thoughts were of betrayal and Matt. How I'd covered his ass for drunk driving on his motorcycle from his parents, made sure he didn't get busted banging a girl not his girlfriend, and didn't tell the cops about his involvement in dozens of minor crimes, and then he gave me up to the feds. More than gave up, set me up with the feds. Fucker. But that's not what Ms. Smith wants. My first thought is never what she's after. She always says, "You need to look deeper." She once said, "Your first thought can be a reaction, a psychic shield to protect the self from the messiness of the truth." The clatter and noise of an easy solution to denial.

Last night after the guard's 0200 check, I knew. I remembered as clear as Ms. Smith's eyes how, once, I had friends, and we'd grown to that age when we started to recognize we could have pals and weren't just a collection of kids in class eating paste, playing tag, and imagining ourselves flying on the swings. Our world began to widen. We'd started to become individuals, and there were others besides ourselves we could band together with as a group.

I open the door, and frosty air rushes out. I step into her office. She looks up from a book she's reading. Her light blue blouse has these giant magnolia blossoms that seem to pulse under the fluorescent light.

She motions to the seat. I sit in the same wooden chair as always. I stifle a yawn. Ms. Smith closes her book and smiles. I think about how I never see her arrive or leave this office. A couple of months ago, I asked how she liked living out here in the staff housing so far from everything. She said she didn't live there but commuted from a small town about an hour and a half away on the other side of the Air Force base. An hour and a half of open road and not one stoplight between her home and this office in the desert where she talks to convicts all day.

She asks, "How have you been? The journaling going well?"

"Yeah. I thought about the last question. I think I figured something out."

She looks excited as she flips open her legal pad and clicks her pen. "I'm interested to hear what you have to say."

I told her my story from the fifth grade.

We lived in the newer suburbs of Phoenix back before they paved over the alfalfa fields and the smell of smog replaced the honeysuckle. My old man had worked at a foundry, then he became a cop for one city, then our town, then he'd become a local judge. I'd had the same group of friends since the third grade. All through our school years, we talked about cars, classic horror movies with Boris Karloff or Bela Lugosi, and some of us played in the band, so we talked about how beautiful our music teacher was with her miniskirts and dark hair. During the summer, when my old man wasn't taking me out chasing gold in the mountains, my friends and I got together and played war or football across the neighborhood. All those fresh cut lawns and sprinklers going for us to run through.

A new kid moved to town and was in our grade. He had a shock of white-blond hair and spoke with a German accent because he'd just moved from West Germany. His dad had been an American soldier and his mom a German national.

I don't remember how it came about, but we were comparing the merits of Bruce Lee and Chuck Norris in *The Way of the Dragon*. We were walking toward the neighborhood after school. A loose gaggle of six of us. I was all about Bruce Lee, but the German kid said Lee could never have taken Norris in a real fight. His dad had trained with Norris and had taught him some techniques. I didn't believe him, and he said he could kick my ass with one arm behind his back. The other kids, my friends, started chanting, "Fight!" I'd never been in a fight or taken any martial arts. We had climbed onto the railroad grade that cut through our town. It had been built up three feet above everything else. From my backyard, we watched the trains go by every day. I crossed the tracks with books under one arm and a trumpet case in the opposite hand. I stopped to let the others catch up and found myself facing the German kid when he put one hand behind his back and kicked me in the ribs. My books went flying, and I dropped my trumpet case. I slipped on the cinder rock and fell down the embankment. My friends kept chanting, "Fight!" As I struggled to get up, the German kid jumped down the embankment and kicked me in the stomach. It made me lose my air, and all I could think of was my trumpet and if it was okay. My parents would be pissed if it got damaged. By now, my friends had joined him in a circle around me.

"There," he said. "Chuck Norris is the best of all time. Admit it."

I got to my feet. I worked my way past kids who I thought were my friends, red-faced, to get my books and trumpet. They all stared at me as I walked along the tracks as we sometimes saw the hobos doing, except I was collecting school papers and not cigarette butts. I heard them muttering and congratulating the German kid for kicking my ass. I wished I had my old man's shotgun. I'd have sent him to be with his Nazi ancestors.

The semester ended, and during the summer, we moved to the southern desert to homestead in tents. I never saw any of them again and never wanted to go back. They were dead to me.

In the chill of Ms. Smith's office, she considers what I've told her. "You've journaled this?"

"Yes. Well, not the part about the shotgun."

"What about a story where someone stood by you?"

"I don't have one. Or at least, I can't remember an instance."

"Your wife didn't turn you in to the police."

I don't know what to say.

She goes on. "So someone can be loyal in one way and betray you in a different way, such as adultery. Did you tell the agents she knew about the gun and lent you the car for transporting it?"

A sudden fear seizes me. I sit, not sure what to say. I betrayed Lynne to Ms. Smith. Over the months, she got me talking, and I relaxed and told her too much. I look at my hands and think of the sutures on my ex-wife's wrists. The only thing I had to give her was my silence, and I blew it.

Ms. Smith says, "It's okay. I'm not a cop, and I'm not legally bound to tell them anything unless it's to stop a crime or prevent injury or death. You are fine here."

"I just suddenly realized I'd betrayed her by telling you."

"You didn't."

She nods and writes. "I want you to think about your need to stand by someone as a friend and how you can avoid being loyal to the wrong people."

I shiver as I think about people who I'd known well, for a couple of years, and who'd betrayed me. How could I have known living in the moment? What if I'm the problem?

She starts to say something but pauses, measuring the pace of her speech, then says, "I also want you to journal about how people have been loyal in some contexts, but not in others. People are complex that way, like you are."

In the quiet whir of her a/c, I scratch my palms as I consider her words. To think of loyalty and betrayal not as mutually exclusive, but as shifting qualities, like love and hate, and the degrees at which each is wrapped up in the same person like in Lynne and me. We are not static, fixed in time, in mind or body, which is why we are all flawed and all perfect on any given day.

Ms. Smith's blouse has wrinkles like she'd left it in the dryer overnight and put it on in a hurry to get to work. The magnolia blossoms on it are creased, and I feel as if I'm looking into some fracture of space. The blouse is light blue and looks like a high desert sky in July at noon when the sun starts to fade the sky to white before it darkens toward the horizon. I hold on to the chair as I dizzy in the distance of her blouse, but it makes me feel like I did when I was chained in a chair looking at the sky through a window in the federal building in Vegas, so I let go. I pat my chest pocket on the flight suit I wear.

"You can't smoke in…" She doesn't finish the sentence. Leaving the last word unspoken, caught in the throat, an unspoken accusation. "Right, you don't smoke."

I think about this morning when, right before dawn, I finally fell asleep and felt as if I were drowning in the blackness and woke with a start, gasping for breath. It was one of those moments where you think you are beyond the point of no return, being swallowed by the black, only to return into the light switched on by a former heroin dealer who only wants to go home to his kids.

Ms. Smith clears her throat. "But back to my suggestion. Journal about it and see where it leads you. Okay?" Her desk chair creaks and clicks as she shifts her weight, and it reminds me of my old man's desk chair and the smell of paperback books, gun oil, and the fuzz of a CB radio breaking squelch.

"Yeah, yeah," I say. I squint, trying to refocus as I stifle a yawn. *Fuck*, I think. "I'll do that."

I march into my last parole hearing. I sit on a plastic chair like those stacked in auditoriums where motivational speakers tell hundreds of people how special they are.

Three suits and one pantsuit stare at me as they read over the paperwork. They have the letters from family and friends saying I'd have a possible job or two lined up and a place to stay and eat and not be on the street. Lynne even wrote a glowing 'I'm his ex-wife and still love him enough that he can stay with me and my new husband' letter. Even her mom wrote saying how much respect I showed her and her parents, how I was always such a hard worker, and that she'd be available to give me spiritual guidance at any time. Three guys from my platoon wrote letters, as did the recruiter, Sergeant Von, telling the board how much I loved my country and would still be willing to lay down my life in defense of freedom and liberty.

The four hold copies of my file like poker players with a bad hand who suck at bluffing.

They decide I'm not ready for early release. The warden thinks releasing me early sends a wrong message, just like when he refused me permission to deploy with the fire crew beyond the boundary of the prison grounds. *So much for fourteen months of good behavior*, I think. So much for breaking down and getting the letters and testimonials of family and friends only to be rejected out of hand. I wonder, why didn't the warden just say he'd passed judgement when I first arrived and nix this charade of justice? Just to fuck with me? To force me to go through all this fucking bullshit and headache? A wrong message to who? Nobody knows who I am, and nobody pays attention to if I have to stay here another four months or not. Inmates joke that justice wasn't "just for us."

But they have me and are not letting me go. Menace to society. The relativity of time dawned on Einstein after he imagined himself riding a beam of light, but to explain time's perceptual relativity, he used an afternoon with a pretty girl or sitting on a hot stove to illustrate his point. We inmates know exactly what he meant—the insurmountable minutes in the dark or the way visiting time ends. You no sooner sit down than the guards announce the time has come to drag your sorry ass back to the cellblock. All the months blend into one long day and, like you are on Einstein's beam of light approaching a black hole, time slows down for you while all those you left behind on Earth move forward in time by attending school, starting careers, getting married, having families, and living into the future while you are not. The mass of incarceration has stopped time. Upon your release, you will travel to the future and always be out of time—the quaint time traveler arriving in a different era, not so distant as to be in an unrecognized time but far enough to be the awkward outsider.

No worries, I think. This is how it was going to be.

I feel a shift in my attitude. I can't say what it is, but years later, when I reflect on those last months, I see a kid tempered by the violence of the state, the violence of inmates, the violence of society, the violence of men and women in his life, the violence of his delusions, and violence he rages upon himself.

I spend these last days reading, doing fire drills, washing the truck, and pissing off two urban goat ropers on the crew by playing rock 'n' roll on the engine bay radio. One of the guys says, "Only two kinds of music: country and western," and changes the station back to some K-RDNK station. I like some country music in general but rebel and turn the station back to rock. I grew up in the country, in mining towns and farms and in long stretches of desert where, without a visible electric light at night except for jetliners flying the dark skies, it might as well as have been 1876 instead of 1976. I bristle against those songs as country as the Las Vegas Strip. I call them dude, and they bitch, "I'm not a dude!" They whine incessantly like prissy school children. I can't catch a break in this system of petty tyrants, so anyone trying to put a thumb on me without weight can go fuck himself. They won't fight with being so close to going home on their horizon. They see the end of their time. This is the real power of time.

This camp is like no other prison I've been at because the violence isn't physical. All a person needs to do is show they don't care if they get sent back to the coast with a few more months not worth living. All those motherfuckers count the days like rare coins, and to threaten one makes them back the fuck down. No one is going to challenge me over changing the radio station.

Then I dial in the classical music station.

I do as little work as possible. I do pull-ups. I do sit-ups. I do push-ups and then lift weights and run. I never talk to the guards unless asked a direct question. I keep learning to play the guitar. I learn to make guacamole. I read *The Odyssey*, *Tao Te Ching*, *Seven Years in Tibet*, *The Razor's*

Edge, and *Two Years Before the Mast.* I do whatever I think is good for me. All the while, I walk around with a hard-on. This is doing time. Time waits for no one.

Ms. Smith has on a beige blouse that reminds me of a summer sandstorm that rolled over Vegas and brought the city to a crawl. I had been on Bad Bob when it hit, and I fought to keep upright as I made my way home. The blouse is embossed with posies, which gives it a snakeskin texture. So when she moves, it seems to be alive and swallowing her. On her desk, she has what I always suppose is my file, a stack of legal pads, and a pale blue book that says *Diagnostic and Statistical Manual of Mental Disorders DSM-III* on the cover. "I've been going over our conversations."

I scratch at my palms. I'm not sure if I should say something. This is our last session. I am going to be released in a week, having served my full sentence after being rejected for parole a second time. The banal inquisition of bureaucrats could go fuck themselves.

She smiles. "One story is missing, and I want to hear it from your point of view." She taps the file. "I know the official record, but that has its own purpose and is told from a different perspective."

I like Ms. Smith, and she is the only one I talk to without the imposition of force. This will be the last story I tell her. It will also be the last time I tell this story along with the story of the crime in full for decades. I think about how Matt came over to my apartment a couple of days after I got back from getting rid of the machine gun in the desert.

He was jacked up. "Bro, I got a line on going to Pakistan to help with the Mujahideen fighting the Soviets."

"Serious?" We'd been talking about serving our country in a bigger way. I was going to transfer to an active-duty unit after my divorce was finalized, but this seemed like a sweet opportunity to get into the action.

"I know these CIA guys. One was helping Gritz up by Hawthorne, and he asked if I was interested in really serving my country. I told him you might want in, so he said to ask you."

"No shit?" Ronald Reagan said the Mujahideen in Afghanistan were just like the Founding-fucking-Fathers.

"You still have the weapon?"

"No." I told him about the guy and the sketchy trailer.

He looked like he was considering something heavy.

I asked him, "What's the problem?"

"Nothing," was all he said.

That weekend, Matt introduced me to his contacts. "This is the big deal, man. Just like we talked about. C-I-fucking-A, man. C-I-A. No worries, man. You'll meet the case officer. You'll be transferred from the Guard to a unit on temporary duty just like when you go out with those other units."

I met the case officer at a one of those Great American family diners staffed with uniformed waitresses and offering food that didn't come wrapped in paper but was not served on china either. A cool dude in aviator shades, beard, lean and hard. Another guy with one of those brimless hats, a suit, and a close-cut beard was introduced as the nephew of a tribal elder. I wanted to appear the real deal, like I could be trusted beyond the wire. The case officer talked like he'd seen shit and knew shit and tossed off names of places I knew about. "You'll do great, man. C-I-fucking-A. We get shit done and—say, have you read Machiavelli? Matt says you're a reader…" I had. "Get shit done for the prince. You won't be able to brag about it, but you don't strike me as one of those guys who needs a bunch of medals and ribbons. But like in Machiavelli, everyone knows, but no one knows, and they all fear you coming into their hooch and cutting their fucking throats while they're dreaming of their fucking workers' paradise, man. Last years of Nam were like that. No shit. More violent than all the '60s put together. Just not enough press. C-I-fucking-A, man. I was there."

The nephew leaned forward, his accented voice low with an air of a man of station asking a favor, and said, "It is for my father and family honor. The Soviets murdered my mother, sisters, and all the women in the village when we were in the mountains. I need this help from you." As a boy, I loved the stories of covert operatives in WWII and Vietnam, and now these same operations were taking place in other regions. It was my time to serve. I was also raised on tales of blood feuds and honor codes like these tribal men in their turbans and robes. His words coiled the spring in me. Fuck yeah. An affair of honor and still fighting communism? "Hell yes," I said. "I'm your man."

The CIA guy said, "Excellent, but first, you need to earn our trust."

I nodded.

He lowered his voice and leaned close to me. "Matt says you delivered a weapon to a guy helping the Contras. I'm here to tell you he's a fucking Nazi and taking that weapon to start a race war."

Wetz, that piece-of-shit motherfucker. "Fuck." I glared at Matt with a 'what the fuck, that was between us' look.

"Yeah, fuck. We need to get it back."

"I'll take care of it myself." Fuck Nazis.

"Matt's already told us it was out by Mesquite. We got a team in place ready to take the motherfucker down. Just nod."

I looked at Matt again in disbelief and turned back to the CIA guy. He looked me in the eyes. "Just nod and it goes away, and we go to Pakistan in a month. You do love your country, don't you?"

You bet your ass I love my fucking country. I'd die for it.

A couple of days later, on my last day in the free world, the phone rang. I had no time, so ignored it. I had a woman to see. I needed to bicycle my butt across town, but I answered on the fourth or fifth ring. The major wanted to see me. Okay. I'd pedal right by the armory. Wouldn't miss a click to stop in for a few minutes.

No time to tidy up now. Clothes on the floor, pressed uniforms in the closet, my knives and guns and books, food in the fridge, the cupboards were not bare, an empty whisky bottle and crumpled beer cans, half a loaf of bread, and dirty dishes on the table. All the stuff a twenty-year-old left when it was time to go get shit done. To go see a woman. I had no time to straighten things up or make it right. I stepped into the Vegas heat. My head filled with images of Bonnie's sweet body bucking against mine.

I double-checked the deadbolt and hit the road. My commanding officer wanted a face-to-face. *Must be good news*, I thought. Good thing he caught me before I left. I thought of my girlfriend as my legs pumped the pedals. After the armory, it was on to Bonnie's house where we'd finally spend the night together now that her husband had moved out. I couldn't wait to see her, but for my commanding officer, I'd wait a little longer. What was a few minutes? The commanding officer, Major Robinson, looked like one of those super fit fathers, gray at the temples, who ran 5Ks in his spare time when he wasn't planning to kick Soviet asses through superior fire power or prepping for flash floods in the city and engaging looters who should be shot on sight and asked questions later. I admired him a lot. I cut my hair like his, but mine was blonder. He liked me. Wanted to promote me, give me a full-time position in the armory and then send me to more training so I could get ink on my records for Airborne School or Ranger School someday. I wanted to keep my options open here until my transfer came through. I hadn't heard from those guys in a week.

I rode my Schwinn. It kept me fit. Besides, Lynne kept the car when she moved out, and my motorcycle was not running so well. This weekend, I planned to give Bad Bob the motorbike a tune-up, make it scream like a hysterical sinner crawling on the floor of hell. Screaming, and all part of my new life as I shed the old.

The shabby roads beat the hell out of me, the shitheads crowded me against the gutter, and it was going to get hot again soon. It was only April, but the heat was coming. I thought of Bonnie's long hair, auburn and shimmery in the spring sun, and her small breasts with big nipples. I loved her body. She loved my body. She loved me to get behind her so she could fling her hair and buck against me and scream like I hoped Bad Bob would scream after the tune-up. I coasted up to the big yellow cinder block National Guard armory and chained and locked my bike. The armory was not in a good neighborhood. Criminals prowled these streets.

They lurked everywhere. A month ago, two dudes tried to shake me down for money a few blocks from here, but I told them I had no money. They told me they saw me in 7-Eleven. I said, "So the fuck what in 7-Eleven? I still ain't got no money." They towered over me. I looked them up and down. I knew they could've killed me on the street that night, and it would've been all over but for the body identification, or at the very least, a hospital trip after they beat the ever-loving shit right out of me before taking my $13.00. I mentally prepared to fight. What the fuck else to do? If I went down without a fight, I'd bring shame to my family. Couldn't have that. No one in my family ever went down without a fight. I looked them up and down again. They just looked down on me and smirked. "See ya," they said as they shuffled off. I checked the bike lock again for good measure.

I calculated the distance to Bonnie's apartment. Not far. A fifteen-minute ride. I thought of her wild auburn hair flinging in the incandescent light of her bedroom as I pushed open the armory door. I walked across the armory assembly area where they had awarded me certificates and medals.

The major's door was open. Two men in department store suits sat in the major's office. They stood when I entered. They had great haircuts. They asked if I was who I was, and I said yeah. They told me I was under arrest. They Mirandized me. Something I'd heard on TV cop shows thousands of times. My dad had been a cop before we had moved out to the desert to homestead. I knew for sure he'd read rights to criminals just as sure as he gave me a taste of mace, tossed me on the floor, and slapped cuffs on me before searching me for weapons and drugs when I was in the fourth grade just to show me what it was like. My guts clenched, and my heart beat in my throat. Their lips moved. My mind swirled and didn't register the four counts charged against me concerning the machine gun. I caught my breath and asked the major to see the JAG as I followed their orders. I was a disciplined soldier after all.

The major said nothing. He remained steady in his chair like he was in the tank cupola commanding his battalion in the field.

Dizzy-headed, my mind burped and stuttered. The feds led me back through the assembly area and then outside. The sun hurt my eyes. A local news crew stood grouped together on the sidewalk. Where did these guys come from? They were all set up with their lights and cameras and reporters with pancake makeup and microphones and their shrill sense of importance. I figured the agents must've called ahead like ordering for a pizza. I realized they must have watched me ride up and go into the armory.

I was armed, and they didn't know it. They didn't search me in the major's office. Not like my dad. They didn't push me against the wall, spreading me eagle to frisk me, ready to kick my leg out from under me given the least resistance. They cuffed me almost gently. They didn't jack them on tight and cause my fingers to tingle just to make a point. "A little lesson for you, son—to scare you straight." I figured the right thing to do would be to let them know I had a knife. I told the agents I had a Balisong butterfly knife in my back pocket. It felt forty pounds now. I sweated. It was hot, and it was only April.

One said, "What? A knife in the back pocket?" They both looked at each other and shook their heads with puzzled grins. I worried they'd steal the knife. That it'd disappear into evidence. The TV cameras saw them fishing the knife out of my back pocket on the sidewalk. It must have looked like they pulled it out of my ass from that angle. Besides, my dad had made it clear that if I got to the jail and had a knife, the county cops would throw me on the floor and search me with a knee planted in my back and, for good measure, probe me for other hidden weapons. I didn't mind being probed, but only if I got to probe back. One agent asked if I had any other weapons. I said no. They nodded, trusting me by now. Once they had the knife, the agents walked with me between them. I thought about the pistol I sometimes carried, glad it was on the nightstand in the apartment I'd never see again.

The agents looked camera-ready in their suits and great haircuts. They must go to a special class at the academy for looking good on camera. Show only their good sides. I was in jeans and a T-shirt with a screaming bald eagle circled by "US Army" in black block letters. At least I looked like a proud American soldier. I held my head up. I refused to look cowed, and I wouldn't look like those jackasses who tried to hide under their jackets or hold up file folders in front of their faces like toddlers—I can't see you, so you can't see me! I marched, showed fortitude and military bearing. Looked both confident and innocent. Later, on the television, I saw I looked like an unrepentant fuck.

I noticed my locked bike. I started to ask the agents if I could take it along, but some asshole with a microphone yelled a question at me. "How do you feel?"

Seriously?

The agents stuffed me into a nondescript sedan.

In the backseat, I stared out the windshield, stomach churning, not sure how to act or what to say. I wondered how I'd get out. My steel-trap mind seized up. They took me to a federal building and chained me to a wooden chair. They asked me questions about who I knew, and I didn't answer. I learned the CIA guy and the Afghan nephew were BATF agents setting me up with Matt's help. They mocked me for believing I was so important to the United States. They laughed, and I tried to appear stoic, but inside, I screamed. My body struggled with fight or flight, but I was a pinned insect on a card. They allowed me to call Lynne so she could call my parents because it was a long-distance call. Then they unlocked me and took me to the county jail.

I sat in the holding cell for what seemed like hours. The other prisoners of the State cheered and pointed at the TV mounted on the wall in the upper corner when I appeared magically on the evening news being led by two agents of the BATF. I had to admit, the agents looked good on TV, just as good as any actor on *Miami Vice* or *Police Story*. The men in the holding cell noticed how I held my head up. They gave me a thumbs up, but no one offered their baloney sandwich as I was still innocent until proven guilty.

The cops looked at me through the glass with slitted eyes, looking to see if I soaked up the glory of the criminal class or looked embarrassed or remorseful or guilty. Everyone looked from me to the TV and back to me and back to the TV. I never got used to this in the coming weeks.

From the hallway, a Black guy banged on the safety glass of the holding cell with his forehead. He flashed a broken-toothed grin and pointed to me and then the TV. His cuffed hands made it look as if he was doing a victory handclasp over each shoulder. Me to the TV, me, TV… I had no idea who this guy was, but he knew me. The cops pushed him along.

A drunk Mexican in frayed jeans pissed into the toilet overflowing with toilet paper. He yelled, "Time waits for no man!" He laughed hard. Sawdust covered his clothes and flecked his hair. He zipped up and wiped his hands on the front of his jeans. "Time waits for no man!" His grin looked like he was spreading the word of God to soothe us sinners in our time of need. Oddly, it struck me as something I needed to hear right then. *Time waits for no one*, I thought. *All this will pass, and all I have to do is endure it.* Or so it seemed.

A guy missing two front teeth broke my thoughts as he asked, "You want that?" He pointed to a chewed-up baloney sandwich sitting in the lap of a guy passed out and drooling.

I just didn't want to cry, and I felt myself withdraw from the world, cut off and watching everyone as if I stood far out on the plains and they were a caravan moving past at the lip of the world. One moment, I was living in the city in an apartment, looking forward to getting laid, and the next, I wasn't. And everything I owned was left behind like I'd been nabbed by aliens and flown into deep space for experiments. I was suddenly absent from classes at the community college and a no call-no show to work. I'd fail and be fired. I wondered what'd happen to Bad Bob the motorbike and Bonnie and my wife who'd left only a week or two before the major called. A clatter of keys and shouts and the scuff of shoes could be heard as cops ran while someone screamed like a werewolf was eating him, or perhaps he was the werewolf in transformation.

I wondered if my dad and mom would catch the news. They did. I was sure they'd wonder where they went wrong. I bet they wondered when I became a criminal. How did the strait-laced boy from high school unravel? Had I always had a criminal's heart repressed, or was I just a good boy gone astray? Maybe some of both.

The next morning, I'd get no bail. The federal agents said I was a flight risk even though I had no passport and my only transportation was a beat-up Schwinn currently locked to a rack at the armory. They said I was a menace to society because I was a highly trained soldier, an expert shot, and a martial artist. They had taken a weapon off me during my arrest. They said I drank too much. They said I was violent. The judge believed their portrayal of me and their fears because they were federal agents, while I was the accused. It was hard not to look like a menace to society when you were cuffed on the evening news both local and national.

When the judge sentenced me, he ordered me remanded to an institution where I could receive psychiatric help. It made me question who the fuck I really was anymore. Was I this dangerous person who deserved no bail? Someone had to tell them stories about me to make this conclusion. Who did? Or did I just shoot my mouth off like a pistol when I thought the BATF agents were really CIA? Was I mad and walked around thinking I was sane?

The guy who'd bought the machine gun got bail and didn't even serve time. The guy who stole the machine gun wouldn't even be arrested. But the guy who held on, who didn't speak up and name names before it was too late, the guy who acted like the image of a stand-up guy, didn't get bail and vanished into the system. Drug dealers, nuke protesters, and murderers would say, "Damnnn, no bail," low and smooth, some with a low whistle as if I'd said I'd gotten it on with Miss America in the bathroom of the Continental Casino.

An inmate whooped and got my attention. I was on the television screen again. I wondered if my informant best friend was watching with a satisfied grin or if he felt a tinge of regret. I knew he felt like a stud. Prisoners slugged me on the shoulder or patted me on the back, sporting silly-ass grins. I had attained hero status—the hero of the fuckups. I wanted to look away but watched the ghost of myself flicker by on the TV until they cut to the weather.

Ms. Smith regards me as I finish. Somehow, I'm leaning forward and feel like I'm about to free fall. I sit back.

"Thank you," Ms. Smith says. "How does it feel to share your story?"

I shrug, not sure. "In a way, it feels good, I suppose. But in another way, it feels as if it happened to someone else now."

"In a way, it did happen to someone else. You aren't the same person."

"I'm the one who confessed, so I must be the guy."

Ms. Smith smiles. "To confess isn't just admitting guilt for your sins, but also asking for forgiveness so you can change and move on."

I think about it a second. "But for all the talk of redemption and forgiveness in this country, we sure don't practice it." I don't tell her I'm terrified at the prospect of never finding a job again. I don't know what to do about it. I know no one I knew would ever look at me the same, and all the people I'd meet would always judge me. The dread I sometimes feel at the future of never finding meaningful work overwhelms me as I lie awake at night. I knew I'd have to leave here and try, but the darkness threatens me always.

"True, but it's enough for you to forgive yourself and move on."

She stares at me for a minute. "I'm not a doctor, so I can't give you a diagnosis, but as someone who cares about your well-being, I'm going to explain a few things that might help you."

She opens the book. "Before your arrest, you told me stories of physical restlessness, sexual indiscretions, reckless driving, engaging in high-risk behaviors without thought to consequences when drinking, the self-harm by burning yourself. And here, when you are talking to me, sometimes your speech is very fast like your voice can't keep up with the ideas in your head or you have this need to keep talking. It indicates your flight of ideas or memories of subjective experience are racing. It's as if you're afraid to take a breath for fear of losing the thought."

This was news to me. "I never felt like I was talking too fast. My thoughts do race, but it means I think fast. So what?"

"It's like when you told the story of Bonnie. You were almost breathless, like you were afraid you wouldn't be able to finish the story. And then when you helped Brenda, you were acting out driving in the chair and your voice increased with the pace of the story. With all your stories, you're very dramatic with your body motions. It's as if you are reliving it."

I try to remember.

"It even shows in your writing. Long sentences as if using a period will interrupt the flow of your thoughts too much. Your topics sometimes switch in the same sentence and then come back a paragraph or even a page later."

She says, "You could have been suffering then, and still are maybe, from an undiagnosed type of manic-depressive illness. You will need to get help, or it will get worse before it gets better because of the trauma you've suffered."

I sit staring at her book.

"I'm just a normal guy. I'm not any different from anyone else I grew up with."

"You're an outlier. How many other guys have done the things you've done?"

That stung.

"Some of them are lucky they aren't in prison or dead."

She closes her book. "You've been going through grief since your arrest. The old you was effectively killed. You're in this in-between world and will need to cope with this grief and create a new life after your release. It'll be good if you got professional help. It will manifest itself in you with all the negative consequences."

I'd seen *All That Jazz* when I was a freshman in high school. I'd gone with my friends, Adam and Jane, and their parents when they drove to the city from the mining town. Joe Gideon staged a production as he popped pills, drank booze, smoked, and slept with actresses. Underlying it was how he went through the five stages of grief before he died. I love the movie because it had Broadway numbers and was intercut with him backstage talking with the Angel of Death played by Jessica Lange. As he goes through the stages, he never gives up the intensity of his lifestyle. It kills him, and I thought it beautiful. I wonder about grieving for the dead when you're the dead. Is there a beautiful Death waiting to help me cross over to this other world? There's a song there somewhere. My dread was to be among the living like a ghost and live a meaningless existence.

Ms. Smith says, "I want you to think about the stories you've told me and what you've written. It's important, in therapy, to make sense of the narratives we tell ourselves. Without guidance, it can be hard to find the emotional truth because we lie to ourselves and tell a slanted story to avoid confronting emotionally difficult memories that we must confront to grow. You only know them from your perspective, and you'll need to try to understand them from the intersubjective experience of the others involved."

"Thanks," I say. "Even if I want, I can't afford a shrink." I pause, trying to measure the speed of my speech. "But if I did go to one, it'd pretty much crush my chances of fighting my discharge. I want to stay in the Guard. A chance to prove myself worthy."

She smiles as she looks down, shaking her head how a parent does when a kid recites some fantasy. She looks up and into my eyes. She holds my gaze a few seconds. I feel her sincerity and know she does care no matter how many whining cons she's had to listen to. "You need to create a new story of yourself and live it. You must, or you will always be here."

The a/c fan doesn't tick but spins smoothly. The air is cold, and I listen for the goon squad, but there isn't a sound to be heard except the ringing in my ears. Ms. Smith sets the book on top of the file and legal pads. Her blouse shifts and folds as if she's about to disappear from the world.

PART IV

THE FREE WORLD

"Old Time is still a-flying;
And this same flower that smiles today
Tomorrow will be dying."

Robert Herrick, "To the Virgins, to Make Much of Time"

Time did not wait, and I walked away from the halfway house without fanfare or a press corps asking me questions. My life officially broken like a fault line shearing the continent of my life from award-winning, decorated soldier and student to felon. I moved into Binder and Jen's spare room, and I kept working at the tire store. I bought a factory orange 1969 Dodge Charger with a 440 Magnum under the hood and used my tire store discount for some sweet Center Line rims and fat racing tires on the back and narrower ones up front. I spent a lot of time drunk—or recovering before payday—and not sleeping. Nodding off felt as if I were slipping into death and waking to a terror of rebirth into this pointless shit life, too sober and too lost to care about anything except getting another drink.

I hung out and ran loose to drag races, casinos, concerts, and stripper bars, especially a seedy little place called Charlie's Chateau that had a pool table and a grill and fryer in the back for short-order lunches. Not a tourist spot, it seemed discarded along the highway like an overheated car that broke down, not quite making it all the way downtown.

I'd gone in there the payday after my court-martial, alone, to watch women dance and get drunk. I sat at a table in the back out of the light with a pitcher of beer and a single glass. When a new dancer came out, I'd get up and toss some bills on the stage and go back to my beer. At least here, I didn't worry about people wanting to chat me up. People left me alone. The dancers would come by to see if I wanted to buy them an overpriced drink, but I said no. They moved on. But I needed to be here, needed the erotic allure of women in this darkened place of sexual desire and false promises. I needed to feel the possibility of something more than despair even if it was an illusion.

One of the strippers, Clarisse, came to my table. She had the showgirl look, a high-tensile, strong body and hair as thick and dark as the insides of the bars she danced in. She had sat with me before and chatted. A single mother who'd had dreams of Broadway and dancing in shows like *Chicago* and lived in a ranch-style house in a respectable neighborhood. I told her I didn't want any company, but thanks. She sat down anyway.

Last week, I'd gotten my Class A dress uniform dry-cleaned, made sure all the patches and badges were in the right positions, and ironed the shirt. On Sunday, I buffed the brass to a shine to blind the unwary, and I shined the shoes with spit, fire, and polish. I got a haircut. The night before, I found my dog tags. Name, SSN, and religious preference, which had No Rel Pref stamped next to it. No religious preference instead of agnostic, which is what I told the clerk taking our information. Agnostic is a preference. It meant I preferred not to believe superstitions and myths and preferred evidence instead of elaborate stories. Also on the chain hung a Saint Christopher medal. I often wondered how it'd fuck with some mortuary affairs guy's mind to see a no religious preference tag and a Saint Christopher medal on the same dead man.

Lynne had given it to me, saying, "He's the patron saint of travelers. Please wear it." I did. Like Carl Sagan felt, who am I to deny her peace of mind? It's working in that way, isn't it? Besides, if there is some divine magic in the universe, it's probably channeled through personal objects like this that are charged with the belief we give them. I slipped the chain over my head. Through the night, I toyed with the tags and medal wishing I could sleep, wishing I was at least drowsy.

My alarm went off the morning of my court-martial. I felt groggy, wanting to lay there in the in-between world of waking and unconsciousness, but got up. I couldn't recall falling asleep. It just slipped over me sometime after three o'clock, the last time I'd checked the time.

I shaved, dressed, inspected all aspects of my uniform and appearance, then drove over. In the parking lot, I sat staring through a dirty windshield at the block building, the empty bike rack, and through the chain-link fence to the assembly area in back. It looked like a school I'd gone to in a desert mining town. No one moved. I saw some others arrive, and they looked at me as they locked their cars and made their way into the armory. My guts hurt, and I wanted a drink. I took a few deep breaths and got out of the car. It'd been just over two years since I'd been led out of there and frog-marched in front of television cameras and reporters with microphones.

I marched in and stood at attention before the tribunal of officers in the Vegas armory, those stony faces of captains and lieutenants sitting on folding chairs around a folding table used at picnics and family days, and pled to be kept. Several crew mates wrote letters or showed up in person and testified on my behalf. My recruiting sergeant, Sergeant Von, strode in with all his combat patches, jump wings, and Ranger Tab and said to give me a chance. He had more combat experience than all the officers put together. His word should mean something. After all the testimony, I made my case. They stared at me. Then they told me to wait in the main armory while they deliberated. I saluted and stepped out. Across the polished floor, the battalion commander's office door was closed. I thought about the disgrace of being led out of there in handcuffs.

I stood in the assembly area. Sergeant Von came up. He shook my hand as he told me, "Good luck."

That seemed like an all clear, and some of the other soldiers I'd served with approached me and asked how I was holding up. I thought I was going to pass out as my heart sped up and my guts twisted. I wanted to run. I knew they'd just chase me down and arrest me, but what drove me more was that I wanted a chance. I'd been thinking of a shogun I'd read about who pardoned the ronin. Pardoned them and made them his personal guards as he knew they would be always faithful. I would be always faithful for another chance to serve the shogun. I managed a smile and said I was doing alright.

I'd answered their questions, and now it was up to them. I thought about when I was in basic training and the drill sergeant told me I had been selected to compete for the George S. Patton Jr. Award. I had to ask what it was and then won the honor. I thought I'd blown it after giving a bullshit answer on what the colors of the American flag stood for. "Red is the color of all the blood of men and women who had been killed fighting for the United States of America. Blue is infinity, like the sky, and the white of the stars stands for purity. Our purity and our country go on for infinity like stars in space. They just go on for infinity, drill sergeant."

"Blue is infinity?"

The smirks on their faces clued me that my wild guess was wildly wrong, but backtracking on a firm answer given would only lead to waffling and looking uncertain. "Yes, drill sergeant!"

Later, my drill sergeant told me no one got the answer correct, but I displayed such confidence in such an obviously made-up answer that I got the most points for it, and my stellar answers on the other questions and commanding presence made me a clear winner. Red is courage.

White is purity. Blue is justice. Figured, justice. "Just us," as the inmates would say. I felt so far away from that private who walked across the stage to be handed the award at graduation.

An NCO emerged and called for me to come back. We knew each other, but they looked at me like a stranger who walks into a party. I swallowed and followed as the others in the assembly area watched on. I was hopeful, but I saw, in their eyes and set their jaws, the no vote. I stood at attention when they gave the verdict that I was to be stripped of my rank to private and discharged under less than honorable circumstances. I saluted when they dismissed me and executed an about face, facing all my life from twenty-two on as a felon and stained with this discharge.

In prison, Flat-Five and Brew sang the George Harrison lyrics, "If you want to sing the blues, you have to pay your dues." Well, I was a dues-paying son of a bitch.

I wondered if any of the officers had argued to keep me, wondered if my old platoon leader thought I might be worthy of a second shot as I had carried our tank crew to the top gunnery award with my gunnery skills. I hit every target in record time—fastest gun in the West. Surely, that was worth keeping me. My mind reached out to all the things I'd volunteered for and how I had lifted other soldiers in the field in all the small and large ways. It was like a mad accounting of good deeds against the one bad thing that canceled everything out. Did anyone say I was a good guy and worked hard, that I was confident I'd learned my lesson from falling so far down?

The deliberation and vote were confidential. I'd never know. These men had been like a family, and now I was an outcast. I was dead to them.

On the street, under the hard desert sun, the city went on about its business unconscious of one more criminal having been served justice. I wanted to get a beer and forget and wanted to be both alone and lost in a crowd. I wanted to sit in the dark and stare into a light I can't enter. But I was broke and forced to live with my hunger until payday.

In the Chateau, Clarisse sat next to me. Only a few day drinkers sat at the bar, and a couple of out-of-towners sat at the stage waving dollar bills like flags on the Fourth of July. We sat in shadows and didn't speak. We'd talked more than a few times in the past, so I supposed it was the familiarity of talking about ourselves to each other that made the silence between us not awkward.

When I was signed out of the halfway house, I'd slipped further away from any sense of normalcy. Alone, the nights became endurance tests. My room's flimsy walls more confining than concrete, giving me the jitters. Sitting in the living room making small talk with the television on made me fidget and look to the door like an escape pod. My mind was a lake of fire that popped and snapped from thought to thought, my breath the wind making it burn hotter and my pumped blood the fuel from the heart, until I drank enough booze to dampen it down and fall into oblivion. My mind finally quieted. In the mornings, after three or four hours of sleep, I'd throw on yesterday's clothes and race my car to work by 7:00 am. When I ran out of money, I stayed in and read until the dark hours after midnight. When I had a day off and was not forced out of bed, I slept off the week, did laundry, shaved and showered, and made ready for the evening.

I'd hoped the Guard would give me another chance and help me reestablish who I was, give me a purpose. With them, I knew I'd have a direction to move in with a destination that meant something. There, I'd excelled and could again. What other way to overcome the death of the spirit, my spirit? I'd thought about going back to college. I'd failed my last semester, unable to complete the coursework because I was in jail. Even so, what could I study for four years and hope to be hired to do as a felon? It had been hell getting a job before the tire store, much less some job that required a degree. It felt more ridiculous than believing the Guard would show mercy for my sins against them.

Here I was, in the dark, drinking with a stripper who was nice to me even when I wasn't spending money on drinks for her.

When Clarisse's time to dance came up, she left, saying, "See you later." As she came on the stage, I downed the last of my pitcher of beer. Her baby blue boa ruffled with light and shadow as she spun. I went to the end of the stage. She strutted over and dropped into the splits before spinning to face me with her legs open. Her boa dangling between her breasts to the floor. "Thanks for the company," I said.

She smiled as she spun up onto her heels, so close that her knees were on either side of me. I tucked a twenty into her garter and said, "Later."

In the parking lot, I sat in my car, a convection oven in the sun. My breath felt trapped in my lungs. My mind raced like a muscle car, and some driver had the accelerator mashed down and wouldn't let up.

Under my shirt, I felt my dog tags and the Saint Christopher medal. I hadn't taken them off since the night before heading to the armory. Like if I kept them on, there was some chance the officers of the court-martial would reverse their decision, that by some magic, some divine intervention, I'd be forgiven and reinstated.

When I was a boy, my dad had given me a rabbit's foot. He gave one to my younger brothers too. They were garish colors: fuchsia, chartreuse, and lemon. I'd never seen rabbits that color and wondered where they'd come from. He'd just landed a new job and told us, "Rub 'em for luck, boys. Our fortunes are changing." Five or so years later, after another layoff, I lost the rabbit's foot in the move. I asked my father if he'd seen it. He said, "The rabbit had four feet, and his luck was none too good."

Through my shirt, I rubbed the Saint Christopher medal between my thumb and forefinger. Patron Saint of Travelers. Where am I traveling to? I wanted so much to believe, like my ex-wife did, in the power of talismans to channel divine favor or some cosmic energy to protect us as we move through this uncertain life. Even small things like carrying the little slips of paper from fortune cookies or a coin from another country or a stone caught in sunshine or whatever token strikes a vibration in us to fill the void. Anything. But in my heart, the dog tag stamped No Rel Pref still had more power to me than all the good luck charms, mojo bags, or religious medals in the world. Disbelief and skepticism would never let me down. How many travelers have been killed along the road with their patron saint looking on?

Ever since I'd left the armory, a line from Pink Floyd's song, "Wish You Were Here," ran through my mind. I'd traded my "walk-on part in the war for a lead role in a cage." But where to now after the cage and with nothing left of the former life except these remnants, these reminders that may yet guide me a little further down the road? To where? I didn't even know where I was going next. Sweat stung my eyes, and I wiped the tears away before turning the engine over. I knew I'd have to take the tags and medal off soon. Just not today.

At the tire store one afternoon close to closing time, a woman in cutoff shorts that showed off her tattoos and a halter top that barely contained her huge tits came in looking for a tire. Ron called me up to help her find a used tire as she didn't have much money. As I sorted through the used tires in the back, she chatted me up. Her name was Kate, and she asked if I wanted to go out after I got off. I had nothing going on and said sure. I found a tire for her and put it on.

She met me after work, and we went out to a bar to catch a band she knew was playing. We drank and danced, and at the end of the night, we ended up in my room at Binder and Jen's. Jen didn't say anything the next morning about me bringing her home, but she did give me the look of 'what in the ever-loving hell are you doing bringing that skank into my home?' I hadn't even thought about it.

That evening, Binder had come home. We went out to get some beer, saying we'd be right back, but we stopped in a bar on the way back and lost track of time and got back right before midnight. Jen and Kate were watching television when we staggered in laughing. Jen was livid and told me I needed to fly straight or get the fuck out. Kate slipped into my room to get her stuff, but Jen stopped her. "Not you. You can stay, but you," she pointed at me, "need to go if you can't wire your shit together."

Binder started to speak, but one look from her and he closed his mouth. She fumed. I understood why she was so upset, and I felt both bad and helpless at the same time. She relented, but I didn't get better. I didn't stay the same either.

One night at the Chateau, Clarisse asked me and Binder for help moving, offering us money that we refused. She only had three hours to get her stuff out of the house; she didn't want a confrontation with her ex. I understood. Relationships end in stages similar to death: anger, animosity, sense of failure, reunion delusions, resentment, and, depending on the couple, lifelong bitterness or an eventual realization that the other person was never that bad—acceptance.

I was all for no confrontations. My uncle assumed that because we were two guys who had been in a few fights, her ex wouldn't want a confrontation either. After all, he may not want her to go, but odds are he wouldn't risk an ass kicking when he could wait until we were long gone. Vegas was all about playing those odds. Being drunk, though, you can never figure all the possibilities, especially in the erratic nature of broken relationships.

I had worked with a guy, Red, at the tire shop. He helped a friend retrieve some possessions from an ex-wife one night after swing shift. Night is not the time to move. New boyfriends can be armed and jumpy, knowing husbands might be in the anger stage of the breakup. Red took two bullets to the head. His twenty-three-year-old widow, ashen, blonde, and stoned, wore his motorcycle jacket and pushed her fatherless two-year-old twins in a stroller to the graveside. Guys became anxious to console her grief.

On a sunny, hot Vegas winter day, we pulled up in front of a single-story, half-acre house in Binder's '64 Dodge Dart. It was a nice neighborhood. Kids played on quarter-acre lawns of imitation ranchettes with split rail fences with wagon-wheel accents. Landscape trucks crowded curbs, and tanned men and women pushed mowers, raked gravel, and clipped hedges.

We each had bottles of Gatorade—trying to soothe dehydration headaches and three hours of sleep—and black rock 'n' roll T-shirts and jeans, torn and dirty. Clarisse had a small moving truck and was carrying a box with a pale blue boa hanging out of it. She walked in heels across the lawn. Her face showed no marks of rouge or lipstick, and she wore an oversized sweater that fell mid-thigh, making her shapeless, although her jeans were tight enough to show she had strong calves. After loading the box, she gave each of us a big hug and said how happy she was we'd showed up. She smelled washed, free of perfume, cigarette smoke, and the stink of drunks. We helped her with small items: a rocker her mother had given her when her first son was born, pictures of her two kids and family members, hand-carved salt and pepper shakers, a small sculpture of Don Quixote, some books, travel magazines, a record player, and a few Frank Sinatra albums. I was going to ask about her kids when her husband showed up. She was packing dishes for one.

Tall, Italian, and he wore a suit that needed to be a little bigger in the shoulders. On his left cheek was what looked like cigarette burns. Smooth scar tissue puckered and broke the contour of his profile. The spots were lighter in color than his dark skin, and they trembled over a clenched jaw.

He glared at us as he leaned against a bar off the kitchen, trying to get her to speak to him. He yelled in whispers, his whole body poised as if he was holding back everything he had, but she walked around him without making eye contact. I heard his teeth grind, and as his physical strength did not work in restraint, he became a well-dressed, brooding bronze. We witnessed the end of how he thought his future would be. Until that moment, he believed in the habit of her reconciliation but replaced lost faith with nothing, sacraments of dust and water. He hurt, and I felt like a shithead for being there. I couldn't even reach out a hand and commiserate. As fine as the line between empathy and betrayal is, it is even thinner between a gesture of kindness and an insult. Clarisse followed us to the truck and warned us not to stare at the scars on his face; he had been shot and wasn't too happy about it, although he didn't mind the body scars, she said. The atmosphere thickened.

I worried. The sulking guy by the bar could be calling a couple of business acquaintances. While he was vacationing on a Caribbean beach, my cousin and I would be taking up new digs in a shallow grave. Vivid in my mind was Anthony Spilotro. He was involved with a strip club and was reputed to have ties to the Mafia, even if politicians and civic boosters said, "There's no mob in town." One day, he came up on a missing person's report, and then, on a day much later, authorities found his body in a Great Plains cornfield without his head. An ineffable menace oozed through the room, and however tough I thought I was, I knew I wasn't that tough. I had been shot at before, survived prison where I met mafia guys and their enforcers, and knew the odds of bluffing your way past five guys with forty-fives who fuck people up for a living were the worst odds in town, a shell game where the ace was a real bullet. No witness protection if you're just a dumbass.

I wanted to fold the hand. I wasn't even sleeping with this woman, and here, a guy with gunshot wounds on his face looked at me like I'm the son of a bitch. The acid in my stomach burned down into my testicles, and the air became stale and salty in my mouth. I acted calm until the last box was loaded. Binder moved in the same mode: don't look frightened, and don't stare at his scars; pretend he's a plant.

Clarisse pulled away first. The yellow moving truck blended into the sunlight. As we turned the car around, he walked a measured cadence into the yard to the grass's edge, his right hand twisting a wedding band, and watched as we drove away. A cape of blue exhaust smoke obscured him and the house. A less than perfect day.

Alone out on Blue Diamond Road, I drove. The motor rumbled. It was on the outskirts of town surrounded by desert and the night. The dash lights illuminated my face, and the headlights pushed back the darkness as the car moved forward. I just wanted to drive nowhere, feel the road under me. Somehow, I was out on a long stretch of road that was mostly straight. When a curve or dip appeared, inattentive drivers found themselves rolling into the desert to wait for an ambulance and a tow truck. Anger and frustration hit me from nowhere, like being blindsided in an intersection. Energy swarmed through me and seized me. I felt like my mind was going to explode and my body was charged with the electricity of sudden rage and despair. Already doing sixty, I stomped the accelerator. I pushed my body back into the seat and straightened my arms, holding on to the steering wheel. A heavier car, the old Chargers weren't quick off the line, but, already in motion with the big eight-cylinder motor designed for speed, the car lurched forward. The speedometer needle arced over toward 100 miles per hour. I held on to the wheel as the car shook. The front tires vibrated over the asphalt and felt out of balance. The roar of the engine strained under all the fuel being dumped into the cylinders to be compressed by the pistons and ignited by the spark plugs in coordinated explosions. I wondered about nothing. Not rabbits or coyotes crossing the road or potholes or cops sitting out along some dirt road waiting for speeders and retirement. I focused on the lines at the far edge of the headlight beams where darkness and light meet. I kept the accelerator mashed to the floor, my body rigid with the tension of pushing back with my arms and legs against the seat. What seethed through me, I didn't know. It was an old impulse, and one that'd seize me again and again as inexplicably as reaching for a drink.

The speed topped out, and the car wouldn't go any faster. I still held on to all the speed in my hands for as long as I could. I didn't want to stop the feeling of it, the raw power coursing through me and the machine.

The thump and crash of metal breaking apart inside the engine filled the passenger compartment. The car started losing speed, and I guided the car onto the shoulder of the road where it rolled to a stop. The engine no longer ran, but I turned the key off out of habit. I cut the lights. The fever in me had broken, and I felt empty, flattened. Smoke drifted into the air. Getting out, I went around to the front of the car. The hood was blistering hot to the touch, and the engine ticked and seemed to sigh in relief as it cooled. It smelled of burnt oil and dirt kicked up by the tires.

I looked out toward the city and its towers full of lights and the reflections of lights. I saw the cars along the highway going and leaving town and jets landing and taking off in holding patterns over McCarran International. Binder's place was over twenty miles from me through all of that. A winter breeze came down from the mountains and cooled me. I turned my back on the city and gazed at the night sky, at all those stars, wondering which were already dead, their light still traveling through space like a last breath. The hot gasses given out and their warmth dissipated into space. All that burns dies, but what kind of light did it have before it burned itself out?

A group of coyotes howled and yipped out in the desert. I kicked at the earth. I got my car keys and locked the doors and began walking. I started to shuffle run and was taken by the spirit of my boots on the asphalt like I was during the road runs back at Fort Knox. In my head were the Army cadences I'd learned to call out: Up jumped a monkey from a coconut grove. / He was a bad motherfucker; you could tell by his clothes. Your left, your left, your left, right o' left. Ain't no use in going home. / Jody's got your girl and gone. Left, right o' left. I used to wear my faded jeans. / Now I'm wearing Army greens. / If I die in a combat zone, / box me up and ship me home. / If I die on the Russian front, / bury me with a Russian cunt. / Pin my medals on my chest. / Tell my mom I did my best. Your left, your left, your left, right o' left… And my favorite: Momma, momma, can't you see / what the Army's done to me? / Used to drive a Cadillac. / Now I pack it on my back.

Air, clean and cool from its long kiss with the night, filled my lungs and pimpled my skin.

The drill sergeants' commands brought discipline to my pace and a way to measure time and space. They yelled and cajoled us over miles and miles and made us run step for step. It felt great to have everyone in time, moving down the roadway like a beast on the move. Together, we generated energy like a series of coils generates more power than one alone, a unified field of marching and double-time marching to ward off the nuclear threat. Each one of us was useless alone, the rugged individual a pale myth amongst the camouflaged mass chanting cadences. I was at the head of the column with the platoon guidon, green and yellow, D-4-1, the mighty armor symbol flapping and popping in the wind created by my running, marching, and twirling it like a bo staff, a weapon ready to puncture the heart of the enemy. We must have been worthy in such numbers.

At Fort Knox, three mountains broke the forested horizon: Agony, Misery, and Heartbreak. The culmination of the basic part of our training, before moving on to armor training, was a twelve-mile road march in which we'd climb and descend each of these mountains. As the date came upon us, we worried the mountains might break us. I kept thinking about what my dad had said: "Some sorry specimens of manhood have made it through boot camp. Just keep that in mind." Not to mention how often the Spartan code, "Come back with your shield or on it," the exhortation of the Spartan women, passed his lips. How can you come back with or on a shield if you didn't earn the right to carry a shield? The morning came, and we assembled our equipment and formed up. The drill sergeants, in their pressed fatigues and campaign hats, called cadence. Up we went. Onward we marched and took time out to take off our boots and air out our feet, something I'd never done while hiking. I realized the benefits on not just the physical well-being, but how it also psychologically boosted us. "Yes, drill sergeant! We can climb these fucking mountains and carry on well past because you made us feel loved by letting us air out our stinking-ass feet!" And many did not know the benefits of airing out their feet, just like the many who did not know the benefits of regular toothbrushing and whose gums bled and bled with fetid breath as drill sergeants stood over them and made sure they learned the ins and outs of oral hygiene. Up those mountains we humped our packs, chanting response to the drill sergeant's call: "Agony. Misery. Heartbreak. Feels Good. So good. Ah, give me some. Agony. Give me some. Misery. Ah, give me some. Heartbreak. Ain't no use in going home. Agony…"

But the mountains weren't any worse than ones I'd climbed up and down growing up. We'd let the drill sergeants get in our heads, making us believe we marched into the High Sierra with the threat of a hard winter's storm. The satisfaction of finishing as a platoon, though, felt as if we had.

Out along this desert road, alone, my car in a state of collapse after its supernova, I jogged, airborne shuffled, alone—no platoon peer pressure or the shouts of being a dickless douche bag for falling back—chanting quiet breaths, puffs of frosted air around my face.

Momma, momma, can't you see? What this anger's done to me? Out here in this desert, there was no we on this road, only me calling a cadence without a response. The old sergeant had said, "It is always coldest before the dawn," and it is generally true. But the heat of day lingers long after the sun has disappeared over the desert's horizon. Sometimes all you can do is leave the wreckage behind and run through the dark.

After I spun the main bearing on the Charger, my dad let me use his old El Dorado—a big boat of a Cadillac that fighter jets could land on. I'd try to visit my parents and sister, the last child still at home, on the weekends. They no longer lived on the other side of the state line in California, the mine there having laid off my dad right before fucking Christmas. He now supervised a shift at a plastic injection plant that made buckets and lids next to a state prison and a small casino in Jean some 30 miles southwest of Vegas on the 15. Binder still worked out at the mine in Cali as part of a skeleton crew but knew his days were numbered and started casting about for new work.

I drove out to Goodsprings, which sat northwest of Jean along a two-lane road. It was little more than a collection of single-family houses, mobile homes, a cemetery, a bar, a church, and abandoned lead and zinc mines played out since the 1950s. My parents had a plot of land with one of the last original rock houses from the 19th century in town that was located a dozen yards from the foundation of a hotel that burned down decades before and a bar that was the oldest freestanding building in operation in Nevada. My brothers and I went and had drinks there a few times and listened to the owner spin stories about the old days. Five bullet holes were left over from a gunfight over a poker game and suspected cheating. In short, just another desert town where if it weren't for the automobile and air-conditioning or swamp coolers, people would have abandoned it decades ago.

Mom knew I was coming and had made a dish full of enchiladas and brewed a jug of sun tea.

When I shut the door behind me, mom held out a small envelope. The return address was in Los Angeles and from Jane. Penguins were on the front, and it had been sent to my parents' last address and then forwarded to Nevada. I opened it as my mom dished up some food.

I hadn't heard from her since the morning I'd withdrawn from Cal State Long Beach when I'd left LA.

I'd met her brother first. I was again the new kid, but so was he.

The spring of my eighth-grade year, we lived in the forest on the outskirts of an old church camp in the mountains above Prescott, Arizona. It was just for a few weeks until the school year ended. My parents and sister slept in a small cabin while we boys slept under the pines. We had been living on a small farm in Skull Valley where I milked the cows and my younger brothers and sister collected chicken eggs to sell. But something happened, and we ended up having to leave. When I graduated the eighth grade, we moved to California, our Okie forebearers in the back of an old pickup truck with a camper on the back. My dad got a job at an iron mine at Eagle Mountain as a truck driver. The iron mine was on the eastern edge of Joshua Tree National Park. A company town had been built next to the mine, and the schools were named for the oligarch and his family who founded the mine and foundry. Mountains of discarded rock loomed as high as the pit was deep next to the town.

For the first few weeks, we stayed at a grapefruit orchard where the caretaker kept rattlesnakes in an aquarium and let us ride his three-wheelers in the desert. I began my freshman year, hoping this time we'd stay and not be driven away by layoffs or crooked men or bad decisions. Then a few months into my freshman year, we left the grapefruit orchard and moved into a single-wide twelve miles south of the mine at Lake Tamarisk. On one side of the constructed lake was a trailer park and on the other were single-family homes of lathe and plaster. A golf course that struggled between green and yellow arced around the houses. My favorite place was the library next to the fire station.

Later, my mom became the night shift waitress at the Desert Center Cafe fifty plus miles from any city to speak of along Interstate 10. I later got a job washing dishes there. Desert Center had a post office, a gas station/garage, and a kindergarten. It served travelers between Arizona and Southern California, truckers, tow truck drivers, local miners, and other desert rats. The iron mine was some fourteen miles to the north.

I'd met Adam first when we left a class at the same time and he said with a grin, "I got to get home. It's not good for the super's kid to be caught out after school." His dad was the superintendent of schools who wore tweed jackets, smoked a pipe, and always had a lame joke. I laughed a little. He invited me over if I had time. I couldn't that day because I had to catch the bus home.

The next day, we went to his house for lunch. I'd brought a peanut butter sandwich, some chips, and a banana in a brown paper bag. The house, a small three-bedroom, was one built by the mine to house miners, administrators, support people, and their families. He brought out a couple of plates because his mother, a special education teacher, believed every meal needed to be on a plate. We sat at the dining room table.

They'd moved here from a coastal city in Orange County when his dad took the superintendent's job. He was flabbergasted when I told him we'd been living in the forest above Prescott after we left a farm we'd been working on when it didn't work out before living in a camper here until my dad could move us into a single-wide. He told me he thought moving from the city to this place was a rough transition, but it was nothing like what I'd experienced.

We started talking about science fiction. He loved Gordon R. Dickson's *Necromancer*. I was telling him about *Stranger in a Strange Land* when the front door opened. I looked around and was surprised to see Jane. Adam said, "This is my sister," and introduced me to her.

She waved and said, "Nice to meet you," as she disappeared into the hallway toward the back of the house.

Dumbfounded, I took a bite of my sandwich. I'd been enamored with Jane when I saw her coming out of the girls' locker room, still in her PE clothes and carrying her band uniform, flute, and books for the English class we shared. Her sandy-colored hair had been tied back in a ponytail. She was flushed and in a hurry. Even though I'd seen her in class, something made me stop in that moment and think that if I wasn't such a dork, I'd try to strike up a conversation about English and the way Ms. Mac played Pink Floyd's *The Wall* in class or even ask her to one of the school dances. Now I'd discovered she was my new friend's sister and therefore off-limits to ask out.

We all became friends, though. Adam and Jane had taken me as I was, a gawky guy who was the definition of an unsophisticated hick. Although well-read in the sciences and history and in fantasy and science fiction, it seemed I knew nothing of the culture I lived in. Outside the country and western music my parents listened to and the standup comedy albums from Steve Martin, Richard Pryor, Robin Williams, and Cheech and Chong I'd listened to with friends from my last school, I knew nothing. Adam and Jane showed me a range of things I'd never heard of, like Broadway show tunes, *The Rocky Horror Picture Show*, Mozart, Wagner, Van Gogh, Monet, and Abstract Expressionism. In general, this thing called the Arts. They enlightened me with the power of the arched eyebrow.

The first time I heard Jane use the phrase, *je ne sais quoi*, I had to ask what it meant. When she told me, I wanted to use it in casual conversation. Unfortunately, that was in front of my dad. "Clint Eastwood has a certain je ne sais quoi as an actor."

He looked at me as if I'd farted at the dinner table. "Knock it off with the fancy French phrases. People'll think you don't belong to us."

Toward the end of the fall semester of my junior year, my dad got laid off. We'd have to move. Luckily, dad found work further north at Mountain Pass, a rare earth mine. When it came time, dad decided to tow our single-wide with his big '64 Dodge truck. We had three vehicles—the truck, a station wagon, and my Scout—and only my dad and I could drive. My mom had never gotten a driver's license. We'd make the trip in a couple of rounds.

We packed the house by strapping the furniture in place and spreading the load to balance the trailer. I had planned to return to Eagle Mountain once the family was situated in Mountain Pass. We lit out from Lake Tamarisk after midday. Then someplace along the Desert Center Road as it bent north around a spur of a mountain headed to Needles, a tire on the single-wide bounced away. Following behind in the station wagon, I watched it roll out into the desert as the brake lights flashed a Morse code of stopping. The tire disappeared a hundred yards away. At first, I thought only the tire had come off, but I discovered the center of the wheel was still held down by lug nuts on the hub and the middle of the wheel was mangled. I wondered what weakness caused it. What caused this forged steel to give way?

I'd already seen one trailer scattered across this stretch of desert when my dad drove a tow truck to make some extra money. All the possessions of the people exposed to the elements and scavengers both animal and human. I saw two yarmulkes, the first I'd ever seen, and thought they went to a bra. What did I know, sheltered agnostic/Protestant I'd been?

Dad took the rest of the family onward, and I stayed with the trailer. He said he'd be back the next day if things went right. My job was to protect our possessions. After they disappeared down the road, I set up a campfire ring and gathered some wood. Darkness loomed not far off.

Much to my surprise, I heard Adam's VW Bug pulling up behind the trailer on the shoulder of the road. Almost like the sound of a cavalry troop coming upon a stranded pioneer. Somewhere along the way, my dad had called Adam and Jane to let them know I wouldn't be returning as soon as we thought and where I was camped out along the road. I became unbelievably happy. I finished readying for the night with their help. The sun broke against the jagged mountains and spread the blood of sunset over the sky. Long streaks of smog blown over the sky from LA reddened like long scars, faded to gray, and then blackened to shadows obscuring the stars.

We sat around the fire of mesquite, chatted, and ate some food they brought out. The wood popped and cracked, and our laughter echoed with the coyotes' yips in the distance. I felt like I had when my family and I gathered around the campfire down on our attempted homestead close to the Mexican border in 1976. We had all the hope of a new country in that Bicentennial year. Even though I couldn't name it then, we had been filled with the hope of Jefferson's yeoman farmer, Emmerson's self-reliance, and Thoreau's living deliberately. How much laughter had we echoed across an empty landscape?

With Adam and Jane, I didn't know what things were important to us then as a trio to talk about, but the joy we shared filled me. The desert night chilled, and even as I thought I'd have enough time to say all the things I wanted to say, they had to get back home, leaving me along the dark highway to Needles.

The next day, dad showed up with a new rim and tire.

I returned to Eagle Mountain within a couple of days. We had a couple of weeks until the fall semester ended, and Adam and Jane's parents let me stay with them until it was over. We hung out and talked about getting an apartment and being roommates in Los Angeles and going to college. Adam would already be in art school and situated there. I imagined us the very picture of urban hipness.

As the semester wound down, we went to football games to watch Jane in the marching band. One night after a game, Jane and I sat on her bed and kissed for like an hour, surrounded by the hand-painted rainbows on her walls, but I was paranoid to touch her. What if it upset her and she screamed at me? I'd find myself turned out into the desert with no place to go. I'd be a feral boy kicked off the wagon train to be either taken in by wolves or eaten by them.

Once, Adam and Jane's mom took me with her on a trip to LA. She treated me to my first Chinese food. She made me laugh when she said with a wry smile, "God, I thought having kids in high school would make me feel old, but it was the gray pubic hair that did it." She liked to drink wine and talked about books with me. Although I didn't drink, I could imagine myself in Los Angeles having a glass with her as we chatted about events of the day with a pipe. So sophisticated I'd be.

After I left Eagle Mountain when the fall semester ended, Adam and Jane and I wrote each other. Adam and I, inspired by *The Lord of the Rings*, constructed an elaborate written language and mailed letters written in it to each other. Adam always enclosed a few exquisite ink drawings with each letter. He was going to college to be an artist. Jane wanted to be a teacher. These were both careers my dad and mom disdained. My dad had said teachers only taught because they couldn't make it in their field and were in the bottom 10 percent of their classes in college. I had no idea where he got his information from, but as a boy in elementary school who'd had one bad experience with a teacher when he started saying this, I believed him. When I'd repeated this to Jane, she lost her temper and explained to me all the education her parents and others had to do to become teachers. Her anger stunned me, but what also stunned me was the way I felt about what my dad had been saying. Only years later would I see how the effects of class and self-worth were tied together by diminishing other professions. Like how I wanted to be a writer but then was torn by my dad's insistence it was a stupid waste of money. I needed to study chemical engineering if I went to college, something I could get a job doing to make a living.

At the high school in Baker the spring of my junior year, I did well in classes and won election for student body president for my senior year. This school bussed some of us in from Mountain Pass thirty miles away as well as other kids living in remote desert towns. It was much smaller than the one at Eagle Mountain. Instead of a class of a hundred or so students, we were sixteen. The vibe was different, and there weren't the bullies that had been at Eagle Mountain, so I loosened up and started to do more things, like play sports and join groups. But one thing was missing—my heart was still to the south.

Jane and I planned to go to prom in May—a double date with her brother and his date. I borrowed a car from a friend my dad had helped get a job at the mine and who was part family by marriage. A factory blue 1969 Chevy Firebird with a 350-cubic-inch engine ready to race.

The prom's theme was, "It's Just a Fantasy," inspired by the Aldo Nova song. I'd rented a tuxedo in Las Vegas and made the long drive south. They held it at the Lake Tamarisk rec center. All the way down, I had the stereo cranked up over the sound of wind through open windows and the roar of fuel being guzzled to Journey's *Captured* live double album.

I kept daydreaming, in the hypnotic thrum, of finding the guts to kiss Jane again. I had it all planned out. We'd roll from Eagle Mountain in the Firebird, and I'd play it cool so as not to start the evening off with a major indiscretion. Then after a night of dancing and maybe a stroll around the lake to test the waters, so to speak, we'd end with a kiss. If the kiss went well, maybe I'd suggest a side trip along the way back to her home. A spur road by a railroad crossing just out of sight of the blacktop. I imagined being James Bond smooth in the muscle car. Licensed to kill it. After all, I had a tux on and that awesome early '80s Prince Charming hair. Just a casual swing off the two-lane road onto the gravel road to watch the stars, talk about something, and hopefully make out. I imagined my awkward teenaged shyness dissolved into a more confident man who knew the right things to say, the right things to do, without being foolish or some cheesy douche bag.

I tried to think of some lyrics or lines from a smooth song like my grandfather had used to sway my grandmother. "Hey, good-lookin'. Say, what's cookin'?" But rock anthems with lines like, "You ain't a beauty, but hey, you're alright" or "I'm your ice cream man" seemed out of sync, and all the other songs I came up with were about already getting ready to have sex or straight up asking for sex. Marvin Gaye's "Let's get it on," which was smooth and cool coming from him, sounded dorky and borderline perverted coming from me. I figured something would come to me.

I drove down, looking forward to prom night, hoping for the best and hoping to recreate making out like we did in her room only a few months before. "Maybe this time," in the words of Sally Bowles, "I'll be lucky." After all, if they threw me out this time, I had the Firebird to fly me north at a hundred miles an hour and not worry about being horseless and afoot in the desert.

Her parents thought it a great idea we ride along with Adam and his date in his VW Bug. Why take two cars? Be environmentally conscious, they said, be responsible and carpool. Why not save yourself a little driving considering you've already driven so far and have so far to go, they said to me. What I heard was: We don't want you alone with our daughter in the back of a muscle car. We crammed ourselves, tuxes and rustling prom dresses, into the car, and up the road we went.

At the rec center, we milled about, got our picture taken, and danced. I ached to stroll with her out along the lakeshore walkway and find a dark spot to make out alone, but Adam kept following us around and talking to me. He was my best friend, and I was there only a short time. Before I knew it, the dance was over. Jane and I had squeezed into the backseat of his VW Bug, and we motored back to their house. I've often wondered if Adam's date felt frustrated with my inadvertently cock-blocking her.

We got to their house and talked for a little bit before turning in. Jane gave no indication she wanted me to follow her. I lay on the couch awake for most of the night, wondering if I should tiptoe to her door and check to see if the knob turned. How many movies have we seen where would-be lovers waited for the other in separate rooms, hoping? Did I miss her signal? I wondered if she didn't want to say anything in front of the others and waited as awake and full of desire as I was, waiting for dawn. The stupid dawn where all hope ended but the desire remained.

I left Eagle Mountain that morning. Some of the young miners I'd made friends with at Mountain Pass ribbed me—a tux and a Chevy Firebird and you still didn't get laid. Hahaha. I grinned and felt like something slipped by and it'd never come back around. It was a weird sense of loss. Can a person lose a thing he'd never had?

Within the next year, Eagle Mountain would slowly become a ghost town as it emptied of miners, their families, and others, like the teachers. Sometime later, a private minimum-security prison was built. And after an inmate riot over a baseball game and a murdered prisoner, the prison closed. After that, someone floated the idea to convert the old open pit into a high-tech landfill, but lawsuits over environmental concerns stopped it. They gated it off with No Trespassing signs and a phone number to call for inquires and a few live-in caretakers.

Some years later, Jane and I would go back to see what had become of the place. The company had sold the houses of the community. They cracked them in half to load onto railcars. It was something to see a train on a siding loaded with half houses. The neighborhood had gaping holes like missing teeth in the jaw of the streets. Some halves remained on their lots, open to the weather and wildlife, waiting for the next train. Jane's room had been split down the middle. The looping rainbows she'd painted missing half their arcs in the desert sun. She cried at the sight, and I held her.

In the Green Rocket, the miles ticked by, and I closed the gap between two versions of my past. My stomach felt queasy thinking of Jane and if our year and a half of letters meant more than just two pals getting together in the big city of LA and if we'd kiss like we did the time I'd stayed with her family—long and unsure of what it meant.

I pulled onto their block and parked. Jane answered the door and welcomed me in with a hug. She smelled so nice, like spring and flowers. I gave Adam a big hug. On the couch sat Ricardo, a guy from our high school. *Weird*, I thought. What was a perpetually failing special education student doing here? He had never figured into any of our conversations.

"We got to talk," Jane said.

My guts dropped. Had Jane and Adam replaced me with him as a roommate? Was he with Jane now? No. It was much weirder. Their mom had dumped their dad and moved back to the coast, dragging the high school dropout with her when the semester ended. I was dumbfounded.

"Don't worry," she said. "We're still on." We would move out to a different place after I found a job and registered for school.

Through the front window, I saw a traffic cop writing a ticket by the Green Rocket. I went out, and he told me I was parked facing in the wrong direction on the street. Silly country kid. What a way to start my first day away from home.

The next morning, I woke up on the couch and got ready to look for a job. The night before, I'd gone through the classifieds with Jane by my side. I loved being close to her, and she knew what to look for. "No, you're not qualified for that. No, that's too far away." I'd held four jobs in my life: farm labor in Skull Valley, dishwashing at the cafe in Desert Center, and pumping gas and checking oil at the filling station in Mountain Pass and at Stuckey's on the western slope several miles before reaching the summit. No classified ads involved, just a word from my mom or dad that someone was looking for help. Jane made sure I had all the right documents and, after breakfast, drove me around in her Toyota. We hit the places in the ads, and we stopped anyplace I was qualified to work: oil change shops, gas stations, pizza joints, fast-food restaurants, and as a dishwasher at cafes.

As she drove, she got me up to date about all the people I'd gone to school with in Eagle Mountain. Who'd gotten pregnant, who'd gotten scholarships, who'd gotten held back in a school that was rapidly being shut down as the mine slowly died for lack of investment so the owner could buy a professional football team. I asked about how her father was. He was still out in the desert, alone in an empty house, overseeing the school district's death throes. His wife leaving had crushed him. I imagined him like a marooned administrator of an old outpost on the frontier the railroad had bypassed. Out there alone. His kids all gone and his wife moved back to the big city with an illiterate young lover. The exile of the left behind. We talked a lot about the past but little about the future except for what classes we hoped to take or what movies we'd like to go see.

I had this strange sensation. I'd wanted Jane bad, but I had a girlfriend, Lacey, still in high school. Since I'd been a freshman, I'd had a crush on Jane but didn't know how to make my feelings known, just like I didn't know how to break up with my girlfriend without being a dick about it. There were no high school classes on it, and my parents, who had remained married their whole lives from the time they were teenagers, were models of how not to break up. Lacey and I had some rocky moments that summer. We broke up and reunited, but like in many small towns, it was hard to stay apart. I worried I'd miss my opportunity with Jane only to be dumped later by Lacey.

Jane and I went to some movies, and one night, we held hands through *Conan the Barbarian.* By the time Conan and the two thieves he had fallen in with were captured by a king, I began caressing Jane's leg. I didn't rush my hands over her like Conan might have done. I wondered if she might respond back to me. She did in a halfhearted way that left me puzzled. I could feel her desire to do something and her restraint, so I didn't do anything beyond the caresses and holding her hand. This was no one-day-and-a-night turn and burn between mining towns like when I had visited her for prom. We were going to be around each other a long time now, roommates with her brother. In retrospect, she might have been going through what I was. Maybe she had a boyfriend in the old mining town, in another desert, waiting to come to the big city. She too might have been caught in an old desire, one where the years between the last hot kiss and the present bent together and touched. We got up and walked out with the crowd into the warm California night like nothing had happened in the barbarian darkness.

On another night, Jane and I went to the mall and people-watched. It was the era of big hair, lip gloss, and lots of blush, mall singers, girls in fingerless lace gloves and short skirts, boys in Members Only jackets and parachute pants, and an array of gag T-shirts. We walked around doing nothing in particular, holding hands a little bit as we moved in and out of crowds and got an Orange Julius. Sometimes we'd just sit on a bench and concoct stories for the people who went by us. She always made me laugh with her wit and how she saw the world. I'd wondered what life here would be like when I'd left Mountain Pass. I had all these notions, instilled by television and films, about apartments and possessions in the city, none of which were realistic. But I started to feel the rhythm of life and started to consider its boundaries and its shape. Right now, it felt like I was visiting and sleeping on a friend's couch and hanging out, but also felt like I was headed in the right direction.

After a couple of days of looking for jobs, I got into the Green Rocket and drove to California State University in Long Beach and registered for classes. I cannot tell you why I chose that school other than they accepted me and allowed me to register. When I asked the registrar what I should take, she handed me a course catalogue. "Something from in here would be good. Stay in the 100s." I asked to see an advisor to help me enroll, but she said none were available. The catalogue was huge and full of information. My high school teachers had never explained how this worked, and my family had never let on if they did know. My dad had taken some classes at Arizona State in the early '70s but didn't graduate. I leafed through the catalogue, reading the first section with the instructions. I flipped to the back and used the index to find classes I thought I needed to take to be a good student. I was a curious kid, given to copying out things I'd read in notebooks and researching things I wanted to know more about. I'd been in a writers' club at Eagle Mountain and the editor of the school newspaper as a senior. I wrote fantasy and science fiction stories in longhand in spiral notebooks in the style of authors I loved. Once, I had my father read a story for me. All he said was I'd ripped off a story he'd written, even though I'd never seen anything he'd written and didn't know he wrote stories at all. But his remarks remained with me about pursuing electrical or chemical engineering as a real job instead of trying to become a writer. Those were subjects I didn't want to study. The math needed had been my weakest subject.

As I stood there thinking of what classes to take, I knew the problem was that I was interested in so many things. I wasn't sure where to start. For sure I wanted to take philosophy. In the end, I enrolled in classes I felt all college freshmen took their first semester based on what I'd heard Adam and Jane talking about with their parents, the offhand things my dad had said, and television shows. I signed up for philosophy, sociology, English, and, as an appeasement to my dad, intro to chemistry and basic math.

Even with my confused start, I felt a sense of accomplishment and joy signing up for the classes and receiving my schedule. Although I'd considered joining the military during high school, I didn't want to put off getting a college degree. Four years in the military and then four years in college seemed too long. I knew about the ROTC, but it was just the flip side to joining the service first. Plus, my dad always bad-mouthed ROTC officers as next to useless in Vietnam. He called them Rot-Cees, and I didn't want to be grouped with them. But any military option to pay for college seemed an impossibly long, long time. Besides, there were no wars. I wanted to get on with it and get a job and start making money and build a career, even though I wasn't sure what it meant. I didn't know the difference between a BA and a BS or an MA and an MFA or a PhD and an AA or what it took to get any of them.

As a kid, I had been told college was the thing to do while listening to college being disparaged at the same time, sometimes in the same conversation. They'd say, "Oh, he's a college-educated idiot." "Oh, he's book smart, but he's got no common sense." All this as if it were one or the other instead of the reality, which is a lack of an education doesn't give you any common sense, and being book smart doesn't mean you lack it. It was a strange way working-class folks had of telling their kids to do better, but you'd be a sellout and lose your common sense if you did.

I filled out all the paperwork and signed it in all the right spots and went to the registrar's window. I paid my tuition in cash from the months of helping motorists between Los Angeles and Las Vegas. Elation filled me and carried me lightly all the way home.

I got back to the house, ready to tell everyone the good news. Ricardo sat on the couch as he always did, watching television and doing nothing. Jane took me aside. Jane said Ricardo was uncomfortable with my presence. Maybe, jealous of the guy who graduated high school, he thought I might make a play for his lady? Jane asked if I had enough money in the bank to move out. I didn't have a bank account because banks took your money and then turned you out onto the street while taking your car. I was a cash man and told her I had my share for us to move out. Jane shook her head. Her mom didn't like the tension, the drama. Jane and Adam weren't ready to move yet, so I'd have to go it alone. After a quick search through the classified ads, I realized I didn't have enough money for an apartment, and without a job, no one would rent to me anyway. Money can't buy happiness, someone once said, but it'd sure help to get a studio apartment.

After Jane had uttered those words, a sense of urgency swept over me. I had to do something and do it now no matter what, or I'd end up sleeping in the Green Rocket. I called Blaine. All I needed to do was get there, tank full of gas away.

I spent my last night in LA and, in the morning, said bye to Adam and Jane in the front yard after I'd put my bag in the Green Rocket. The drive was about five hours or so to Las Vegas, and I wanted to get out of town early. I still had to go to the university and withdraw from classes I'd just registered for and get a refund before I could head out of town. We gave each other big hugs, saying, "See you soon." They acted like it was temporary, just a matter of time and we'd get a place, but I was already turning away. Maybe I'd lived through too many goodbyes growing up. This was one of those moments, though, when everyone was lying and everyone knew it, but the truth was too heavy to hold between us and keep the bridge that connected us from collapsing.

I held Jane's card in my hand, and all those years came back to me. She'd just gotten back from Europe and separated from her Army husband. I had no idea she'd gotten married or had gone to Munich. Damn, she got to go to Germany. At the bottom was her phone number, or her mother's phone number, and she asked me to call. She'd love to hear what I'd been up to since we'd last seen each other. Maybe I could come out to Los Angeles. I must've grinned as my mom gave me a smile as if I might be going on a date.

I rolled out of Vegas on a Greyhound headed for Los Angeles, full of hope and cheap booze. The crowded bus was hot and smelled like a bunch of people who had been sleeping in their cars until they were repossessed. Rain had been falling across Southern California, and clouds grayed the light. The inside of the bus hung with the hot breath of dozens of confined people. When we stepped out of the bus at Barstow, the air had the cool, crisp feeling like you get when water hits the back of your throat after having been powerfully thirsty. Relief. I'd left Vegas behind a wreck of troubles worse than I cared to talk about with a stranger in a stinking bus. I just wanted to get to L-fucking-A. City of Angels and City of Dreams.

I'd worked the hot, gritty fall and into the winter at the tire store and was officially released from custody in April. I'd been seeing some women on and off, but nothing was sticking. I was pretty sick of everything in general. My parole officer called to inform me that my ex-best friend, Matt, had complained to the cops I'd been stalking him and I needed to stay away. "What bullshit," I told him. I had no idea where that paranoid asshole was and didn't care. I was minding my own business, and if he minded his business, he wouldn't be minding mine. The parole officer told me it didn't matter a damn bit because it was his word against mine. The cops would arrest me off the street and haul me to county at his whim. It wouldn't go well for me.

The bus stopped for a break and to take on or let off passengers at the Barstow station before heading over the Cajon Pass. It hadn't changed from the last time I'd been there. A squad of us from my Guard unit had been sent to Fort Irwin to act as opposition forces for some regular Army. We'd all been chauffeured out in a couple of vans and had all our equipment, including our small arms and training explosives. When the time came to go, the unit forgot to send the vans back for us. The NCO in charge got us a ride from the fort to the bus station in Barstow to ride the Greyhound back to Vegas. The one problem was that it was illegal to transport our firearms, blank ammunition, and other training munitions, like fragmentation, smoke grenades, and flares on the bus. The sergeant had us break down our weapons, and what couldn't be hidden in duffel bags was hidden on our bodies. We waited for the bus, hot and sweaty, covered with dirt from two weeks in the field, unable to take off our jackets concealing our pistols.

Funny, I thought. I stood by the chair I'd sat in back then while we soldiers waited for a Vegas-bound bus. It had only been about two and a half years ago that I was smuggling guns back to where they belonged. I hoped for a future past all of it. The chair like some relic in a museum of down-and-out places where the past always looked dingier than what the city boosters wanted. Maybe that was for the best. The driver called for us to board. We milled about in the rain as we loaded. Soon, the doors swished shut and the bus lurched forward. We rode westbound through a gray drizzle. For the first few miles, we were aired out from the fresh rain still on our skin and in our hair. Then the heat rose, and the air became muggy as the windows fogged up with our collective breath.

I had on my headphones, listening to my trusty transistor radio, and as we started into downtown LA, the drifter song from The Band, "The Weight," came on. It felt perfect, a song about rolling into town just looking for a place to hide and being asked to help take a load off someone. I guess sometimes it came back to that. You got nothing, and no one will give you a place, but you still have the capacity help raise someone up even when you ain't no saint. I heard it so many times on the classic rock stations in prison. The biker we called Classic Rick for his deep knowledge of rock 'n' roll trivia yelled and carried on about it being better than "Born to Be Wild." Who was I to argue with a guy with "Fuck You" tattooed on the inside of his lip and who had been one of the guys at the Rolling Stones concert in Altamont when they stabbed a guy to death? Hooo whoo, don't you know my name? No, I didn't argue because I agreed. Fuck yeah.

The song finished as the bus parked. I waited for most of the other passengers to file off and then got out and grabbed my duffel bag—the same one I'd used to smuggle the weapons back to the armory from Barstow at the NCO's insistence. I'd never thought about it at the time, but how could I expect to shed the past and start over if I kept carrying it with me like this? I should have burned all that military shit and been done with it.

I threaded my way through the station, slipped by the panhandlers, and went out onto the street. Two Hispanic guys in a Buick asked me where I was going, and I said, "I have a ride coming."

"We can get you anywhere cheaper than a taxi, man." One of the dudes popped the trunk.

Bullshit, I thought. I grinned at them as I scanned the people on the block. "Nah."

Jane appeared out of the crowd. Holy fuck. She had been a smooth-skinned high school girl, awkward in her own body, and now she walked the city streets a woman with blue eyes and hair the color of copper wire I'd stripped out of an old Air Force barracks. It was one thing to think about seeing the girl you'd had a schoolboy crush on, but quite another to see her years later as a woman. She wore a white blouse scattered with small blue flowers that had a ruffled collar and jeans like she'd stepped off a billboard on the side of a bus rumbling by the Buick.

"My ride's here, boys." They looked and whistled, then turned to hustle a mousy blonde gal for fare.

Can someone be more beautiful than you remembered her? Weren't we supposed to enhance our memory, romanticize the unrequited love? Weren't we supposed to see our old love and have our expectations seem a grainy photo found between the pages of an old novel? Not now. We gave each other a hug. We pulled each other close as if closing the distance on the time we'd been apart. I felt her against me, so familiar, yet new. The noise on the street stopped, and I breathed in her hair like I had years before.

She made pasta to go with a swordfish fillet we'd bought at a fish market on the corner for dinner at her mother's apartment in the Wilshire District. I leaned against the counter and took in the apartment tastefully decorated by an educated and sophisticated person—wood floors, books and jazz records, and airy plants soaking up the gold sunshine streaming through gauzy curtains. I worried I'd break something. Her mom and her mom's new boyfriend were out, so we had the place to ourselves. It was a place to crash after her marriage fell apart in Germany. After getting back stateside, she said she wrote me because I'd been on her mind a lot.

That first evening, we drank the first bottle of Blue Nun Riesling we'd picked up at Trader Joe's. After eating, we did the dishes and cleaned the kitchen, then sat on the hardwood floor on a bunch of cushions and started a second bottle of Riesling. She had turned on some Moody Blues and lit some candles. Outside, we heard the cars and occasional horn honking from up the block on Wilshire.

I'd spent all day walking around with her, trying to keep my hands to myself and play it cool. I didn't want to have any expectations so I'd have no disappointments. But I wanted her, and it's one thing to have no expectations, but quite another not to have desire. I thought about high school before the layoffs, the prom, my week in Los Angeles, and the sexless days and nights that existed between us. On those cushions, in the flickering candlelight, "Nights in White Satin" on the stereo, she leaned in and kissed me. I kissed her and, after a minute, leaned her back and ran my hand slowly up her blouse. She arched her back, and in minutes, we closed the distance on seven years. Not awkward virgins in our teens, we moved our hands and mouths over each other, sure of what we did.

I'd hoped when I'd caught that bus to see her on that first weekend, we'd drink and end by ravaging each other in her mom's spare bedroom. We'd had a lot of pent-up sexual desire since our unrequited high school years, and we both felt like we were reclaiming something from the past to create a future. Memory is a mosaic, broken fragments making the present. We see all those images and events as they create a picture that is being added to day by day. All those broken fragments of memory all point toward the future.

Later that night, we lay on some sleeping bags and blankets on the floor of her room as she'd left all her furniture in Germany as if fleeing the Chernobyl fallout. She'd lit some candles and an incense stick and put on Mozart's *Jupiter Symphony*. Moonlight, streetlights, and a patrol car light's rolling colors streamed through the second-floor window and broke the grappling darkness. I didn't want the weekend to end, but it did. Time waits for no man, so the saying goes, but we planned for me to work in Nevada for three months, save some cash, and come back for good.

It wasn't without some doubt even though all I could think of was being with her. Our plans had not gone through once before because of her mother, who we'd have to stay with until we got enough money to move into our own place.

The memory of loading the Green Rocket with my stuff, the sad drive over to Cal State Long Beach to withdraw from classes, and the long highway to Vegas was like biting into a cookie only to discover it full of salt. All told, the first time I was in LA was a week, maybe more, maybe less, enough to confuse the course of my life. The thought of being pointed east again, with the sun setting on me in the rearview mirror, troubled me.

Now, though, it felt different. Did I want to try going back to college? I didn't know for sure what I wanted. For the months I traveled the weekends to LA, it seemed good to just be with Jane. I loved how we snuggled up with candles flickering, incense drifting on the currents of chilled air as Mozart played on the tape deck. We whispered about the future and the past under the blankets as sirens, street noise, and a helicopter thwacked their way across the city like a song.

Instead of waiting on a bus, I'd started driving out to LA in the El Dorado, and I could crawl between the comforters with Jane on Friday night and not worry about what was next. Those small moments were good enough until I moved out there and could look around. I wanted to focus on my future with Jane, but it was hard to focus in the noise of the plastic injection plant where my father helped me get a job. The factory was its own kind of mind-numbing prison. The schlock and suck of machines pressing out buckets and lids. The people shouting and talking shit about others. Some nights, I went drinking after work with the crew. Those evenings, I felt the strange pressure of crowds and casino noise and would get into the occasional fistfight born from my anger like a terrible swift sword when I saw guys talk shit to women or encountered those who thought they could call me out. I felt as confined by it as when I was incarcerated. It was a funny coincidence to me that a state prison was less than a quarter mile away from the plant. This was no life, but I endured it for the promise of LA and Jane. I didn't have the boundless possibility I used to have, but staying in Sin City held the threat of Matt and the persistent reminders of how bad I fucked up. In three months, I was in LA, and this time, I wasn't asked to leave within the week.

I thought about my drag racing cousin and his brother-in-law and if there was some way to make a living doing that. When I'd been in Boron, I'd met a tax evader who was a Ferrari dealer. He said to call him when I was off parole and he'd send me to driver school for the Formula One circuit. He answered the call but told me it was impossible as things had gotten much worse for him and the money was gone to fines and interest on back taxes. I understood.

Jane was studying education at Cal State LA, and I thought about college but was still uncertain what to study. The cost was a big investment, and my record still haunted me. Putting off college was fine, though. Jane and I decided to send her through college first while I worked, and when she graduated in three years or so, I'd go. With three years, I was sure I'd suss out what would be worth investing time and money to pursue. In the meantime, I started thinking about taking martial arts classes but needed to find work first. I wanted to explore more about Bruce Lee and his philosophy and find a way to live a life that was meditative and physical and learn to control my mind and body. Once, I was walking through the day room in a barracks at Boron and, on the television, caught sight of a Korean man in a martial arts studio forcing a spoke through his arm and suspending a five-gallon bucket of water from it before hoisting it up and spinning it in a circle. He did the same with the skin of his neck. Next, he lay on a bed of nails with cinder blocks stacked on his stomach. Another guy in a martial arts uniform broke them with a sledgehammer. It amazed me, and I wanted to learn to control my mind and body like that. But like most things, I turned away, not sure if they'd train me and embarrassed to even ask.

A bonus of moving in with Jane was hanging out with her brother. Adam studied art at a university in Orange County, and I loved seeing him again. We got together at a place called Hudson's where the front end of a Hudson stuck out of the wall. We showed up after dinner, sat in a booth that looked like bench seats from an old car, and didn't even take a menu. We drank coffee served with cinnamon sticks and chocolate chips. All night, we chatted and laughed about our lives since the last time we'd seen each other. We laughed a lot, and it felt like a reward after being so long down. I was still young and in love. Gifted the chance, some said. Jane, Adam, and I regained the sparked air we had when we languished in high school, except Jane and I had a few more sparks than before.

I still felt uneducated and a little backward around them but felt they would help lift me up. I needed more lifting than before. Others had been working onward. I'd lagged and not just by the two years I'd been warehoused. I had longer still yet to go. How long would that take? I didn't know and didn't care. Jane had kissed me, and it was like I was awoken from one hundred years of sleep.

The day I left the artificial lights of Sin City and their false promises of luck for California, I looked out on the familiar desert. The same highway I'd driven on when I left LA the first time in 1982. The same highway on which Lynne had brought me back from Boron. The same highway I'd been bussed to and from high school on. The same highway I'd ridden in buses and vans to Fort Irwin and back to Vegas. There, though, at the junctions of highways in Barstow, I did not take the off-ramp to Needles and down to Eagle Mountain or head north to the fort or take the off-ramp that'd stretch to Boron in the Mojave Desert, but went to Los Angeles, a city of con artists and dreamers and a place of obsessions that can drive you mad. A place where the golden light makes all your despair beautiful.

PART V

COMING CLEAN

"I said that time may change me
But I can't trace time."

David Bowie, "Changes"

DECEMBER 2013

My daughters stand on a terrace at the Getty Villa looking back at me as I frame them in the camera viewfinder. Over the last year, I have turned my old gunnery and target acquisition skills to photography. Sophia is thirteen with long brown hair and, at five-seven, looks old enough to be a freshman in college. She carries a patchwork Nepalese shoulder bag full of art supplies. She had been sketching sculptures in the garden. Her eleven-year-old sister, Maddie, is whipsaw lean. I call her Girl on Wire, after the film about Philippe Petit tight roping between the World Trade Center towers, for her mad acrobatics and yoga skills. The sun fires her copper-colored hair, and her braces gleam. Behind them, the trees sway in the onshore breeze, and further beyond is a replica of a Roman gate. In the distance, the Pacific Ocean fades into the haze of the smudged horizon. Above them, gulls cry in the winter sky. The marble of the Villa, the trees, and the hills blush with the golden California light. The late afternoon warmth still surprises the girls as they have only known the Idaho winters they grew up with. I tell them to smile, show their faces, and they groan, "Daaaad," in the way teen and tween girls will.

I snap the photo. Tell them to hold for a couple of different shots. One more visit to the koi pond in a garden dedicated to the food and herbs of the Roman Empire at the time Vesuvius erupted, covering Herculaneum and Pompeii. The Getty Villa is modeled after one of those Roman villas covered in a pyroclastic flood all those centuries ago. Out of the past, we head for the parking garage.

We drive down Pacific Coast Highway and park along the shore to have a picnic. The waves roll and break on the continent's edge. Traffic trickles up and down the coast like so many minutes in a day. My girl posse spreads blankets on the big boulders that keep the highway from slipping into the sea. We sit and listen to the waves as the sun goes down. We joke and tell stories and eat sandwiches, avocado, grapes, and cheese with crackers. Their mom, Kathy, lives in another state and is not coming back. I'd met their mom in Boise in the summer of 1996. I'd just got back from commercial fishing in Alaska and was out drinking with a friend before planning my next move. I'd just gotten divorced from my second wife who couldn't leave gambling behind in Vegas even after we'd moved to Idaho to get away from it.

Kathy trained racehorses at the Le Bois track and cooked in the off-season. In April, we moved to north Idaho so she could be close to her father. In June, we were married in the front yard of her stepsister and brother-in-law's cabin at the fire camp where I worked, surrounded by miles of mountains and forests. It had been seven years since I'd left Los Angeles because Jane and I no longer lived with the same purpose. Now in California where I'd moved to work in an oilfield as a chemist, it was just me and the girls. We three alone. Life has been difficult, and at times it feels like the earth might split open and swallow us, but we manage. Day by day. And some days, I feel as if awoken from a lucid dream and still groggy.

Almost fourteen years before, I worked at a remote station with a small fire crew on the edge of a vast wilderness. By day, I hiked mountains, constructed firebreaks, and fought fire—the hard sweat and labor of living the dream. At night, I read the classics and philosophy and wrote surreal poems and fiction and nonfiction about martial arts. I still had the high school hope of finding other writers to hang out with.

After a summer of forestry work and fighting fires, I waded winter snows logging and doing other odd jobs, not knowing how to join those writers and too timid to try. That changed the night I sat and held Kathy's hand and watched as she struggled in labor for hours. We didn't know the gender of the baby, so I kept talking in the general—the baby or the kid. You can push this kid out no problem. I felt it would be any second, but each drew out in the darkened room until it became limbo. Each squeeze of her hand I thought would break this moment into a before and after with the birth of our child. But it wasn't to be so. The doctor came in and took me out to the hallway. He explained the baby's head had stuck somehow in the mother's pelvis. He needed to perform emergency surgery to save her at least, but without surgery, odds were they'd both die. I said to get to work. Please. My heart thumped hard in my chest. Save them from Death. Please save them from oblivion.

They outfitted me in scrubs and a mask. I stood at her head. Breathing deep to stay focused, I tried not to appear nervous or useless, even though I felt both. A nurse told me to just touch Kathy's shoulders as it'd help calm her. I did and felt her body trembling. I watched as the nurses swabbed her abdomen with antiseptic. They placed some kind of material over her with a little gap in it. The doctor stood by with his gloved hands in front of him like a supplicant. The nurses parted, and the doctor stepped between them. One nurse took a scalpel from a tray and handed it to him. He lined it up over Kathy's belly and hovered it. I waited for the blade to come down. It looked like he wasn't sure. He lowered the blade over the gap in the cloth. Her belly, reddish with the antiseptic, looked fake, but when the blade cut her, blood came. A nurse next to the doctor looked up and smiled with her eyes over her mask at me. I saw them pull Sophia from Kathy like a magic trick and announce a girl. I heard her cry. Of all the odd things, I noticed for the first time that they had been playing Elvis Presley over the speakers in the surgery. A nurse rushed off with my daughter to check her over. The nurse came to me and handed me Sophia swaddled and with a little cap on that her fine dark hair escaped under the edge.

Stunned by the emotional upwelling, I whispered Walt Whitman's poem, "O Me! O Life!" over Sophia's head in the darkened room hours past midnight, not knowing what else to do. Who knows what soft syllables lodge in an infant's brain? For years, I'd wandered, confused without knowing it. What was it to think you knew what you were doing only to discover you had been living in a lie? Living someone else's version of you? For years, I'd chased jobs and adventure, still believing I needed to go out and experience things to write. I was so busy experiencing I wasn't writing and still felt no one would care about what I had to say anyway. It didn't help I was still under the delusion that going to school for writing was a waste of time. Some failure of character, I'm sure.

The baby in my arms broke my head open and shined a light in it. Epiphany, revelation, enlightenment, a sudden striking of consciousness. It was surely what the Buddhist heroin smuggler meant when he said enlightenment will come when you're not looking for it. It'll just be there. Like the full moon. I vowed to return to college for writing. To be the man I was. I needed to do it for her too. How could I tell her it was important if I didn't earn a degree? Eight years later, I walked across the stage at the University of Idaho with a Master of Fine Arts degree and a 4.0 GPA and was an alumnus of the Jack Kent Cooke Foundation with a desire to teach and find the confidence to write and send it out. I had forsaken a career in wildfire, leaving a permanent position to take this chance. This was what I was supposed to do. Teach writing, storytelling, and pass the love of the story to others. I couldn't help but think of Lynne and her encounter group telling me to take off the mask I'd been showing society and show my true self to the world. The guy who needed the courage to admit he needed help. What had taken me so long? Had I never stopped long enough to really know myself?

Light lingers on the Pacific Coast as the sunlight spreads itself across the sea. The darkness flows out of the canyons and foothills, and we find ourselves sitting in the shadows. Headlights switch on. Brake lights cast red warnings behind them. The girls' faces flash with light and darken with the passing of cars. Jets orbit and land or take off and depart LAX to the south. Freighters and tankers ride anchor chains, their shadows against the sea like hulking leviathans from far ports. Where they've come from, I wish I knew. The poetry of girls' laughter mixes with the swells washing ashore. We sit in the dark in the flickering of car lights. They love to ask me questions about my past before they were born, or as they say, "When we floated around in the stars." I have told them stories of the National Guard, of getting a black belt, of commercial fishing in Alaska, what it's like to work logistics at South Pole Station, of repossessing cars, of hotel work, of surfing, scuba diving, hiking, and how I started fighting fire. They love hearing about my childhood in the desert. I have not told them the story about when I lost it all at the age of twenty.

Through no plan of my own, we now live in Tehachapi, California. It is about an hour away from the prison Lynne picked me up from. I have traveled a great distance around the world and, through decades, landed back on the edge of Death Valley with my daughters. We have taken trips with a rock and mineral club to within the shadow of the mountain. As they looked down for rhyolite, jasper, opal, and obsidian, I could have directed their attention up to the east and said, "See those buildings in the haze? That radar dome?" Instead, I pointed to a rock outcropping within easy reach.

I've told very few people this story. Well, until now, that is. I held it in the magma chamber of my guts. How to tell it? Why tell it? It is not enough to want to tell a story, but what difference does it make? What thing can it bring to the world? Does this story bring a boon? So many questions, so little answers. I tried fiction and poetry and even a screenplay. All fizzled. Then two things happened.

After my collection of essays came out, I heard from a brother who'd quit speaking to me some years before due to political differences. I was walking between my apartment and a dive bar along the railroad tracks by the oilfields when the text came. Mad about my essays, like it seems all writers' families, he texted me that he was going to tell the world I'd been in prison and how would I like that? Why didn't I tell that in my silly-ass writing? He was right of course. It stung because he, like only family can do, struck right into the heart of my fears. I lived in terror of being unmasked because I was too much of a coward to come clean. It would take years of traveling to find my way out of prison's shadow and speak the truth. The journey started on that dark street in Oildale.

The second thing happened in the same night or a night soon after. I was alone. My girls were with their mother in Idaho, and I'd talked with them on the phone. I sat in a one-room dump in Oildale, California. After I hung up the phone, I recalled those moments when Sophia was born, and later when Maddie was born (in the same hospital with the same doctor and nurses who would again witness my reciting Whitman to a newborn and holding her in my arms for hours because this was what I had been built for), how I felt I had done the right thing by quitting a career in fire to go back to college. I remembered the commitment to them. How could I tell them to be honest with themselves if I couldn't be honest with myself? I suppose one can, but it ate at me. I confided in my friend, Kelly Blikre, from grad school, and she told me to write it real and own it.

Even though I wasn't all the way convinced, I began to write in first person, using my name and my memories, changing salient points to protect the guilty and innocent alike. To cover up, some might say. And I say it doesn't matter. The truth set my story free, and it flowed out of me thousands of words at a time. Unstoppable. I finished the first draft in weeks and had a workable draft completed a year and two months later. I felt I could fly.

No one wanted to publish it, and no agent wanted to represent me. So I rewrote it differently a year later, the same story. No one was interested or cared. I'm waiting for responses, but it is a fact that no one responds back. And after a time, you just give up hope, like waiting for parole when you already know the answer is fuck you. I consider what I can do next with the manuscript.

My daughters laugh in the LA night as the tide starts to flood. Maddie jumps rock-to-rock looking for crabs and other creatures to capture as Sophia watches her. They will know my whole story eventually, but now, who cares? I'd covered it up for years to get jobs and avoid the shame of my disgrace, but I always felt the terror of discovery like the shadow of a shark in open water. No more. My girls have given me that courage. If not them, then who? I have never been that brave.

We pack up to leave. They help clean up the trash, believing those who don't pick up their litter are scumbags. They are excited to get on the road and see the Walk of Fame. The last time we went to Hollywood, it was after we'd visited the LACMA and the midtown fossil pit at the La Brea Tar Pits. Much to their delight, we saw the Oscar Mayer Wienermobile on a side street and "a hobo cat" riding on the back of a rolling suitcase. They are in a perpetual state of discovery and love both the cityscapes and the wilder lands. We climb into the truck and buckle up.

Before I start the engine, Maddie points to the south. The Santa Monica Pier lights the night and shimmers colored streaks over the water. We can hear the screams of people from the roller coaster and bumper cars. I tell them Route 66 starts and ends there. They say, "Cool," not really knowing what it means, but I know they will learn. Sophia and Maddie want to go to the pier first and walk through the carnival lights, past the street performers, the trapeze act, the rides, the magicians, and artists, until we come to the end over the ocean where fishermen huddle against the rail. I say sure. Why not? A person should always take the time for a side trip because even if we pass that way again, we won't be the same. I stare a moment at the Ferris wheel as the spokes spin like the hands on a giant clock at the end of the road. It pulses the neon colors of an unnatural rainbow, bright as all life, streaking the sea with undulating light and only visible because of the dark. Much like life.

Perhaps that is my boon to the girls. Transcendence is a matter of how you look at the world. You see the sacred in a pile of rocks, then it is sacred. The sacredness is the breath they breathe, the hope they have. We have seen the artifacts of long-gone civilizations that ruled the known world for centuries and the bones of animals once loose in the

Los Angeles area millennia before. We picnicked next to the Pacific rising and falling under the influence of Earth and moon. Everything, in time, perishes, never to exist again, whether it's the lifespan of a butterfly or the geologic motion of mountains finally wearing down. But even if time waits for no one, each still has sentient life, no matter where or how it arises in us, and we can do good with it. Like Whitman wrote: "That you are here—that life exists and identity, / That the powerful play goes on, and you may contribute a verse."

The revelation I had was to resolve to let go of all else and to seek everyday wonder if I could. Life and a mind coupled to a furious body allowed a person to slip into life's worry, but that was part of the challenge, wasn't it? Slip the chains of the body and glimpse the infinite in a grain of sand on the palm of the hand. I searched in meditation, trying to escape myself in a flight of the soul when all there was to do was be present there. Meditate and look at the sunset burning the sky over the wire. There was no need for supernatural divinity. That concept has always led people away from the real, the here and now, and they miss the life they should be living. Worse, it led them to cruelty in the name of the divine. Maybe that old chestnut of whether human nature is basically good or evil is null. It is neither, but degrees of both. Psychopaths and saints haunt all of us as surely as the faithful will commit evil in the name of good. The nature of a thinking animal is that it still has the body driving it, biology that creates consciousness and colors our perceptions.

Some could say that'd lead to nihilism because without the supernatural, there is no value in life. It would be meaningless. "What good amid these?" Whitman begs to know of all the injustice and chance traumas of the world. But I'd say no. It's precisely that there is nothing that gives life meaning. We should be in awe of the sacred in the transient. Make the best of it because the afterlife is the sleep of atoms. The sleep from before we were born. Is this the extreme end to self-reliance? That we have to find our own life's meaning? At least we can draw on the thoughts of artists, writers, and thinkers of cultures living and dead to guide us. We are a part of a community of ideas that exists in both time and space, just like light reflected off the ocean is still light.

I encourage them to explore, question, experiment, create art, and see the beauty around them. It's hard. The world is full of ugliness, suffering, and hate, but that doesn't mean we shouldn't try to pull back the despair and injustice to see the beauty. This is our only chance. I tell them it's okay to completely ball it up as we work through our imperfect grace. They can find redemption in life, and there is a dignity in recovering from a setback. I know. We all must suffer through some things, but that's the nature of life. I didn't escape prison by sending my soul to another place through mediation. Instead, I turned inward with music and the holy services of the disk jockey. I shunned religion and metaphysical worlds of ghosts and spirits and all those lonesome gods wandering the wastes and archangels with flaming swords but embraced Life. Capital 'L' Life. They needed to find their own rituals, and they have, whether it's drawing, crafts, music, or petting the cat. Will it last them throughout their life? I don't know. I'm just a single dad trying to keep it together. My trial in the desert.

Maddie snaps me out of my staring at the Ferris wheel, chiding me. "What are you waiting for, Old Man?"

Sophia says, "Yeah, Old Man. This truck isn't going to drive itself."

They laugh as a duet. I smile and start the engine. When a gap in traffic appears, I floor it hard. The truck burns out and rolls full speed ahead.

OCTOBER 2018

I turn off the two-lane highway onto a rough road the desert has started breaking down. The last time I rolled up this road was some thirty-three years ago, chained up in a US Marshal's van. Ms. Smith would have been proud. Me on a pilgrimage of sorts. I've resisted coming here but decided I needed to make the trip. Still, I tremble.

Of course, we've had some difficult years with medical problems and the general life as a single dad and working a job an hour from home as well as trying to keep my two daughters healthy, entertained, and educated and, importantly, teach them how to bake the perfect chicken. So who can blame me for not coming out to this abandoned, graffitied, window-broken, half-boarded-up camp where the cypress trees planted in the 1950s die of thirst? Yet one other American ghost town, except in this ghost town, my ghost walked and wondered if it'd ever be free.

In May, I'd applied for a PEN America Writing for Justice Fellowship. I hoped winning the Fellowship would make an agent or editor notice me. I also promised if I was selected, I would tell my daughters about my arrest and incarceration. I had thought when any one of the three manuscripts I'd written were published, I'd tell them, but so far, no takers. When my oldest daughter was born, it had been fifteen years since my release from prison, and as she and her sister grew, I knew of no way to tell them. It just doesn't come up in casual conversation, especially when I'd been suppressing my memory of it for so long. As they got older, I started to wonder, if I told them now, would they'd ask why I didn't say something sooner?

As I waited to hear from PEN, I started writing a new manuscript, an autofiction novel, to get a jump on it. My memory bugged me. How much I'd willed myself to forget. One night, I stared at the computer screen with a notebook open on the desk, trying to sketch the layout of the camp. I tried to visualize the place and how I'd moved through it and those I was there with. I started to remember the conversations with Ms. Smith and all I'd forgotten and realized how much she'd said to me that made sense now and wished I'd overcome my upbringing to find help after my release. Still, though, the gaps became this barrier to writing a true story, so I decided to drive out to that remote desert camp.

The outpost from the Cold War converted to a prison still stands out here, visible from miles away like some fort on the frontier between the wild and the civilized. You can see the buildings hugging the bluff, weathered and abandoned as if fading into the rock. The radar dome still towers over the camp. You can see it for miles from any horizon. I'd forgotten how big the concrete building is that the dome sits on. How many loops had I walked around that monolith on the bluff as it tracked aircraft back then? I think about how it's a ruin in waiting like the camp below it is now.

At the end of the broken road, one and a half miles from the two-lane US 395 bisecting the dry lake, you come to a dirt softball field to the south and a large parking lot and administration building to the north that looks like a Forest Service welcome center. The road necks down to one lane to enter the camp proper where we walked from admin past two palm trees to get to the barracks. Palm trees were transplanted all over Southern California as real estate boosterism to make Midwest Protestants feel they were entering the Holy Land. What is holy about any of it? Nothing, but the illusion of it worked.

I stop and park in the big lot. I walk about and take some photos.

I am particularly interested in the crumbling concrete Department of Justice—Federal Bureau of Prisons emblem next to the steps to the admin office. Relics and symbols of failed empires always fascinate me. I climb back into my car and drive up the single-lane road past the dying trees, the rubble-strewn spaces, the sun-burdened buildings with broken windows that haven't been boarded over, graffiti, and the remembrance of months upon months I spent living here. I take a photo of the building where Ms. Smith's office had been and the line of phone booths on two sides of an open courtyard. I drive up the road and around the radar installation, stopping to take photos from the bluff where we played guitars and I learned the 12-bar blues shuffle. I survey the miles of dry lakes surrounding the bluff, thinking of how walking in the desert is like walking through a dream. I walk to the edge of the bluff. The wind fills my ears as it washes over my face. The landscape hasn't changed. The desert an ancient seafloor between the mountains. I feel old. I feel strange, out of time or maybe out of place. Closing my eyes, I listen, imagining the music, people chatting, and the footfalls of guards and convicts. The wind vibrates the power transmission wires, sounding like the spirits of prehistoric whales swimming through mirages on the playas.

I drive back down past the double Quonset huts that had been the factory and the old workout area before going back through camp. I stop to take photos of the building we used as the firehouse, where I spent my last months working as a member of the emergency squad and the only member not allowed to leave the compound on a call. The warden thought I didn't deserve the privilege of saving the lives of the public or going out to the airbase and assisting the Air Force. I leave, not sure of what to think or of what it means to come here to this desert prison after all the decades except that now I know I have the layout of the camp, so I can write my story.

I didn't get the Fellowship, and I didn't tell my daughters.

I did keep writing.

OCTOBER 2019

Night closes in as I sit on the couch. I'd made a promise to myself, and now with phone in hand, I prepare to call my oldest daughter. My youngest is out and about, and I can't remember if she is with her boyfriend or with her squad. Her squad is a group of girls she's been friends with since we moved here when she was in the sixth grade some six years ago. It's funny to think I've been in this town that long and have no friends. I know some people, but I'm an older father. All the parents of my daughters' friends are in their late twenties to mid-thirties. I was forty-nine when we first moved here. We also don't share many interests, and most of our politics don't align. Some are prison guards or work for the prison in other ways. In talking with the other dads, there exists those guarded looks from me to their wives as if I might be looking for a stepmom for my girls. Are they measuring me against the imposition of time in asking favors to help with my daughters or fearing seduction and imagining themselves in my sorry lot as I cook dinner with their ex-wives? Nobody wants to be that guy.

But maybe there is the other thing—my own distance with people. The interiority of barbed wire and chain-link and block walls and safety glass. You are all out there; I am in here.

Although I have friends from the past, I also have some reason to believe I've never developed close friendships, no matter where I go, because of my secret. The same secret I'm going to call my oldest girl about and then, later in the evening, talk to my almost seventeen-year-old about.

There might be other reasons for the grand loneliness I've often felt, but I wonder. Secrets are like friction. They slow you down, retard your growth, and, if you keep pushing, heat up and incinerate you from the inside. So you try to put the fire out with booze, and like any fire where fuel is added, it burns bigger and hotter. People avoid you because they can smell it.

When I moved to LA to live with Jane, I started to learn martial arts from the grandmaster I'd seen on television. It was just luck that his dojang was in the LA area. At first, I wasn't going to, embarrassed and nervous, but Jane encouraged me. I spent the next three years studying martial arts. It would destroy our love.

I became an instructor and started teaching in the studio. Some of the other instructors had come from other states and countries to study, and all of them were former military. I didn't tell any of them about my incarceration out of shame and instead only talked about being in the Guard. I thought I'd put my desire to prove myself honorable to the country through military service behind me, but it came roaring back. There's no one thing I can point to other than the obsession to be seen as good enough, tough enough, and worthy of their respect. But it was also for the adventure. No place else could I get the training or the opportunity to parachute from aircraft, ride around in helicopters, shoot machine guns, blow things up, and travel in the name of adventure. I started trying to get back into the military—any branch that would take me. Also, in my mind, I still harbored the desire to be a writer and still believed military experience would give me experiences worth writing about. First, I tried the Army and went to a different recruiting station when the first fell through. Then I went to the Marine Corps, the Navy, and then the Air Force. Months of processing, physicals, hearings, interviews, and the long wait to hear if my waiver would be approved only to be denied each time. I'd been reading a lot of *Soldier of Fortune* again and reading books about the French Foreign Legion and famous mercenaries. One of the legends of my martial art had been a mercenary and taught a close-combat style of the martial art to the Green Berets and other special operations forces. He went to Nicaragua to train soldiers and ended up dead when an aircraft he was in blew up in flight.

I decided if the US didn't want me, then I'd go to France. By this time, Jane and I were frazzled as a couple. She announced she was moving to an apartment to be on her own but really moved in with a guy from the college. I left for Europe about a week later to wander cobblestone streets with a backpack that held more books than pairs of socks. At first, I went to Spain to visit my youngest brother and traveled about Spain, Gibraltar, and Morocco. Before taking the train to France, I stayed drunk and got in a brace of fistfights with knife-wielding gypsies, local tough kids pissed off I'd flirted with local girls, and US sailors or marines who'd fight fire hydrants on a dare. My sudden rage uncontained like a sudden quake along a fault line. When I arrived in Paris, I saw legionnaires at the train station in their sharp uniforms and the iconic *kepi blanc*. Tomorrow, I'd have a taxi take me to the recruiting office. That night, I made it to a hostel, and the Vietnamese guy at the check-in said they had no bunks available. I stood a moment and asked if he knew another place I could go. He thought a moment and said I could sleep on the floor of his room.

He had pictures of his family from Vietnam. I thought about how my father had fought in his country. I imagined his father probably fought as well. It didn't matter if it was with the South Vietnamese army or the Viet Cong. What I saw was a civil war and knew his family might have had combatants on both sides fighting and killing each other. Of course, his family might have skipped out to France in the wake of Dien Bien Phu, leaving the American war behind for others to fight. In the night, I was awoken by him masturbating to a porn magazine by the light of a table lamp on the floor. *Just a regular guy*, I thought. I turned over and went back to sleep.

The next morning, I had to leave through the window so he wouldn't get in trouble with the day supervisor. Once I was outside, he hoisted my pack to the windowsill. He gasped and asked why it was so heavy as he dropped it with a thunk on the sidewalk. "Books," I said. He shook his head. He wished me luck, and I waved to him as he shut the window.

On the street, I thought about what I'd read and how the legionnaires had to fight for France against any enemy, even their own country of origin, like the German legionnaires in World War I and World War II or any other number of nationalities. Last night, as I tried to go back to sleep after I'd been awakened, I thought more about families fighting wars against each other. Even though France was an ally, in history, it is not uncommon for alliances to change. Not only did I start to feel uneasy about the idea of bearing arms against my country, but also my brothers and all the friends I had who were still in the service. Civil war is tragic enough with families killing each other over ideologies, but to kill your family because of a contract and an irrational need to be a soldier at all costs seemed suddenly pointless. I needed to stop with this madness. Ms. Smith had told me that part of my life was over and I needed to grieve for that dead boy and find a new way of being in the world. I felt the clock again. Not the time that we measure, but the quality of time as we perceive it as it is felt. It changes the pace of life to where you feel your striving years are compressed into a minute and it has all been a hallucination. But it was real. My life had spiraled to this point, and I wasn't any better off than the day I'd left the halfway house. Time crept on the sidewalk. The sky was cloudless and the air crisp. Coincidentally, it was April, almost to the day of my arrest five years ago. I turned away and went to the Louvre.

But this night, with the phone in my hand, is my moment of truth. How long the years to find myself in my mid-fifties, a single dad to two teenaged girls, one still in high school, and the other in her first year of college. I feel the weight of my unemployment and obligation to keep my youngest in the same school until she graduates, even in this small town with limited opportunities. I lie awake at night hoping I can manage something. I hope this is the start of getting out of this hole.

At the beginning of the month, I learned I'd been selected and was to go to New York City to meet with the other Fellows and with the people who ran PEN America's Prison and Justice Writing program. I almost didn't apply a second time, but I'd written a draft of my incarceration narrative, still stuck between writing fiction and nonfiction, and had just been laid off, so I figured I had nothing to lose and much to gain. When I talked with Caits Meissner, the director of Prison and Justice Writing at PEN America, all I could do was tell her how honored and grateful I was to have been chosen.

Our first day in NYC is scheduled for October 31, my youngest daughter's birthday. She is turning seventeen. When I explained to Caits about my situation, she said if I paid for the flights, then my daughters and a friend to guide them through the city could stay in the hotel no problem. But before I can plan for my two daughters and my friend to explore NYC as a birthday bash on Halloween, I need to have a conversation about my past and hope for some measure of understanding.

As I prepare myself to have the conversation with my kids, it makes me take stock of all the ways, small and large, incarceration has impacted my life. My family kept my imprisonment a secret from my grandmother. They wanted to save her the shame of knowing. The last time I saw her alive, Jane and I had ridden out on my motorcycle. Jane almost died of dehydration. We stayed the night but had to head back the next day. My grandmother had gotten up early to fix us breakfast, but Jane really wanted to get back and didn't want to wait. I could see the disappointment in grandma's face. I should have stayed at least through breakfast, but coulda, woulda, shoulda. Grandma took a picture of me swinging my leg over the motorcycle and sent it to me. She died soon after, and I rode back to Glendale to attend her funeral…alone.

As I hold the phone, getting ready to call my daughter, I think of the long years I haven't spoken about it. To plead guilty in court is not only a confession of guilt. It is also asking for forgiveness and for mercy.

To confess one's sins is seeking absolution, to be cleansed of sins. Or as Walter Benjamin said, "The most sacred…act of the…ritual is the erasing of sins from the book of memory." But you also confess to confront the stigma by vocalizing it, putting it out there in the world, so you can begin to stop doing violence to yourself. But it's not a switch, not a sudden conversion. It's a process where the body and mind and the competing desires, obsessions, and addictions must battle it out. I want to believe it's like the five stages of grief but can't quite visualize it.

But here, this night, I wish I could talk with both of my daughters at the same time. My first confession of crime changed the course of my relationships for the rest of my life. Not just with the people who I knew then, but everyone I'd ever meet in the future.

I dial her, wondering how to say what I need to say. With confessions, they strike at the center of who you think you are or who people think you are. It's one thing to admit to a crime, but quite another to admit to the madness that went with it. I'm on the cusp of two more confessions to each of my daughters, not knowing how I got here. The phone rings. I catch my breath and steady myself. I have to find the words now.

She answers.

It is difficult, but not the worst phone call I've ever made. For that one, I was chained to a desk chair in a federal office building in Las Vegas thirty-four years and some months before. I had to call my hostile wife, Lynne, to call my parents to tell them and hope they heard from her before they saw it on the news. I can't remember how I found the words.

I still have a hard time sleeping. Sometimes I'm awake until the sunrise. I joke that I don't go to sleep but pass out. When I was writing about my experiences in earnest, I began having nightmares about being arrested and locked up. Not dreams of times past, but of the present, of me being hauled out of my house, off the streets I now walk, or from my car as I sit at a red light. They are vivid, and I am told my body trembles and shakes and my breathing changes with my racing heart. At least I've stopped screaming in my sleep.

But they have subsided now, and I no longer feel trapped in the past. That boy is long dead, grieved for, and reborn. Maybe I had to pass through that underworld of nightmares to transform my waking self.

Maybe this is why I am not as subject to sudden anger as I had been. Over the years, I learned not to just start fighting even as I yelled at some asshole. Now too, when confronted with a fight, I don't. I de-escalate, using my martial arts training for peace. Once, on a bus in San Francisco with Sophia, someone who was clearly disturbed confronted us and started yelling. He threw a punch at me, but I slipped like I'd been taught in prison. In the old days, I'd have throat chopped him and swept his feet from under him, but then, I just talked. I told him to take a breath. There was no money fighting me. One bystander said to Sophia, "Did your dad just ask how that guy was feeling and if he'd like to talk it out?" Yes, I did.

Maybe I'm just old and burned out and don't have the energy to fight anymore.

But worse for me is my shame of the times I let the anger out on my girls at whatever disobedience they committed. I'd even see it like an observer off to the side, saying, "Stop this!" They don't get it, and this isn't that serious. These battling voices between the irrational and rational roared in my mind. In the wake of those moments, which weren't often, I'd apologize to them and talk about trying to do better. I never struck them, but angry words do have a weight that needs the salve of contrition. I started to try to mitigate it. I tried to catch myself and breathe. I tried so hard to modulate my voice to try to sound less mad, to walk away to let it subside, and in so doing, try to be a better dad for them. But the suddenness of it made it hard. I didn't know where it came from. It was as hard as anything I'd ever tried to do. The exception is the rage I feel toward petty tyrants. Those who think they can crap on others with impunity. I don't react with violence but unleash all the forces at my disposal in the civil and legal system. Yes, I have changed policies, the system, and had people fired for their arrogance with nothing more than writing and moral outrage.

And about that phone call and subsequent conversation? It went well. My daughters didn't abandon me but forgave me and were loyal to this flawed man who was loyal to them as best as he could be. How could I have ever doubted it? There you have it again. The monster of self-doubt. Once, I heard someone say you must forgive yourself before you can ask for forgiveness from others. I don't believe that's true. It was only through the forgiveness of others that I learned to forgive myself. I also learned, as I researched psychological trauma, that Judith Herman's second stage of healing is being able to tell the traumatic story to those who have been through traumas themselves or those who accept you for who you are and listen without judgement. Confession, if you will, as a way toward healing through the narrative.

After visiting the other Fellows in NYC and returning home, I took another drive out to the abandoned prison camp. I'd brought my Nikons—a film camera and a digital camera. The first time, I relied on my iPhone, not really thinking about seriously photographing the place. I'd just wanted the layout. This time, though, I planned to take a lot more photos. I discovered as I pulled up the old road that they'd put up a fence with a No Trespassing sign at the parking lot entrance where the administration building used to be. Beyond the sign, I saw a work crew had come out and demolished the camp and hauled away the debris. Some road signs were left lying around, foundations exposed to the world, a low wall, brush. The empty lots where homes used to stand occupied with families. Scattered all around like bombardment rubble were the detritus of busted concrete, brick, and rocks. Scraped from the earth and left like a filled-in mining pit. It filled me with a strange desolation and disappointment.

A cold wind blew. I walked the perimeter taking photos, lost in that familiar place. I didn't know what I was looking for there. I gazed into spaces where buildings had once been and where men had worked and lived for years as prisoners. A strange connection struck me in that emptiness. Not long ago, I'd learned the concept of prison rose with the first city-states and the rise of social classes and the haves and have-nots. But instead of keeping someone locked down for years, they were holding places until judgment could be passed and one of two sentences handed out if the person were deemed guilty—death or slavery. Things haven't changed much.

In the late fall light, I just kept snapping photos and wandering the perimeter. I expected a security truck to show up and ask what my business was. After all, there was an operational radar dome for tracking aircraft, and in our paranoid nation, everyone was a threat. Fuck them. For miles around, though, no one was headed my way or even driving along the 395 cutting across the playa. Just me at the end of the road.

At the car, I secured my cameras in their cases and put them in the back seat. I leaned against the fender. I wanted to come back at night and take a series of long exposure photos with the stars spread beyond the bluff. I wanted to stretch time out in a single frame—seconds of clock time, geologic time, the light years of traveled starlight, and the eternity in the void. How long the time and how far the distance in those dark spaces. My past and the present intertwined with the future—"a traveler of both time and space." Contemplating the night sky, I thought about the stars in the ever-expanding universe, how they would eventually be alone in a lightless cosmos.

Before leaving, I walked back to the chain-link fence barring the road. I stared through the wire. This place had no fence when inmates haunted this bluff. I grasped the cold metal as if I were at a border waiting for a guard to let me cross over to the other side. The palm trees stood alone with their Holy Land promise over the rubble. They waved in the late fall breeze, the clatter of their fronds the only noise on the wind. Beyond them, on the bluff, the radar dome sat silent and stark against the sky. I remembered sitting up there surrounded by the incense smells of dried grass, creosote brush, and baked earth on the updrafts. There was only the wind over the bluff, humming through the wires like whale songs.

Was this the kind of pilgrimage Ms. Smith said I needed to make? To arrive at an inner revelation by a journey to an abandoned pile of rocks, the ruins of an ancient site? I thought of Brew and Flat-Five up on the bluff helping me to find the one, marking time, and making music out of my life. There is meaning in suffering, and if we give it voice, it can be transcendent, mystic. I turned from the fence. Out of some compulsion, I stepped in time to a long-ago drill sergeant's cadence call and response. I felt it like an old blues number sung in the dry air under a desert sun. "Your left, your left, right o' left. Momma, momma, can't you see? Your left, right o' left. What this prison's done to me?"

Acknowledgments

Kimberly Verhines at SFASU Press, I give you my deepest thanks for your support and seeing the value of my work. Karina Chacon amazed me as she edited this manuscript with a masterful eye and posed the right questions to make this memoir better. Sophia Mathes created eye-catching cover art that embodies the mythic emotions of the imprisoned. You are awesome.

This book would not have been written if I hadn't been selected for a PEN America Writing for Justice Fellowship. Caits Meissner and Robert Pollock, you will always be the ones who helped set my voice free.

As I worked on a short script and film with Dawn MacDonald and Kate Kennedy at Rehabilitation Through the Arts to be shown to inmates about to be freed from prison, the structure of this memoir came to me. This realization was a gift, and one I wish I could reciprocate.

All writers have guides who help them get further down the road. I need to thank Claire Davis, Kim Barnes, Mary Clearman Blew, Luke Whisnant, Daniel Orozco, Ben Fountain, Lan Samantha Chang, and all the living and dead writers whose words inspired and taught me from the page. I appreciate my fellow students of writing and impromptu writing groups over the years.

I must also mention the Jack Kent Cooke Foundation and the scholarship they saw fit to award me, making it possible for me to study writing at the University of Idaho and earn an MFA.

In becoming a writer and getting to the point of being able to write this book, I can't stress how much my daughters, Sophia and Maddie, are the engines that drive me forward. They have been there through all the work, disappointments, and accomplishments, so I share this with them.

To my wife, Heather Moe, a special thanks for the magic we share. Writing is hard, and with her encouragement and love, this memoir made it into the world.

Essays excerpted from this memoir have appeared:

"Rough Road." *The Sun Magazine*, 2025.

"The First Day of Everything After." *The Fourth Genre*, 2025.

"In Strange Company." *Wordrunner: 2024 Nonfiction Annual Anthology*, 2024. Nominated for a Pushcart Prize 2025.

"Shadow Boxing in Lompoc," *Gold Man Review*, 2024. Nominated for a Pushcart Prize 2025.

"On the Origin of Time: A Meditation." *Ploughshares*, 2024. Nominated for *Best American Essays* 2025 and the Pushcart Prize 2025.

"Before I was Free." *Agni*, 2022: Semifinalist.

"The Long Road to Fresno." *ReSentencing*. Selected best story of the issue, 2022.

"On Halloween." *Litro*, 2022.

"Moving in Gangland." *Talking River*, 2006. Nominated for a Pushcart Prize 2007.

The in-text photographs are of the abandoned Boron Air Station/Boron Federal Prison Camp and were taken by the author.

Photo by Heather Moe

J.D. Mathes grew up a feral child in the deserts of the American Southwest who loved to read library books and take photographs. In 2019, he was awarded a PEN America Writing for Justice Fellowship. *Of Time and Punishment: A Memoir* is his fifth book. He has worked as a field hand, a martial arts instructor, an armor crewman, a construction worker, hotel auditor, car salesman, repo-man, delivery guy, cable guy, went logging, worked in forestry, crewed on several types of fishing vessels, fought wildfire on a helicopter-rappel crew, has taught writing at the university level and for literary organizations, and led the Southernmost Writers Workshop in the World at Amundsen-Scott South Pole Station, Antarctica where he worked in logistics. He loves his two daughters and wife very much.

jdmathes.com

www.ingramcontent.com/pod-product-compliance
Lightning Source LLC
Jackson TN
JSHW022253240925
91600JS00007B/46